Praise for B and *Angels*

. . . .

This book is an excellent heart-warming account of a humanitarian operation that provided life-saving safety and future care for thousands of infants and young children. International in scope amid a wartime environment, the operation known as "Babylift," which took place in Southeast Asia during April 1975, presents a Herculean effort without equal. Angels Flying Out of Hell *will hold your interest and remind the world that the seemingly impossible can and will be accomplished by diligent, dedicated and determined rescuers.*
-Lt Gen LeRoy J. Manor, *USAF (Ret.)*

. . . .

Angels Flying Out of Hell *is truly the most compassionate book about the whole Babylift experience I have read. It recognizes so artfully and gracefully the unsung heroes of Babylift. No one involved with the Babylift mission was left untouched by the experience, and the tragedy called forth overwhelming compassion from those who participated in it in the midst of great personal grief and untold courage. Thanks for writing it!*
-Col Regina Aune, *USAF (Ret.)*

. . . .

This is wonderful work! Reading through it several times, with new insight on each, brought back a flood of memories. We were so involved in our small part of the experience that there was no way for us to know what so many others were doing. The breadth of involvement reflected here brings, even now, deep gratitude for all the people and effort involved in bringing our dear Marcie to live with us. Many, many thanks!
-Ann and Bill Say, *FCVN Volunteers and adoptive parents of Marcie Say*

. . . .

I consider myself very fortunate to have been placed in such a loving family who have always supported me through my life events whether they were good or bad. You do not choose who your family will be; on that note I am the lucky one. I was surrounded with a very loving family and a lifetime of friends whom I dearly love. I feel extremely honored to have this book written about me. Bette Milleson James has done a superb job of capturing the events and the emotions that people were dealing with during this time. I feel grateful to be a part of this wonderful book.
-Marcie Say, *Babylift child adopted by Ann and Bill Say*

. . . .

Bette Milleson James

Angels Flying Out of Hell

Printed in the United States of America

Discounts are available for orders of certain quantities.
Contact the publisher.

First edition

Designed by Paul Rodriguez

ISBN 978-0-9776906-7-1

Blueline Publishing LLC
1539 Platte Street, Suite 204
Denver, CO 80202 USA
www.bluelinepublishingllc.com

This book is printed on recycled paper.

To all the children,
and in memory of those who were lost.

Table of Contents

Introduction

In April of 1975, as Vietnam was crumbling from north to south, a massive humanitarian mission was carried out in Southeast Asia, achieved by a combination of military and civilian efforts. The compassionate, heroic, daring civilian volunteers and American military staff accomplished an unprecedented feat, unique in the annals of war: they brought out of the tragic, collapsing nation thousands of destitute orphans, transporting them to homes in the U.S. and other countries. From Saigon's embattled Tan Son Nhut airport through U.S. Air Force bases in the South Pacific and finally to the mainland and adoptive parents, these infants, toddlers, and young children traveled the 7,000 miles to safety. *Angels Flying Out of Hell* tells the story of the children's journey: how they traveled so far while so young and so helpless.

Prologue

Frantic activity at An Lac Orphanage exacerbated the exhausting effects of Saigon's hot and steamy atmosphere, which lay over the area like a blanket in April of 1975. Volunteers that included orphanage caregivers, nurses, doctors, and even flight attendants loaded infants and children onto trucks, buses, or vans—anything that would transport them to Saigon's Tan Son Nhut Airport. They were working against time. Vietnam was falling to the Communists, and everyone knew that the loss of the city itself was imminent.[1]

Inside the orphanage, workers engaged in triage, a sad but necessary process to determine which of the infants were least likely to survive the two-hour flight to Clark Air Base in the Philippines. The main criterion for transport was weight; experience of the past few weeks had taught the volunteers that infants under ten pounds were unlikely to live through the journey, so the tiniest infants were to be left behind to a questionable fate, with the few local Vietnamese staff who were left.

One young woman, normally a flight attendant, today a volunteer, knelt before a cardboard box being used as a makeshift crib. "Bye, Sweetie," she said to the tiny infant it contained. "I wish you could come with me." She snapped a quick photo and turned to go, tears starting to flow.

In an instant, she changed her mind. Turning back, she whispered, "I cannot leave you, baby girl. I know you can't weigh more than a few pounds, but I won't leave you here in this hell of a city." And with that, she removed her spare clothing from her flight bag, tucked the baby inside, and drew the zipper partially closed. It was a good trade. There would be one extra child on what would be the last rescue flight out of Saigon. At that point, the baby would be safe from abandonment, for there would be no turning back.[2]

1

The Beginning

Saigon, Vietnam, in early 1975 was chaotic and growing more so with every passing day. By the end of March, "Things looked very black indeed in Saigon. The Central Highlands had fallen and so had the great airport and sea terminal at Da Nang. The U.S. Congress had made it clear that there would be no additional emergency appropriations. The crisis in neighboring Cambodia was at its peak and competing with Saigon for American resources and attention."[1] The North Vietnamese Army (NVA) was pushing south, making steady progress toward the city. At Tan Son Nhut Airport, commercial flights carried on with their schedules amid increasingly difficult conditions. As April approached, the NVA was into South Vietnam, past Da Nang and moving rapidly toward the capital, leaving death and destruction in its wake.

In response to this threat, volunteers at the Saigon orphanages, in an effort that would come to be known as "Operation Babylift," were desperately trying to evacuate as many children as possible before the city fell.[2] They would, as history played itself out, have less than the month of April to carry out this task, as far as it could be carried out, and then, ironically, their chance to save children would end with the end of the war.

In Honolulu, assistance to orphans had been ongoing for years, having begun long before the crisis of April 1975. Despite claims that the Vietnamese people take care of their own, and despite the probability that there is some truth in those claims, orphanages had been operating in that country for decades before the crisis of 1975, many established by French nuns long before the 1954 demarcation line at the seventeenth parallel divided French Indo-China into North and South Vietnam. In the confusion following the division, streams of refugees, many of them abandoned children, flowed to the south.

At that time, An Lac Orphanage was established by a well-known North Vietnamese woman who had been the minister of social welfare (and a former tennis champion), Madame Vu Thi Ngai, assisted by a young humanitarian, Navy Dr. Tom Dooley. Dr. Wayne McKinny, a Honolulu pediatrician who worked with the orphanages throughout the sixties and early seventies, and through the weeks of Babylift, had assisted Dr. Dooley in building hospitals after the partitioning of the country. He remembers well the efforts to establish a place for the masses of children arriving in the south in 1954. Madame Ngai found an abandoned French army post, and she and Dooley began moving children into the post even before she had established permission to use it. Eventually she negotiated with the French government to pay one dollar per year for the use of the building.[3] By 1975, An Lac Orphanage, like all the others, was in dire straits, made more desperate by the added numbers of children arriving daily, again from the north.

In Saigon in the 1960s, American GIs volunteered at orphanages throughout the city. In 1965, as only one example, the Hqd Hq Company, 18th Engineering Brigade of the U.S. Army, adopted a large orphanage within the city to which they rode in motor pool trucks from their location at Tan Son Nhut Air Base. There, they assisted the French nuns by making repairs, building latrines, playing with the children, and delivering clothing (much of it sent by the men's families in the U.S.), food, and other supplies as they became available.[4] About 200 healthy orphans were in residence and another 100 or so in the orphanage hospital. A highlight for them (and for the soldiers) was a Christmas party at the orphanage that year.[5] The overcrowded orphanages were an accepted feature of life in South Vietnam throughout the country, and even then small groups of children were regularly escorted from them to waiting homes around the world.

In 1975, the *Honolulu Star-Bulletin* reported on such groups on April 2: "Groups of babies pass through Honolulu from Saigon twice a week. All have been adopted. All are going somewhere." There at the Honolulu Airport to help were representatives of Friends of the Children of Vietnam (Denver, Colo.) and Holt International (Eugene, Ore.). The article also recognized that island volunteers "down on the rug changed diapers, slipped juice bottles in little mouths, tickled tummies."[6] Even as late as that date, ten years after the work of the 18th Eng. Brigade, no one imagined how suddenly the twice-a-week rescue routine would become intense, chaotic, and massive, both heartwarming and heartbreaking, although prescient reference is made in the article to "those children abandoned crying on dusty roads in a Vietnam gone mad."

Along with many other volunteers, Honolulu residents Ann and Bill Say had been giving time and care to the small groups of Asian children as they came out of South Korea, Vietnam and Cambodia for adoption by American families whenever visas were allowed to them. The necessary stopover in Honolulu was routine, and local people were assisting by caring for the children during the hours they were in the city while their escorts deplaned for customs and other requirements.

"It all started as a lark, a fun thing to do, a mom's day out…we would go and take care of the children and then go out to lunch afterwards. It was a nice thing to do," Ann said of her experience as a resident of Honolulu assisting with those Asian adoptions during the Vietnam War. "It was about an hour, hour and a half that they were on the ground," Ann said. "When the sponsors went through customs, they just had to have someone to take care of these children…oftentimes the children were sick, so we would go take care of them. I was the person in our chapter of Friends of Children of Vietnam (FCVN) who was in charge of scheduling the airport sitters, so I was calling volunteers and going out every week, while someone else was watching my kids for me, and it was just…a change, a social event, and I became very involved."

By early 1975, Ann and others were continuing their 'mom's day out' activities as volunteers, and adoptive children were still being brought out of Southeast Asia in small groups of eight to twelve traveling on commercial airlines with agency sponsors, to be delivered to mainland families who had completed home studies and were awaiting their arrival. Honolulu was the point of entry into the United States, and the Honolulu chapter of FCVN, an agency established in 1967[7] dedicated to saving the children of war, was one of the groups assisting the sponsors while they deplaned, sometimes serving the children on the plane, sometimes in the airport.

At the same time, Ann's husband Bill worked with another organization, Vietnamese Immigrant Volunteer Assistance[8] (VIVA), which was formed by Dr. McKinney and others in the Honolulu area to alleviate the difficulties of Southeast Asian refugees. McKinny for several years had been flying back and forth from his work in Honolulu to Vietnam and volunteering his time at the orphanages there, giving medical care, helping with supplies, and working very actively in the relief efforts.[9]

McKinny, by April of 1975, was well prepared to understand the needs of orphans and to support the work. He had begun even before receiving his medical training by assisting the young Dr. Tom Dooley in establishing hospitals in Cambodia as early as the 1950s, and An Lac Orphanage in 1954, experience that served him well. By 1970, McKinny was back in Vietnam with a medical degree and was already well known for his dedication to the children and to several of the Saigon orphanages.[10]

These experiences that the Says had with FCVN and VIVA, and with efforts to assist orphans en route and to provide for orphanages in Vietnam, directly affected the young couple's plans to have several children. With two small children and a third on the way, they realized that adoption might be the best and most responsible means to have the fourth child they wanted.

"It was a time in the history of the country when there was a great concern for overpopulation," Bill recalled, "and there was some sense of being responsible citizens and not filling the place up with babies and so that was kind of an awareness for us…We got involved with the Southeast Asians concerns group, and actually I think probably the most stirring thing we saw was a Robert Northshield television documentary called *Sins of the Fathers*.[11] It was about the U.S. military personnel who were serving in Southeast Asia fathering children by Southeast Asian women, and then leaving."

The documentary was an NBC Report that featured social workers, directors of aid organizations, representatives of a children's fund, and others who were involved in South Vietnam. In it, Northshield looked at the plight of the racially-mixed children in South Vietnam. (Referred to as Amerasian children, they are half-Vietnamese, half-American, of any race.) The report presented examples of whole families who were shunned and deliberately limited to menial work because of their mixed-race child or children; often, the mother simply gave the child to an orphanage, hoping for a better life for both the child and the family. Racism, Northshield said, was rampant, and the thousands of unwanted children were crowding the overburdened orphanages. No one wanted the racially-mixed children singled out (they were, inevitably), and social workers wanted the adoption process simplified and accelerated (it was not).[12]

The Northshield documentary itself was broadcast at a time when anti-war sentiment and flat-out anger were rampant in the U.S., with a populace who were actually spitting upon returning service men and women as they arrived at ports of entry. Characterizing the American military men as 'sinners' simply fueled the flames of protest, intensifying the nation's struggle with the entire war and anything associated with it. Still, the report did raise awareness of the Amerasian children and sympathy for their helplessness in the midst of the war.

Both Ann and Bill were deeply moved by the documentary and by the plight of the Amerasian children left behind. Because of their desire for a large family, they were motivated to begin the long process of adopting a Vietnamese child. Generally, after a home study was completed, eighteen months to two years would pass before a child was designated for a couple, and after that, the necessary procedures for immigration could extend the time of receiving the child to two and a half years. So, soon after Matt was born in February of 1974, with Susan at four and little Bill at two years, the Says began the journey that they hoped would take them, in time, to their fourth child.

Bill and Ann met in college in Southern California, where Bill's family had lived briefly during his high school years. Having returned to their native Hawaii, his parents left Bill in California to attend college, where he met and married Ann. The young couple stayed on the mainland long enough to graduate and to get Bill's career in banking started. During this time, they had two children, Susan in 1970 and Bill in 1971. Eventually, they felt the time had come to move to the islands, where Bill continued his career in banking. The young family lived in Honolulu for seven pivotal years, years that saw a series of events that changed all of their lives. By the spring of 1975, they were committed to offering a home to one of the Vietnamese orphans, though they knew the process to do so would be a long journey, and perhaps a difficult one.

"I was interested in the Vietnamese children and in the stories that we were hearing on documentaries on TV about these children, so we proceeded to get a home study done…which was very difficult in Hawaii," Ann recalled. In the cases of adoptions that had been ongoing for several years, with a few children at a time coming out of Vietnam on commercial airlines, children were placed with families on the mainland. There had been no placements in Hawaii, which was merely a stop on the journey.

Adoptive parents needed to be able to give certain assurances to the South Vietnamese government, and the Says were disqualified on several counts. They needed to be over 35 years old, which they were not, and they needed to have no other children, or be unable to have children. Having failed these requirements, the Says simply wrote a letter of explanation, imploring the South Vietnamese government to grant a waiver. Meantime, the public agencies would not do a home study for foreign adoptions in Hawaii, so the Says ended up having to pay Catholic Social Services, who, Bill says, "…were very gracious and helpful and encouraging through the whole process." The Says were the first ones in Hawaii to complete the process for a Vietnamese child, and the public agencies weren't pleased about it, since, ironically, though many Hawaiians were working so hard to save them, the Southeast Asian children were not welcome in the state at that time. With the study completed in 1974, the family was put on the list with FCVN, though there had been no response to their letters to the government of Vietnam, where, as Bill realized, "…they were up to their elbows in things much more important than our adoption request."

At this point, there was nothing more to be done but to trust the process and the FCVN leaders, Cheryl Markson and Cherie Clark, who Bill felt "really seemed to understand the politics of the adoptions." Ann and Bill continued to raise money for FCVN, thinking that one of the children who would benefit from the volunteer efforts might be theirs and realizing that, in any event, the need was overwhelming. In addition, Bill was working with VIVA to try to ease the transitions of whole families who were able to get out of Vietnam, who later came to be known as "boat people."

"I was making patchwork quilts and tying them and we were reselling them," Ann said. "People were bringing us old blankets and so we would cover them with patchwork and go down to the swap meet and sell them, and send the cash to Vietnam for buying medications, or whatever we could get to support the orphanage and their needs at the time. We were a service organization as the Honolulu chapter of FCVN; we were raising money and getting donations of supplies, and doing this airport babysitting for them."

By April of that year, with the fall of Saigon to the Communists imminent, Ann's 'nice thing to do' became a desperate effort to save thousands of Amerasian children who were caught in the war zone. No one could have anticipated the amazing massive humanitarian effort of 1975 that was about to begin and to sweep the Says, the FCVN volunteers, the orphanages, and the military along with it.

2

Vietnam: A Country in Transition

In 1973, a cease-fire agreement between the China-backed North Vietnamese Army and the U.S.-backed Army of the Republic of Vietnam was formally signed in Paris on January 27 after a years-long and very difficult negotiation. In the end, it was Vietnam's special adviser Le Duc Tho and America's national security adviser Henry Kissinger who signed the hard-won agreement, an achievement for which they shared the Nobel Peace Prize in 1973.[1] (Le Duc Tho declined to accept the prize, however.[2]) As part of the agreement, American troops began to return to the U.S., and the last prisoners of war were released and transited through Clark Air Base on April 1.[3]

Within a year, the North Vietnamese were already violating the agreement by pushing into positions south of the demarcation line at the seventeenth parallel, originally established by agreement at Geneva in 1954 and included in the 1973 Paris Peace Accords.[4] South Vietnam became increasingly unstable as 1974 saw movement of troops from the north crossing the dividing line and encroaching upon northern areas of The Republic of Vietnam by early 1975.[5]

The situation in Honolulu at that time remained somewhat routine in the assistance to small groups of adoptive children and their sponsors, but when the Communists pushed south into Da Nang in late March, that event changed everything, both in Saigon and in Honolulu.[6] Once Da Nang had fallen, the enemy "continued down the east coast, the major cities falling like dominoes." Da Nang had become a hotbed of panic when President Thieu moved his Airborne Division south to protect Saigon. Refugees from farther north had already fled southward from the Quang Tri area to Da Nang, turning the city into "a madhouse of a million extra panic-stricken people, all seeking escape to a haven farther to the south."[7]

On March 23, 1975, "the situation in Da Nang was pandemonium." The consul general of Military Region 1, Al Francis, ordered the evacuation of Americans and selected others from Da Nang on March 25. Some evacuations occurred that day, but by the evening of the 26th, panic reigned at the airport. A World Airways Boeing 727 landed to take out more people and was surrounded by a crowd and vehicles. "All sorts of illegal persons crowded on board, making it impossible to stay within either legal limits for emigration or those for aircraft loading." On the 27th and 28th, several pilots "complained that their aircraft had almost been swamped by the sea of humans." On the 29th, a World Airways 727 made one last run into Da Nang to take civilian refugees out, but ended up loading some South Vietnamese Army soldiers who pushed aside civilian passengers and forced their way onto the overloaded and damaged plane. Finally, Ed Daly, president of World Airways, himself a renegade adventurer, blocked their way so the door could be closed.[8]

At the same time, refugees flooded the roadways, southbound in families, large groups and small, many of them children of all ages traveling alone or in groups, trying to stay ahead of the North Vietnamese Army. Many of the children coming from the north were brought to Saigon orphanages by anyone who could bring them, sometimes simply by older children who helped small ones along. "Our understanding at the time," reports Ann, "was that when (the NVA) got into those orphanages, they killed all the staff and left the babies...just left them." Abandoning the children in the terrible conditions without food or care may have been literal truth or not, but the reports from the north kept coming, and the appalling possibility was there.

For those who love children, there is an inexorable progression from filling small needs to recognizing and filling the larger needs as they become apparent. Bill and Ann are people who love children, and so when the needs expanded to enormous and desperate proportions, they became completely committed to supplying those needs. At one point in the early days of 1975, Bill and Ann had discussed the possibility of Ann's going to Vietnam as an FCVN escort. Such a trip would have involved the time-consuming process of obtaining a passport and visa, and doing all else that was necessary to travel internationally, and the situation was growing more and more heated in Vietnam as time passed.

In the end, with three small children of their own to consider, they decided against escorting, in part because it was dangerous, and becoming more so almost daily in the early months of 1975, but also because the delay for paperwork would simply have made them too late—and time was a critical factor. Instead, the couple stepped up their volunteer efforts, raising money and meeting the commercial flights that were still bringing small groups of children and babies out of the war zone.[9]

Like the rest of the country, everyone in Honolulu was watching the progression of the Communist march to the south. Ann and Bill, with other members of FCVN, VIVA and other relief agencies, became more and more intent on raising money, and they were needing more and more people to go into Vietnam to escort children out of the country. Among the volunteers provided by the Honolulu chapter of FCVN was a flight attendant, Doris Witt, who was single, had all of her travel documents, and was able to go, so she volunteered to help. Her presence on the last flight would change the lives of the Say family.

By this time, the situation in South Vietnam was beyond desperate. Children, even infants, were being abandoned on roadsides and on the doorsteps of orphanages by unknown and desperate Vietnamese.[10] Parents were "flocking to orphanages to give up their children in hopes of getting them accepted for transfer to the United States," reported the *Honolulu Star-Bulletin*. "Babies are dying of exposure, malnutrition, disease as they wait in the open, travel the miles toward Saigon, or are transported in open barges to safer haven in the south."[11]

As the Communists moved south, the relief agencies and volunteer organizations in their path, hearing this distressing news, were frantic to accomplish as much as possible in the little time that was left. Though opinions varied on whether Saigon would fall in days, weeks, or months, it was obvious that it would fall. Children were still being brought south from the northern orphanages at an astonishing rate to the overburdened volunteers in Saigon, and the commercial flights carrying small groups of children with their escorts left so many thousands remaining, and so great a need, that some alternative had to be found. Sen. John De Camp of Neligh, Nebraska, in Honolulu on business, told the *Star-Bulletin*, "We're trying to get as many out as we can. We're concerned that they might be slaughtered. We're trying to get organizations to charter planes to bring out 1,000."[12]

Although President Ford responded to appeals of the Vietnamese Ambassador and humanitarian agencies on April 3, Secretary of State Kissinger had already "asked the Joint Chiefs of Staff and Secretary of Defense James R. Schlesinger to move the Vietnamese orphans from Saigon to San Francisco, after the Agency for International Development signaled the children were ready to leave."[13] In making this request, Kissinger certainly must have been thinking of an orderly removal. Such a move would involve the use of the Military Airlift Command (MAC), which had a long history of non-combatant evacuation operations. Most of the MAC airlift structure was in place, with C-5s and C-141s flying into Tan Son Nhut on a regular basis, delivering war materiel and returning to Clark Air Base in the Philippines, empty. These aircraft could be used to take the children out to Clark, which had long been a staging area for Southeast Asia during the war and was only a 2 ½ hour flight from Saigon.

Still, Babylift would be unique in MAC history. Differing responsibilities belonged to different individuals and agencies, both military and civilian, including the MAC commanders, the generals in charge of different areas of Southeast Asia, the defense attaché in Saigon, American Ambassador Graham Martin, Maj. Robert S. Delligatti (supervisor of airlift in Vietnam), the operators of the orphanages, and several others.[14] Coordinating this massive operation with its disparate elements—along with evacuations of "non-essential" employees of the American agencies and endangered Vietnamese, followed in just weeks by the fleeing population of South Vietnam— became increasingly difficult as the war drew closer to the airport, yet the military, the volunteers, the medical teams, and the flight crews all would accomplish their missions.

In addition to the military preparations, the civilian agencies caring for the children in Saigon were actively planning any means of escape possible. Fraught with the knowledge that time was running out for the orphans, VIVA and FCVN, along with other agencies such as Holt International and Catholic Relief Services, got involved with finding airlines that would be able to transport the children out of the war-torn country in greater numbers, whole planeloads at a time.[15] The suffering and losses of the abandoned children in the north haunted the volunteers and gave a constantly increasing sense of urgency to the immense project.

3

The Daly Flight

As often happens in the ongoing drama of human events, one remarkable person with a zest for life and a strong sense of decency stepped into the void and became a catalyst for action. Ed Daly was a well-known figure in Southeast Asia at the time. Daly was a colorful character who, because he was president of his own airline, often ran it by his own rules, flying for years as a contractor taking cargo in and out of Vietnam, and on the "rice run" taking rice into Phenom Penh in Cambodia during the siege of the Khmer Rouge. He had successfully commanded the last flight of refugees out of Da Nang a week earlier without authorization from American Military Airlift Command or from the airport flight control, and against the advice of pilots and relief services, although South Vietnamese soldiers created havoc in attempting to board, and others on the tarmac tried to blow up the plane with hand grenades before it was airborne.[1]

At this point, on April 1, Daly pledged to fly 1500 orphans out of Saigon with or without permission. He planned to fly nearly 1000 infants to the U.S. in a DC-8 that he had removed from the rice run, and a group of 400 to 500 babies to Australia in a Boeing 727, paying the cost of both flights himself. "We're going to move out tomorrow," he declared. "Let 'em stop us."[2]

Having accumulated considerable wealth and influence by this time in his life, Daly was free to provide assistance to organizations in need, and he was known to have a soft spot for children, including those far beyond his Oakland, California, home: He had reportedly built an orphanage in a village in South Vietnam, had provided circus tickets for underprivileged children in California, annually sent 1000 children to the Oakland orchestra's Christmas performance, and supported a Colorado research hospital for respiratory illnesses, many affecting children. According to a friend in Oakland, he flew into Saigon that April because "he was emotionally overwrought about the children there."[3]

Daly's reputation as a pistol-packing pilot who carried a .38 caliber when in Indochina, and the history of his rogue airline, suggested that he meant business when he said, "Let 'em stop us." Though neither the United States nor Australia had given him permission to enter with orphans, and the South Vietnamese government had not said that children would be allowed to leave, Daly was adamant that his plan was doable: "Do you think any government in the world would block these planes?"[4] As it turned out, the Australians planned their own lift, beginning the next day with 200 orphans going to adoptive parents in Australia and Europe, and Daly modified his plans, reducing the number for the first flight.[5]

Ed Daly was well known to Major General LeRoy Manor, Commander of the 13th Air Force at Clark Air Base in the Philippines. Though that first flight went through Yokota Air Base in Japan,[6] Daly's later 747 flights, along with many military flights, stopped at Clark, where Manor's people were ready for them. Daly had been a presence at Clark for years in his position as contractor for the U.S. military. "I got to know Ed Daly quite well in dealing with him at Clark," Manor recalls. "He had equipped a 747 as a hospital airplane with nurses on board, and his crew included medically trained members. He performed a great service for us and for the people."[7]

Daly's status as a colorful character preceded him wherever he went. It was widely known that he "flew around for years in a lime green Convair 44 dubbed 'Jolly Green Giant,' a plane graced with a leprechaun on its nose and a shamrock on its tail."[8] With his company's competent pilots in the cockpit, Daly flew along as a volunteer with most of the World Airways Babylift flights, responding to a question about that participation by saying, "Why do I personally go along? Because I enjoy life and enjoy excitement."[9] Oakland friend Charles Finley remarked, "He's that kind of a man, a very determined person. If someone tells him something can't be done, that's when he's most likely to go out and do it." Almost anything could be expected of a man who wore a green plaid safari jacket and pants, brown cowboy hat, a Papal medallion and a silver pistol charm around his neck.[10]

So it was that on April 2, 1975, one of Ed Daly's World Airways DC-8 planes was to be the first to fly out a load of refugees, authorized briefly by the government of Vietnam, but with authorization withdrawn because of 'safety issues,' (it was actually a cargo plane) and without permission from the United States to take the refugees to the mainland. A spokesman for the State Department's United States Agency for International Development (USAID) said that Daly "was planning to use a DC-8 cargo plane without seats, little cabin heating, no toilets, and no personal safety equipment."[11] This judgment of the questionable safety of Daly's DC-8 became the ultimate irony, in light of what was to happen to the first authorized aircraft, a C-5A Galaxy, which was also a cargo plane.

After hours of confusion, frustration and delay in attempting to load orphans and other refugees, caused, Daly believed, by the U.S. Embassy (who denied it) and USAID (whose spokesman commented that there were "adequate alternative ways to transport children from Vietnam to safety"), Daly located two orphanages that were prepared to load their children within hours onto his World Airways DC-8 jet. According to AP correspondent Peter Arnett, who flew aboard the plane on the trip, the orphanages were run by the Seventh Day Adventists and World Vision.

LeAnn Thieman, an American in Vietnam waiting to take home her adoptive son from FCVN's Thu Duc Orphanage, recalls that a group of FCVN toddlers were also on the unauthorized flight. Of the 218 refugees who ultimately boarded, 57 were children, with about 20 adult passengers and 2 physicians caring for them. Tan Son Nhut Airport had been closed just before takeoff because of a feared Viet Cong attack, and non-military people had been ordered off the base. As he prepared for the controversial flight, chief pilot Ken Healey was told by the Tan Son Nhut control tower not to take off, but later said, "I just didn't get the message in time."[12] When he radioed the U. S. Air Base at Yokota, Japan, for permission to land, the tower operator told him, "Gee, you can't land here, because you never left there. So welcome to Yokota."[13]

An official at USAID, commenting on Daly's flight, said the agency "was flabbergasted" when the World Airways DC-8 left Saigon without Vietnamese or American permission. It was due to land at Oakland Airport with 57 orphans. At this point, with the plane in the air, it was decision time, so USAID, immigration and State Department officials met and decided to accept the children in Oakland without the normal paperwork.[14] Because Daly had not received permission to land in the U.S. before takeoff, and because the passengers lacked U.S. visas, he was fined (amounts variously reported as $218,000 to $243,000) by the U.S. Immigration and Naturalization Service (INS) for illegally bringing 218 refugees into the country.[15] This action by INS elicited a chuckle from Daly and a public outcry from the American public, and the fine was later dropped.[16]

After the stop at Yokota,[17] the refugees landed at Oakland, California, where they were met and transported to the San Francisco Presidio, an Army facility near the Golden Gate Bridge.[18] In caring for the children, Daly's daughter Charlotte was a key player, having called Col Robert Kane at the Presidio, as well as World Airways staff, for assistance in preparing to receive the children and other refugees.[19]

Arnett, having traveled on to Oakland and then to the Presidio with the children, reported from that location that they were doing well, playing with toys and "chattering excitedly." Most of them had slept through the flight across the Pacific and were ready for this new adventure. Sgt Ronald Renouf said, "It was like a giant playground. I never saw so many happy kids in my life. Many were looking at and playing with toys they didn't even know existed. It was like out of a dream for them."[20]

Two of the orphans had been left at Yokota in Japan. "They were malnourished and dehydrated and I didn't want to risk them on the long hop across the Pacific to the States," said Dr. Gene Hilderbrand, one of two physicians aboard the flight. Four children were also hospitalized on arrival with possible pneumonia, fevers, or body sores, but in general most of the others were in good condition. After sponge baths and medical checkups, the children were fed a snack of bananas, apples, rice, and soy sauce. Some were transported to their adoptive parents the same day.[21]

In the final analysis, this rogue flight inspired an editorial in the *Oakland Tribune* in April 1975, using the stirring words of lyricist Joe Darion's "The Quest." The article is a fitting tribute to Daly's life and reflects the feelings of editor and publisher Joseph W. Knowland and many other Daly contemporaries about this remarkable man.

"To Dream the Impossible Dream, To Fight the Unbeatable Foe…"

After a decade and a half of that dreary war in Southeast Asia, we needed something uplifting to show for history that we did something right there.

Perhaps that's why a pistol-packing airline owner, wearing a green beret, dreaming an impossible dream and slicing through red tape with DC-8s and 727s seems more like a swashbuckling "Man of La Mancha" than a millionaire businessman.

The phrases from that Broadway musical seem to fit — **"To fight for the right without question or pause, to be willing to march into hell for a heavenly cause…"**

In one sweep, Ed Daly, the rough and ready president of World Airways, has focused world attention on the plight of Asian refugees. The 57 orphan children he brought into Oakland were a living plea for help.

Using his own money and airplanes, without regard to personal risk, Daly started the movement that has led President Ford to speed up the evacuation of Vietnamese orphans.

"To run where the brave dare not go…"

While State Department officials in Saigon were criticizing, Daly was acting.

Maybe he bruised a few rules. His methods may not have been orthodox, but a nation under siege can't always be handled with ordinary methods. His airlift was dramatic, and despite what critics said, safe.

With some cooperation from American and South Vietnamese officials, Daly might have done more.

There has been a lot of pettiness in the actions of John Bennett, deputy director of the U.S. Agency for International Development and U.S. Ambassador Graham Martin.

They were piqued by Daly's "get a move on" attitude, but it was time for a man of action and not a debater.

"And the world will be better for this, that one man, scorned and covered with scars, still strove with his last ounce of courage, to reach the unreachable star…"

Ed Daly, together with pilots Bill Keating and Ken Healy, brought some real compassion into a war that has been dirty, has cost America 55,000 dead and billions of dollars.

It was a spark that kindled a fire in the hearts of the people of the United States. Without an Ed Daly, it is doubtful that the bureaucratic tangle would have been undone.

He reached his star, and we are better for it.

Knowland's words brought to the forefront the plight of the orphans and the need "to fight for the right without question or pause…to be willing to march into hell for a heavenly cause." Because of his personal fight for the right, Daly was regarded as a hero by most Americans, many of whom had seen television reports showing the chaotic conditions at the airport. Around the world, people watched as confusion reigned in every graphic, violent report that came through to worldwide television. Daly had set the stage for an unprecedented performance, and it would begin within days.

4

President Ford and the Commitment to Babylift

Following Daly's breathtaking illicit rescue, a public outcry and pleas from humanitarian groups to save the children were ringing across the country. Responding to the national demand of many humanitarian groups, and to the April 1st pleas of the South Vietnamese Ambassador to the United Nations, Nguyen Hu Chi, for assistance in evacuation and resettlement of refugees, President Gerald Ford, an adoptee himself, authorized, on April 3, Operation Babylift, a massive effort to save the children of war.[1] This unprecedented authorization allowed U.S. Air Force aircraft to transport large groups of refugee children into the United States, waived the need for visas, specifically directed American officials to cut red tape and other bureaucratic obstacles, and authorized 2 million dollars for aid and resettlement.[2]

The moment that President Ford made his pronouncement establishing Operation Babylift, the American Military swung into action to perform a humanitarian mission as only they can do. Not only at Saigon, but at Clark in the Philippines, Hickam in Hawaii, and other bases from Guam and Wake Islands to those on the mainland, preparations began to receive the children and send them on to the United States and ultimately to homes in Canada and Europe as well.

Offers of assistance poured in. Veteran U.S. relief officials reported, "No international disaster in the past has produced a similarly strong desire to offer succor to foreigners in need as have the sudden military calamities that have enveloped South Vietnam and Cambodia in the past three weeks."[3]

At the State Department's International Disaster Relief Center in Washington, D.C., Vernon Lyon told the *Washington Post Service*, "The response has been greater than any we've ever received. People are calling in with all sorts of ideas. They watch pictures on television, see a hell of a mess, and they want to help." The department received 200 phone calls about adoptions the day of Ford's announcement, when normally there would be 5 a day. "We've been getting doctors volunteering their services, offers of food, and tremendous interest in the plight of the orphans," Lyon said. The relief center added 10 telephone lines to the dozen they were using to handle the offers of assistance and the questions about friends and relatives in Vietnam.[4]

On April 4, possibly to divert the offers of help to appropriate agencies, the State Department requested that the State Civil Defense Agency in Hawaii make public the names and addresses of 10 of the leading relief organizations to which money could be sent to aid Vietnamese civilians. Agencies listed were The American Friends Service Committee, CARE, Catholic Relief Services, Church World Service, Community Development Foundation's Save the Children Federation, Seventh-day Adventist Welfare Service, International Rescue Committee, Lutheran World Relief, Mennonite Central Committee, and World Vision. The American Council of Voluntary Agencies for Foreign Services was also offered as an agency that would answer questions. At this point, civil defense spokesmen stated that donations should be in cash, as supplies of food, clothing, blankets and medical needs were sufficient at that time.[5]

At the same time, the U.S. INS in Honolulu revealed that it had been told to expedite immigration requests made by persons with relatives in Vietnam, a well-intentioned order, but one that, as the nature of the emergency unfolded in the days and weeks to come, would fall by the wayside. Requests would become irrelevant in the frantic effort to save not only orphans, but whole families, in the desperate days to come.[6] By April 8, a representative from the State Department was expected to deliver a list of Hawaiian spouses, parents, siblings, and children to the American Embassy in Saigon. The sponsoring organization, Concerned

Vietnamese-Americans in Hawaii, asked American leaders "to do for our relatives what our government is now doing for the orphans of mixed origin—offer a safe haven free of war and death."[7] Thus, the official effort to save the children of American fathers became a stimulus to action on behalf of others.

In the U.S., announcement of the planned evacuation had brought a flurry of activity among all those Americans who had any reason to follow daily information coming out of Vietnam or Washington. In announcing the commitment to fly 2,000 children to the United States, President Ford stated bluntly, "To get these children out—that is the least we can do, and we will do much, much more."[8] Perhaps taking Ford at his word, and realizing as well as anyone that the fall of Saigon may be imminent, Hawaiian Islanders with relatives in South Vietnam "acted swiftly...to organize efforts to evacuate their kin to Hawaii" if the city fell. Members of Concerned Vietnamese-Americans in Hawaii, who earlier had already begun compiling lists of people to bring out, went in droves to the Kalihi-Palama Immigration Center to fill out "emergency evacuation requests" for 1,200 children, wives, parents, and other relatives.[9]

James Morrow, a Vietnamese-speaking volunteer who assisted with registration, reported 234 applicants had filled out requests for families in need of evacuation. Many of the requests concerned relatives who were "already American citizens" with requests in all cases "sponsored by U.S. citizens willing to be responsible for the refugees." The list was to be hand-carried to the U.S. Embassy in Saigon and given only to American officials. "They will see that it does not fall into enemy hands, because it could become a reprisal death list if it did," Morrow said.[10] By April 14, the list had grown to more than 2,400 names, though J. M. Rolls, Jr., president of the group, believed that many people on the list, especially the elderly, might choose to stay in Vietnam. Still, he believed, they should have a choice.[11]

In the matter of children, Morrow's Vietnamese wife stated, "They ought to get the mixed Vietnamese-American children out first. The pure Vietnamese youngsters probably will get along somehow, but those mixed kids are likely to die at the hands of the invaders," she said.[12] Sadly, this viewpoint reflected a lack of understanding of the dire straits of the orphans in a country that was disintegrating. "Pure" children probably had no more chance of survival than any others, though it was true that mixed-race children were referred to in Vietnam as "bui-doi," meaning "dust of life," or "dust of the earth"- a pejorative term showing lack of respect.

In South Vietnam, FCVN, which had been active in Vietnam since 1967 and operated 15 orphanages in the south, stepped up efforts to remove children from Saigon. Cheryl Markson, Agency Director, said rescue flights would be coordinated by USAID. FCVN had "lost contact" with all but six of its orphanages, since they were located in the northern part of South Vietnam where the NVA had swept through, but would continue efforts to rescue orphans until ordered out of the country. "The situation is desperate," said Sally Bergner, mother of an adopted Vietnamese boy and a coordinator for FCVN. "We don't know how long we'll continue to get cooperation from the South Vietnamese government."[13]

At Clark Air Base in the Philippines, General Manor received the order to prepare for planeloads of children in transit to the United States to arrive at Clark, possibly within 48 hours.[14] Manor had entered the service in 1942, had flown air fighter patrol at Normandy on the morning of D-Day, and throughout the following months had flown support missions, including 72 combat missions as a P-47 pilot with the 358th Fighter Group in Europe, subsequently serving in several positions in Europe and the United States.

In 1968, he assumed command of the 37th Tactical Fighter Wing in the Republic of Vietnam, where he completed 275 combat missions in North and South Vietnam. Manor later commanded the U.S. Air Force Special Operations Force, where he served as commander of a joint task force to search for and rescue U.S. military personnel held as prisoners of war.[15] In this position, he was the architect of the Son Tay Raid into the Hanoi area of North Vietnam.[16]

As a veteran of these operations and tactical evaluations assignments, and thanks to his experience in receiving the returning POWs at Clark in 1973, Manor knew what the needs would be, and as Commander of the 13th Air Force, he had responsibility for, and access to, ten bases in the region, including assistance from the commanders of those bases and from their medical teams. "My command included all the bases we had in Thailand, and each of those bases had medical facilities, so I brought in some of the nurses and doctors from those bases. We really didn't need a great big force, but the influx that was anticipated, and the one that turned out, was real young children, quite a number of infants and smaller children that needed quite a bit of attention."

With that age group, he recalled, there was not much need for large equipment such as x-ray machines, a fact that simplified preparations.[17]

Manor contacted Col Donald A. Michela, commander of Clark Air Base, and the commanders of other bases in the region to set in motion the transport of their medical teams and supplies, and ordered immediate setup of a hospital facility in the gymnasium at Clark. The large room was filled with cots, mattresses and blankets on the floor, cribs set up in rows, and stations for supplies arranged around the perimeter. The participation of the officers' wives group, headed by Manor's wife Delores, and of the Non-Commissioned Officers' (NCO) wives as well, was crucial to the success of the necessarily rapid preparations.[18]

"The organization was excellent," recalls a member of Clark's 1st Test Squadron, Major Thomas P. (Tuck) McAtee. "The base set up the gym with small cots on the floor, and food, medicine and supply dispensaries around the sides. We could see a doctor on an instant's notice, especially if the child was having trouble."[19]

While the setup was being organized and the volunteers informed of the care plan, others on the base were preparing to send for the first load of children. Mavis Pearson was a civilian spouse working for the 374th Wing Commander when the initial plan was developed to fly into Vietnam to bring out the orphans. The medical crews to all humanitarian or regularly scheduled aeromedical evacuations were coordinated through the 9th Aeromedical Evacuation Group, stationed at Clark. In this case, the crew and medical team were called in and the entire mission was briefed, including selection of crews and positions for the flight.[20] The aircraft assigned for the first Babylift flight was the C-5A Galaxy, at that time the largest airplane in the United States Armed Forces inventory, capable of carrying hundreds of children and their escorts in an enormous cargo bay area and an upper deck troop compartment.[21]

Preparations at Hickam Air Base in Honolulu differed from those at Clark in that direct communication was with Clark rather than with Saigon. In addition, it was assumed that the condition of the children would be somewhat less precarious on arrival in Hawaii, with seriously ill ones left in the hospital at Clark. Initially, at least, the children were expected to remain on the planes at Honolulu, and the volunteers would care for them there while the escorts deplaned, a procedure that had been in place for years as the small groups of children had been transported by commercial airlines to their adoptive homes. General Louis L. Wilson, Commander of Pacific Air Forces (PACAF) at Hickam, a West Point graduate who had served with Manor in Europe during WWII,[22] received information similar to that of Manor, and responded in much the same way with supplies and volunteers. Armed Forces radio on both bases asked for volunteers to help with the incoming flights of babies and small children.[23]

Temporary care centers with food, diapers, and other supplies were set up at Hickam and in the new passenger lounge at Honolulu International Airport, and volunteers from Honolulu as well as from the military bases on Oahu were recruited to assist the crew and escorts of each plane. Through the coming weeks, Ann Say's responsibilities for FCVN would expand daily. With efforts to earn money, with her own shifts at the airport as a volunteer, and with care of her own young children ongoing, her duties would make for frantically busy days and nights as the Babylift mission developed.

Within 48 hours, both Clark and Hickam were prepared for the influx of children that would prove both enormous and unpredictable. Seemingly prepared for any eventuality, none of them—the commanders, the officers, the doctors and nurses, the military wives and other volunteers—could have forseen what they would see, what they must do, and how they would feel in the next 23 days.

5

. . . .

Preparations Everywhere by Everyone

Security would be an issue from the very beginning, and would become more difficult as the evacuation proceeded. Initially, the 7th Air Force Supervisor of Airlift was assigned "a complement of 11 security guards, 1 customs official, and 8 maintenance specialists for the processing of evacuees and the flight line operations." In addition, 2 U.S. Air Force (USAF) officers from Clark were sent to Tan Son Nhut to supervise the unloading of supplies and the loading of passengers.[1]

Evacuating thousands of orphans would be the most difficult and rewarding undertaking that most of the orphanage workers and other volunteers would ever accomplish. LeAnn Thieman checked with workers at Thu Duc, an old two-story French villa that had been turned into an orphanage by FCVN. On the 4th of April, numerous orphans lay or sat on the floor crying, playing, or sleeping while the workers prepared diapers and other needs for the evacuation. These were to be the first orphans on an authorized flight, and Thieman had already informed her husband on the mainland that she and their son would be on this plane. However, in a twist of fate, she and the Thu Duc orphans were bumped to a later flight, in part because the orphanage had sent their toddlers out on the unauthorized Daly flight earlier.[2] This somewhat punitive action became, in the light of what would finally happen, a heartbreaking stroke of good fortune for Thieman and the Thu Duc orphans.

At Clark, the Saigon-bound C-5A Galaxy was to pick up a medical team headed by Medical Crew Director Lt Regina Aune, who had completed Flight Nurse Training at the School of Aerospace Medicine at Brooks Air Force Base, Texas, a year earlier and was then assigned to the 10th Aeromedical Evacuation Squadron as a flight nurse stationed at Travis Air Force Base in California. Aune was thirty years old and just eight weeks married.[3]

Loadmaster SMSgt Ray Snedegar was awakened at 3:00 a.m. that day, "a typically normal day in the life of a flight crew member during the Vietnam era," and was told that a C-5A was being alerted to fly into Saigon to drop off a load of weapons and fly out "any retrograde cargo made available to them." At that point, Snedegar declined, though he changed his mind later when another loadmaster called to suggest that there were rumors about something unusual on the return trip, and he "made a decision to fly with them based on what I was told in the wee hours of the morning. That decision to accompany a routine C-5 mission," he says now, "turned out to be a trip that has affected the rest of my life."[4]

For Lt Aune, Flight Nurse Capt Mary Klinker, and the other members of the medical team, the experience they were about to undergo that April had begun even before the outset of Babylift, before Daly's flight, before President Ford's order of the humanitarian mission. Events that would affect the operation were set in motion early in 1975, when transitions in the aeromedical evacuation systems were begun. By April, the Air Force was already in the process of aligning the systems under the Military Airlift Command. Aune's group, the 10th Aeromedical Evacuation Squadron (AES) based at Travis Air Force Base in California, flew regular C-141 flights between Clark Air Base in the Philippines, Andersen in Guam, Hickam in Hawaii, and Travis in California. The 10th AES at Travis was being merged with the 9th AES based at Clark.[5]

Medical crews from both squadrons were flying with each other on both the C-141 Starlifter missions of the 10th AES and the C-9 Nightingale missions of the 9th AES. This transition required a constant effort involving many aeromedical evacuation crews for the two months preceding the Babylift missions and into that experience. Few people

during Babylift, or after, realized the enormity of the commitment
to transition and retraining required of the men and women of the
aeromedical evacuation groups. And none of the experience and training
up to that point involved a C-5A Galaxy.[6]

When Babylift was imminent, Aune was at Clark with a team from
the 10th AES and another from the 9th. Neither crew was familiar with
the C-5 when the group was informed at Clark that an aeromedical
evacuation mission involving some children from an orphanage would
depart for Saigon and that the plane would be a C-5. Training would
take place aboard the aircraft on the flight to Saigon. It is a testament
to the excellence of their discipline and training that by the time they
arrived at Saigon, the medical teams were entirely familiar with the
aircraft, although until they landed, the crews were not aware of exactly
what their mission would involve.

The giant cargo aircraft was not equipped for medical evacuation,
its cockpit crew had never flown such a mission, and few of the medical
team had been in a C-5 before. In 1973, Aune had flown back to Dover
Air Force Base, Delaware, from Europe on a C-5 as a Space Available
passenger, and one or two others had minimal experience with the
aircraft, but basically the crew and the team would be learning on the
job. The preparation at the briefing before takeoff for Saigon and the
training on board the aircraft en route, when the loadmasters briefed the
team on the plane's facilities and systems, prepared them for the use of
its features. Aune planned to put the orphans on the upper troop deck,
where seats, seatbelts, and oxygen masks were available, not dreaming at
that point that there would be as many children as there turned out to
be. The extemporaneous on-board training and the medical team's plan
for loading were completed as the aircraft approached Vietnam to land.[7]
In the event itself, when the time came to load and depart, everyone on
board, from flight crew to medical team to loadmasters, did exactly what
they were trained to do.[8]

"Saigon was dead ahead," Aune reports. "You could see when we
were coming in that Saigon was about ready to fall—you could see all the
ground fires. The North Vietnamese were already within the city limits
of Saigon." At that point, with violence at Tan Son Nhut an obvious
possibility, Lt Col William Willis, on board as ranking officer and mission
observer, said, "I need to tell you how to find the bunkers at the airport
if we need to find them." He described the location of the bunkers to the

medical team and gave a quick combat lesson on the way in, in case they encountered combat conditions on landing.[9]

The C-5 landed in the midst of chaos at the Air Base. Planes were everywhere—planes from Australia, from the South Vietnamese Air Force, from the U.S. and Europe. The C-5 was parked just off the runway in the stifling heat. "Noise from the constant traffic on the runway blended with the hot, humid conditions of the day and the smells of the jet engine fuel," recalled Lt Aune. "Bathed in sweat, I felt as though I was eating all the grime and dirt of the airfield. From the cargo ramp of the C-5, I watched the activities swirling about the field."[10]

It was at this point that the medical team and flight crew learned their specific mission, when the aircraft commander and the copilot went into Base Operations Office to get details. They discovered that there were 200 to 300 orphans, many more children than expected, and made plans for how to use the lower cargo deck as well as the seats in the troop compartment. In the circumstance, just moments before take-off, Aune's medical team was augmented with the members of another team from a C-141 that had landed after the C-5. That team had been assigned to a flight with adults, but assisted instead with care of the large number of orphans.[11]

With security problems rampant at the airport from the outset, every precaution possible was taken at this early stage of the Babylift effort. After Daly's harrowing experience at Da Nang just days before, when so many panic-stricken refugees and soldiers had attempted to flee by forcing themselves up a ladder into the aircraft, or by hitching a ride in the wheel wells of the aircraft (successfully, but fatally, in one case), a guard was placed at each wheel well of the C-5. In addition to other assigned guards, TSgt Bradley was assigned to the right wheel well, MSgt McAtee to the nose wheel area, and TSgt Parker to the left wheel well.[12]

The C-5, standing 65 feet—as high as a six-story building—with a wing span of 223 feet and a fuselage length of 247 feet,[13] was large enough to carry oversize equipment such as helicopters in the cargo compartment, where nearly 150 children and attendants were installed. Though there were cardboard bassinettes on later flights, the babies on the lower deck of the C-5 were lying on blankets and pillows in small groups on the floor, along with the women accompanying them. All were strapped to the floor with litter straps and cargo tie-down straps, which were attached to rings on the deck.[14]

Loadmaster Snedegar, responsible for all aspects of the loading operation, moved wherever he was needed both inside and outside the aircraft. On arrival of the small passengers, he assisted with setting up the cargo floor with straps to secure adults and children, moved to the bottom of the ladder to the upper troop compartment, and finally climbed to the top to receive the children there.[15] Nearly 150 more children, mostly infants, and their escorts were placed in the rear-facing seats in the troop compartment. Because of their small size, these children were carried on board up the rear loading ramp and handed from one crew member to another up the aft ladder to the troop compartment. The infants and smallest children were checked for medical needs by Lt Aune at the bottom of the ladder before she handed them up the crew's "baby brigade" to waiting escorts, who strapped them in, two to a seat, with pillows between them.[16]

Twenty years later, the moments were still vivid in the mind of Lt Aune, who wrote in a 1995 commemorative article for *Military Medicine:* "What I remember most about the process of loading the plane is not the sheer magnitude of the enplaning, but the pathos of the moment. Many of the children were brought to the plane by young Vietnamese women who were sobbing inconsolably as they handed the children to us, strangers and foreigners from another country, speaking a language they could not comprehend. As I took each child from the arms of each anguished woman, I, too, wanted to cry. Their pain was palpable and I wished there was some way to ease it and to assure them that I would care for these children with all the tenderness and concern that they had for them. It was with a heavy heart that I took my place along the left side of the fuselage once we had finished loading and were ready for take-off."[17]

With the flight crew of 16, the 44 escorts (including 37 secretaries and analysts of the Defense Attache Office), 4 flight nurses, 6 med techs, a few other adults, and the many children, the C-5A Galaxy carried 305 souls that day.[18] (Official Air Force totals would later put the total at 314.[19]) Capt Klinker and Lt Aune, with the other medical team workers and the escorts, must have felt some trepidation as they belted themselves in and prepared to take off. As for the children, most were too young even to realize where they were, and even those a bit older could have had little realization of what was happening to them.

Pearson, who had been aware of the preparations when the C-5 left Clark for Saigon that morning, describes vividly the news of the imminent return. "My first notification of the flight was when the

Command Post (Base Operations) was notified from Saigon that the aircraft was in the process of loading, with the manifest for passengers and crew, and was ready to depart Vietnam. In addition to the normal crew, a C-141 aircraft had landed," she recalled, "and some of the crew from that aircraft augmented the C-5. Once those people were on board, the aircraft took off from the airport and was bound for Clark Air Base. A position description of the flight plan was transmitted to the Command Post by the flight crew."[20] All was in readiness to receive the C-5, both on the tarmac and in the gym at Clark.

The aircraft was in the air.

In the midst of the weeks of frantic endeavor, one woman with the heart of a volunteer and the soul of a poet kept a diary of her daily activities at Clark, activities that were duplicated by many others both at Clark and at Hickam. Jean Fox Holland was living with her daughter Patte and her son-in-law Col L. D. Folts, Division Commander, 375th Airlift Wing at Clark when this incredible series of events began.[21] Holland involved herself from the first moment and recorded her experiences as they happened. Her writing is consecutive, dated, orderly, yet full of emotion, very revealing of the tone and the heart of Babylift, beginning with the very first day:

> *OPERATION—BABYLIFT*
> *APRIL 1975*
> *CLARK AIR BASE—PHILIPPINES*
>
> *Years hence I may recall with calm*
> *The Babylift from Vietnam,*
> *But now it makes me weep to tell*
> *Of angels flying out of Hell.*
> > *-Jean Fox Holland*
>
> *OH, LORD, WHAT AN APRIL!*
> *I MAY NEVER STOP CRYING.*
>
> *Thursday, April 3, 1975, Clark Air Base, P.I.*
>
> *BULLETIN: FALL OF SOUTH VIETNAM IMMINENT.*
> *2,000 ORPHANS TO BE FLOWN OUT OF SAIGON*
>
> *The telephone rings.*
> *History is calling.*

Come ON! HURRY! Your hair's O.K.! Let's GO!

Alerted in the early afternoon, 40 or 50 assorted Air Force dependents drop bridge cards or bestsellers or bikinis or bonbons and report to Chapel 1 for a briefing on BABIES. My Patte knows the short way to the Chapel, so we are among the first arrivals.

Electric excitement charges the room. Even voices crackle and sparkle. Not every day does the word go out to expect 2,000 BABIES! WOW! That does something to a woman's mind.

"Ages three months to ten years," the chaplain says. (Actually, the youngest is only three hours into life when evacuated.)

BULLETIN: CRITICAL NEEDS: DIAPERS, TOWELS, WASHCLOTHS, SOAP, BOTTLES, FORMULA, CLOTHING, TOYS. BRING DONATIONS TO CHAPEL 1.

Remember RICE! Warns a thoughtful Filipino.

A Family Services Representative recommends that Baby Care Shifts run 5 to 11 and 11 to 5. Each Volunteer will take one baby off the plane, take that baby on a bus to the improvised Super Nursery (Base Gym) and stay with that baby, completely responsible for its well-being for six hours.

That sounds O.K., but looking around the room and dividing the possibly 40 people present into 2,000, one attractive gal asks another, "Think you can handle 50 babies?" The quick answer is positive, "Absolutely! My five often make me feel that I have 50 of my own."

But Clark's bamboo telegraph is spreading the news. Soon the Chapel is full of eager Volunteers signing up for unlimited duty. Women are coming out of the walls. Men, too. The final count of volunteers is 3,500.

Sometimes I'm not ashamed to be a people.

The response is terrific, stupendous, colossal. Choose your adjective, all are inadequate. I shall never again spell Volunteer with a lower case v.

Someone sums it up, "Whatever the need is, Chaplain, we'll meet it."

On that critical day at Clark Air Base, the chapel, and later the gymnasium, were filled with people excited at the prospect of the job that lay ahead, who would, in later years, have been called "a thousand points of light," when President George H.W. Bush would acknowledge in his 1988 nomination acceptance speech and again in his 1989 inaugural address that there is a need for such "points of light" in a dark time.

Throughout Vietnam among the orphanage workers and the American dependents, and across the globe at military bases—Clark in the Philippines, Hickam in Hawaii, Travis and the Presidio in California—in San Francisco and Seattle and Denver, and in homes across the United States, Canada, Australia, and Europe, the world was ready and waiting for news of the first authorized flight, the C-5A Galaxy that everyone believed would take hundreds of infants and children to safety.

C-5A Galaxy

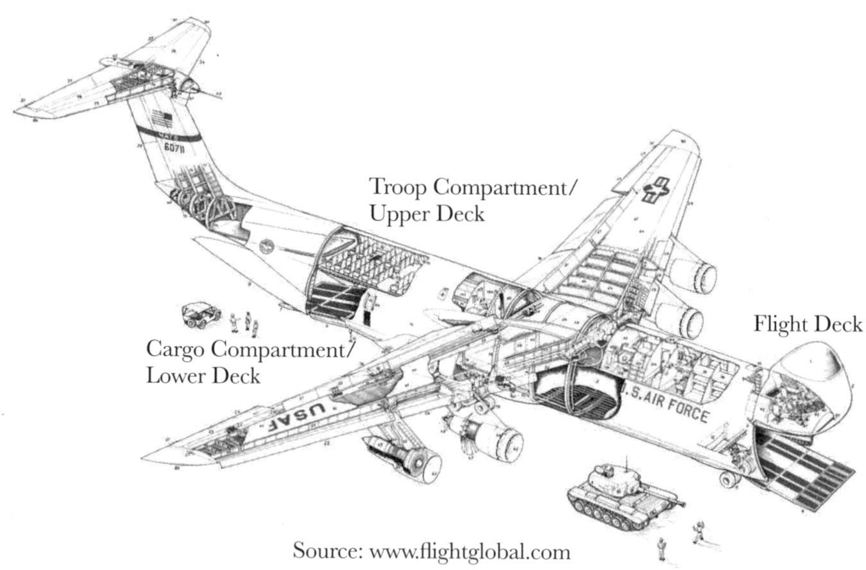

Source: www.flightglobal.com

6

Devastating Heartbreak

Throughout the days of preparation and waiting, Holland continued to record the events, her thoughts and feelings, and her observations as teams of workers set up for the care of so many children, until, inexplicably, they were told the flight was "delayed" and to go home.

Friday, April 4, 1975, Clark Air Base, P.I.
Are you still with me?
What a day!
The whole base is buzzing.
Phones ring constantly, maddeningly, gloriously.
This is better than being in the tenth month of gestation after taking
fertility pills.
What will we DO if the babies come NOW—this minute?
Let 'em come. We'll manage.
Where is that plane?
Any word yet?
What's happening in Saigon?
Do you know that Saigon is just 2 ½ HOURS from Clark Air Base?

What can I do?
Stay busy.
What can I do NOW?

Sometimes it isn't easy to find jobs for all the willing muscle. Even so, I assure you that there is PLENTY TO DO, like instantly, on the double, SIGI-SIGI!

For starters, there are 700 mattresses to be located and transported plus three or four dozen cribs for infants, plus sheets, blankets, towels, etc., etc. This proves to be one of the easier tasks. The real hair-puller is when donations begin to come in by the ton and must be sorted and assessed.

BUT WHERE ARE THE DIAPERS AND THE BOTTLES AND THE NIPPLES?

I appeal to Irene and Jo-Jo and Nita, three Filipino friends, "We'd better start praying for diapers and bottles."

THAT takes care of THAT.

Volunteers are working frantically putting newly acquired liners in hundreds of newly acquired plastic bottles — when the word comes: "Flight indefinitely delayed. Go home. Listen to your radios."

You know the rest.

BULLETIN: A U.S. AIR FORCE C-5 CARGO PLANE CARRYING 243 WAR ORPHANS TO THE UNITED STATES CRASHED NEAR SAIGON. MORE THAN HALF OF THE REPORTED 319 PERSONS ABOARD WERE KILLED, INCLUDING AT LEAST 100 ORPHANS.

The plane had crashed.

Two days after Ford's announcement, this first authorized C-5A Galaxy military transport carrying hundreds of children and escorts crashed soon after takeoff. The rear cargo doors failed, decompressing the plane and crippling the flight controls. According to USAF Southeast Asia Monograph *Last Flight from Saigon*, "At 23,000 feet during climbout and 10 miles off the Vietnamese coast near Vung Tau, the C-5 experienced a massive structural failure in the rear cargo door area. In a considerable feat of airmanship, Captain Dennis Traynor and his crew nursed the aircraft back over Saigon and attempted to make an emergency landing at Tan Son Nhut. The explosive decompression had blown out a huge section of the cargo ramp and door and cut all control cables to the rudder and elevator. Using only ailerons (and engine power for pitch control), Captain Traynor was forced to crash land in flooded rice paddies about five miles short of the Tan Son Nhut runway. The aircraft touched down initially on the east side of the Saigon River, bounced, and flew about one-half mile across the river where it touched down again and broke up into four major sections."[1]

Capt Traynor himself relates details of the event: "We took off (from Saigon) and the rear locks weren't sharing the load equally, and then when one of the locks failed, it made the ramp drop into the slipstream and it started the unzipping. As you can imagine, if you picked at a zipper until you undid one of the pieces that was holding, the rest of it's just going to unzip, which it did. It proceeded to unzip the ramp and unzip the pressure door, because each time you would ask the next lock to carry all the load, it says, 'Can't do it!' and boom, the ramp blew out. The real problem was that when the door blew out, it took two of the four hydraulic systems, and what that did was confuse us a great deal, because although I had hydraulic power powering all the actuators to the tail, when the door went, it also cut all the flight control cables. It appeared that everything should be working, but it wasn't. For the next 15 minutes, on the way back, we were trying to figure out what could possibly be wrong.

"In the meantime, I had been stationed over there, so I was quite familiar with where we were, so I said, 'alright, I'll just make a visual approach to the runway,' and did so. With the extension of the gear and the flight controls to the tail, the drag was too much, and it just started to pull us down to the ground. I couldn't turn; as soon as I started to turn, as you can imagine, the wings are opposing gravity, and when you bank, perpendicular to the ground, your wing span is shortened. As you turn, your lift opposing gravity becomes less because of the reduced area of the wing span. At that point, I still thought I could pull it off...but when we got down within a couple hundred feet of the ground, we got 'ground effect,' a cushion of air underneath the wings. I pulled the throttles down to idle and we touched down at a reasonable vertical velocity. The trouble was, of course, it wasn't a runway, it was a rice paddy and we were going 300 miles an hour, so it tore up the airplane. They had helicopters on us in about four minutes. I had been talking to them all the way down, so they were almost waiting for me to come to a stop."[2]

At the time of the devastating Rapid Decompression (RD), which happened when the change in air pressure caused anything near the cargo doors to be sucked out of the airplane, Lt Aune had just climbed up the aft ladder to the upper troop compartment to obtain medication for an adult passenger in the cargo area, where she had been on takeoff. "At the moment of the RD," she remembers, "I was kneeling on the grate in the floor in the aft section of the troop compartment, talking to one of the loadmasters and closing the medications kit. It was a classic RD, and once the fog cleared, and I could look down through the grate to the cargo hold below, I saw the South China Sea, a vast, sparkling prism of diamonds as the sun glinted off the water. The sight was at once beautiful and horrifying."[3]

The hole in the back of the plane allowed sunlight to stream in, and Air Force Sergeant Jim Hadley, a medical technician in the troop compartment, saw things flying around after the Rapid Decompression: "Eye glasses. Pens. Pieces of insulation off the ceiling. The pillows exploded. That went on for a little while until the air stopped. By then the oxygen masks had dropped down. There weren't enough oxygen masks. We had to keep moving them from kid to kid. We kept on our own because otherwise you get drowsy and then you go out."[4]

An unidentified nurse agreed that the oxygen was a problem, saying the children were "getting dopey from a lack of oxygen," but that the adults had time to discuss where to exit the plane on impact, and that they stayed with the children to administer oxygen while they planned their exit strategy.[5] Of course, in the end, it was only those on the upper deck who were able to exit at all.

While Loadmasters MSgt Wendle Payne and TSgt Felizardo Aguillon were administering oxygen and tending the refugees in the cargo compartment after the Rapid Decompression, they reported to the flight deck that "most passengers were imploring them to continue to the Philippines rather than return to Saigon."[6] Desperation is reflected in that request, and an indication of the intensity of the desire to escape the war-torn environment they had left behind. But the return to Saigon was the only option.

Capt Traynor describes his efforts to control the aircraft and land with the least damage possible: "I flew the power for pitch; the copilot flew the remaining aileron for bank. In the turn to final approach, with the gear extending, we couldn't add enough power to keep the nose up and still bank the aircraft. I told the copilot to 'take it straight ahead.' Even at this point I felt we could pull out of it and try again. We were wings level coming through 1500 feet with the nose rising. We pushed the throttles to the firewall, torching the unburned fuel behind us, leading some to assume that we were on fire.

"Around 500 feet, I determined that we would likely impact the ground and slapped the throttles to idle. We entered ground effect and hit about 1500 feet rate of descent. We seemed to glance easily back into the air; I hadn't realized that the copilot put the flaps to full soon after I pulled the throttles to idle. We skimmed over the Saigon River and impacted on top of 4 or 5 men helplessly watching us skim the water.

"After the second impact, the aircraft broke into component parts: The upper decks survived largely intact; however, the Cargo Compartment crushed and was abraded away. The tail dropped off, the wings and Troop Compartment flew up slightly, leaving the flight deck to roll inverted and skid 180 degrees. Unencumbered by the rest of the aircraft, the wings took the Troop Compartment for a relatively gentle 1000-foot skid, broke off, and proceeded further downwind and burned—away from everything and everybody."[7]

In the Troop Compartment, Lt Aune knew nothing of the deliberate and well-controlled efforts of the flight crew to control the descent and landing. She knew only what those in that location felt. "Our first impact with the ground," she writes, "was a hard bump and then we seemed to be airborne again. Our second impact with the ground was much more violent. Although I had secured myself to the floor near the aft section of seats in the troop compartment, I was thrown the length of the aisle, past twelve rows of seats, and ended up at the wall that separated the troop compartment from the aircraft environmental systems and the flight deck. Once the plane, or what was left of it, had come to a complete stop, crew members began to assess the children and the adults for injuries."[8]

Moments after the crash landing, Mavis Pearson at Clark learned that "shortly after takeoff, a message was received by the controller that the C-5A had crashed in a rice paddy; no more information was provided. That transmission was called in from one of the controllers at Base Ops to the wing commander's office via the 'hot line' phone connection direct to the center. The commander was on the direct line to 22AF/CC at Travis and when the 'hot line' rang in his office, he was told the C-5A Babylift aircraft had crashed."[9] That was the only information they had at the time.

"I reported to the Command Post," Pearson recalls, "and assisted the Command Post Operations Controllers with setting up the communications systems that were connected to the American Embassy in Saigon and with the ground controllers. Once this transmission system was set up, information and photos through the media to TV networks throughout the world could be passed safely without a breach of security. Pictures of the crash site were received, rescue plans were briefed and the new mission for evacuation was set in motion." Pearson remained in the control center for six hours helping to monitor the data and re-transmit information to other bases that would be involved in the transit of the babies. She returned to the office to help with the number of phone calls, messages requesting information from the media and the security of information for release.[10]

Last Flight from Saigon goes on to describe details of the tragedy: "From the crew compartment, upper passenger compartment, and the remnants of the fuselage section, 175 survivors of the crash were able to climb out. The crew members, after freeing themselves, assisted in pulling other survivors from the aircraft wreckage.[11] Within minutes of the crash, Air America and Vietnamese Air Force helicopters from Tan Son Nhut and Bien Hoa Air Base were on the scene rescuing survivors, who were taken to Tan Son Nhut Air Base, a small Vietnamese hospital, the Seventh Day Adventist Hospital in Saigon, and to Thailand. Later, they recovered the bodies of those killed in the crash."[12]

Nearly half the children, service members, and volunteers were killed in the crash, almost all of them in the lower cargo compartment. The *Honolulu Star-Bulletin* reported, "Headless bodies were buried in the mud. A baby's bottle, a flight manual, cushions, clothing, and molten pieces of metal were scattered about in the burning grass. 'It was a horrible thing to see,' a witness said, 'Children were crying while the fire burned.'"[13]

Lt Aune, thrown the length of the upper deck main aisle, realized that her right foot was badly broken and that she was bleeding heavily from her left arm and right leg. Not knowing in the moment who was alive and who was dead, she dragged herself off the deck, checked her passengers as best she could, and opened an emergency exit to help the crew and medics remove children from the aircraft. Again and again in this painful condition, she and the other adult survivors, along with rescue workers who dropped from the helicopters, waded through the mud, carrying terrified children to the hovering helicopters.

Adding to the difficulty of the rescue was the backwash from the helicopter blades, which threw so much debris and muddy water into the air that the adults had to walk backwards through the mud carrying two or three terrified children, in order to avoid being blasted with flying trash. Crews on the helos called out to them when they were near enough to place the babies in the aircraft, at which point they would turn around, hand their burdens into the helos, and turn again to repeat the trip. How long Aune struggled before losing consciousness, she does not know.[14] "Finally, unable to go on," Capt Traynor tells us, "she staggered toward an approaching officer. She managed to stand straight and said, 'Sir, I request to be relieved of my duties since my injuries prevent me from carrying on.' She then passed out."[15] The officer caught her and carried her to the helicopter. Later, at a Saigon hospital, Lt Aune learned that, in addition to her bloody lacerations and broken foot, she had a serious puncture wound of the same leg and a compression fracture at L3 in her back. In this condition, she had helped carry 149 children to the rescue helicopters.[16]

The *Honolulu Advertiser* published details of the crash on the front page, reporting that the two huge cargo doors—large enough for three jeeps to pass through simultaneously—had blown off, "suddenly decompressing the cabin, sucking some of the babies outside, and tearing most of the clothing off those strapped down. Almost all bodies brought into Saigon hospitals were naked," reported the article, going on to say, "The rice field was a scene of horror worse than many battlefields. Tiny fingers clutched, in death, a woman's breast. The lifeless arms of a woman still gripped the corpse of the baby she had tried to protect. Their bodies were loaded onto the deck of a Chinook helicopter."[17]

None of the adult survivors escaped unscathed, though some of the injuries were not serious. SMSgt Snedegar, in the Relief Crew Compartment above the cargo area, had very minor injuries: debris in one eye, scrapes on his shins, and a concussion from falling out of his seat onto his head when he released the seatbelt in the upside-down Crew Compartment. The most memorable pain occurred through the next few days, when his body "was excruciatingly sore from overextending every muscle in my body during the rescue and recovery operation immediately after the aircraft had come to a stop."[18]

Injured not in the crash but in the Rapid Decompression, MSgt Perkins had just climbed the ladder to the troop compartment when the door blew. He was reaching over the gate at the top of the ladder clinging to the railing and was not blown from the aircraft when the RD occurred, but both legs snapped in the direction of the hole. Pulled into the Troop Compartment by the adults there, he splinted his legs with a crutch and seatbelts and, after the crash landing, he assisted in the effort to carry the orphans to the helicopters.[19]

Col Aune has vivid memories of her arrival at Clark, late that night with the other injured crew members, to be taken to the hospital there: "Just a few minutes before midnight, the blue runway lights twinkled in the darkness as the C-9 touched down at Clark Air Base. Our arrival was greeted by security police, key officials at Clark, hospital staff, and members of the Clark Air Base family. What I remember most about that landing, aside from its smoothness and gentleness (a feat promised by the aircraft commander), were the people who stood along the fences of the flight line in silent solidarity and unashamed grief."[20] The landing was so smooth that the injured on board never felt it. And the hospital staff included both day shift and night shift—no one went home until the C-9 had arrived safely and the injured had been unloaded and safely ensconced in hospital beds.[21]

The next morning, Capt Traynor, who had stayed in Saigon, relates, "I asked permission to return to the accident site to retrieve the bodies of Capt Klinker and SSgt Paget, both pinned in the forward part of the flight deck wreckage. Permission granted. About 6 A.M. the next morning, I caught a helicopter flight from Tan Son Nhut to the crash site and arrived to find dozens of scavengers in the area." Traynor goes on to describe the difficult extraction effort among scavengers and debris, another sad aspect of the ongoing tragedy. "More Air America folks arrived and we began the extraction effort to free the bodies of Capt Klinker and SSgt Paget. We picked up several aircraft 10,000-pound tie-down chains, hooked them together and with the assistance of about a dozen or so locals, heave-ho'd the piece of the flight deck pinning the two remaining crewmembers and got them out."[22]

In a supreme irony, just a day before the tragedy, USAID "had yanked the same group of orphans from a chartered World Airways plane because it was believed unsafe,"[23] a decision undoubtedly made with the best of intentions, but ultimately with the worst of results for the children and sponsors who would be the first to fly on an authorized flight.

Television coverage and newspapers around the world related the tragedy. According to the *Honolulu Star-Bulletin*, "The first official U.S. evacuation flight of Vietnamese orphans, carrying 243 children in the world's largest plane, ended in explosions and flames today when the plane crashed only minutes after takeoff from Saigon. U.S. officials said nearly half the children survived and the airlift to the United States ordered by President Ford would continue."[24] The crash of the first orphan flight was "the fourth worst aircraft disaster on record," reported the *Honolulu Star-Bulletin*,[25] and "the worst disaster in U.S. aviation history," according to *The Honolulu Advertiser*.[26]

For Aune, Traynor, Snedegar, and the other surviving flight crew and medical team members, the evacuation was over. For everyone else, it was just beginning.

7

....

Speculation

Shock waves flowed over everyone involved in the brave effort. When the emergency was over and the survivors attended to, the losses were found to be enormous. Five of the flight crew were dead. Lt Col William S. Willis, at the request of Gen John F. Gonge, Commander of the 22nd Air Force, had accompanied the flight as a MAC observer. Willis, a father himself and a willing caregiver, was at one point sitting next to Lt Aune on the small bench along the side of the cargo compartment, along with Capt Mary Klinker. After the tragedy, Willis was found on the lower deck with the children he was trying to save. Three of the medical team, Capt Klinker, SSgt Paget, and TSgt Johnson were lost as well, along with many other adults and almost everyone in the cargo compartment. Nearly all of the children there perished.[1] It was a bitter blow to all those who had tried so hard to save the innocent victims of war.

Capt Traynor was praised by U.S. officials for flying the crippled plane the 40 miles back toward Tan Son Nhut Airport; Traynor himself, whose location in the cabin had allowed him to escape unhurt, said he was "about 18 miles from Tan Son Nhut" when he had to turn back, a discrepancy in distance that illustrates the confusion and the difficulty of obtaining accurate information in the tragedy of the moment.[2]

The C-5 crew and medical team "faced the challenges and demonstrated personal valor and incredible teamwork"[3] in spite of numerous disadvantages. Despite their inexperience with this particular aircraft—and despite being unaware of the big picture of Babylift, nor of recent events such as the fall of Nha Trang and Cam Rahn Bay, nor of the fact that five North Vietnamese divisions had amassed 75 miles north of Saigon and were rapidly moving south—despite lacking any of this information about the imminent danger, everyone on the C-5 performed their duties with efficiency, courage, and singular focus.

For Loadmaster SMSgt Snedegar, the hours after leaving Clark for Saigon were "exhilarating, a day of hope and promise, a day of hard work, a day of joy that turned to sorrow, a day of horror, a day of heroism at so many levels, a day of anguish, a day that I wished had never happened."[4] Like other participants, Snedegar would in time find perspective that would help to make the anguish bearable, though it would always be a part of him.

Questions immediately arose as to the cause of the crash, and suspicions of sabotage were common. The *Star-Bulletin* reported on April 4, "Military sources said today there is a 'definite possibility' that sabotage might have caused the crash of the C-5A transport plane loaded with South Vietnamese orphans," adding that the cargo doors are built so that the pilot's controls should not be damaged if the doors blow out.[5] Yet on April 5, Pentagon officials in Washington said, "It is at this time not appropriate to speculate" on what might have been the cause of the lost cargo doors,[6] and the headquarters of the 13th Air Force in the Philippines "refused to comment on reports that the plane's departure from Manila …had been delayed by mechanical trouble."[7]

In fact, the "mechanical trouble" was a windshield installation made necessary when the C-5 "arrived at Hickam from Travis with the copilot's windshield inoperative." The crew carried a new windshield from Hickam for later installation, which was done at Clark before the Saigon flight. The only mention by Col Traynor of the cargo doors' condition on takeoff from Tan Son Nhut is this: "MSgt Payne was administering an evaluation to TSgt Aguillon as he closed the rear doors; TSgt Bradley was outside scanner. Non-Commissioned Officer In Charge MSgt Perkins confirmed all door warning indicator lights were out. Everybody was at the top of their game. Everything—the offload, onload, and passenger preparations—went smoothly and professionally."[8]

A U.S. Embassy spokesman in Saigon ruled out sabotage, saying that the plane's departure from Clark in the Philippines had been delayed because of "minor mechanical problems" that were unrelated to the cargo doors.[9] At this point, one Congressman in Washington, Wisconsin Representative Les Aspin, urged that all C-5As be grounded because the plane "has never performed up to specifications," citing wing problems.[10] Like many of the facts of Babylift, conflicting information adds to the confusion today, as it did in 1975.

Reactions at Clark and Hickam to the tragedy were identical, reflecting the optimism that was dashed so cruelly to splinters. "I've never seen the morale and the reaction of the people on the base so high as it was for Babylift," General Manor remembers. "We got word that this was going to take place and for us to get ready. We devoted one of the gymnasiums completely to the project. We made it a baby hospital. We brought in additional doctors, additional nurses, and…in a matter of two days we had this set up and were ready and waiting, and that was when the C-5 was supposed to come in the afternoon. It was going to be a large group, as a matter of fact as I recall, over 300 babies, and there were many who perished, including some military people and some civilians from the Embassy."[11]

With sadness still, after so many years, Manor remembers, "Everyone was waiting for the first big flight of orphans to come through. We learned late in the afternoon what had happened, and it was a great disappointment and from that point on, of course, the C-5 was never used again for that purpose; other aircraft were."[12] To this day, Manor's most vivid memory of the whole Babylift experience is, after working so hard to prepare, that moment when word of the crash came and the realization of what it meant struck home.[13]

Shock waves reached Hickam with no less sorrow. "The crash killed a number of the staff and many of the babies," Ann remembers, "which just broke all our hearts; it was just devastating to all of us who were working so hard to save these children."

Cheryl Markson, of Friends for Children of Vietnam, in Saigon with Thu Duc orphanage, sobbed, "It's the most horrible thing that could happen. It doesn't matter whose kids died."[14] For parents who already had children assigned to them, the wait following the crash was painful.

Adoption agencies were getting calls from frantic parents begging to know the fate of their little ones after the crash. All anyone knew was that the first authorized Operation Babylift plane had crashed with hundreds of children aboard. Who the children were was impossible to know at that point. For FCVN, it didn't matter in the moment whose children had died—the tragedy was that any of them had. But as the hours passed, it became urgent to identify children and contact their waiting families. For most, the wait was a long one.[15]

In Saigon, LeAnn Thieman tried frantically to contact her husband with the news that she and their son were not on the flight, but communication was impossible, and the original plan had been for the two of them to be on the first authorized flight out. Her husband did not know that their group had been "bumped" to the next flight. Thieman would be in the Philippines the next day before the Red Cross could notify her husband that she was safe, and yet another day would pass before LeAnn could call him herself from Honolulu to say that she was bringing home their son.[16]

Actor Yul Brynner and his wife, Jacqueline, called the agencies, attempting to determine whether their second adopted child, a little girl, was safe. Having already adopted a girl who was now 18 months old, they had applied for a sister for her. Finding no one who really knew the details, Mrs. Brynner said, "We are looking for help—not only for ourselves, but for everybody. Only God can help us all."[17] In the end, the Brynners were among the fortunate ones; their little girl survived.

Like the Brynners in Boston, Edward and Louise Moos in Westfield, New Jersey, sat by the phone in hope of hearing news. "My wife and I began adoption proceedings 18 months ago for our daughter," Moos said. "We feel great sadness. We have no way of knowing whether our daughter is on that plane. She could be."[18]

For Roland and Mary King in Pittsburgh, sadness turned to relief when they learned that their 5-month-old adopted daughter was not on the plane. "The past two days have been an emotional roller coaster," Mrs. King said. "But now I can't remember a happier day in my life."[19]

More than 100 waiting families, of course, would receive the most heartbreaking news, their grief understood only by those who knew how parents could love a child they had never seen, a child they had been promised, a child for whom they had waited in great anticipation for months, in some cases, years.

In San Francisco, President Ford, who had planned to meet the
first plane, announced sadly, "Our mission of mercy will continue. The
survivors will be flown here when they are physically able. Other waiting
orphans will make the journey. This tragedy must not deter us, but offer
new hope for the living."[20] U.S. officials continued their efforts, working
around the clock to plan transport for the orphans. Military Airlift
Command set up military transports, Air Force C-141 Starlifters, to fly the
children from Saigon to Clark Air Base, with plans for civilian airlines to
carry them out of Clark. A MAC spokesman said the command at Scott
Air Force Base in Illinois would contact airlines and attempt to charter
civilian planes for the operation. One airline official said, "It looks like
they're talking to everyone who flies a Boeing 747."[21] Though indeed the
C5-A Galaxy was not used again, Operation Babylift continued.

Oddly, on the same page with the report of the crash, the *Honolulu
Star-Bulletin* included an article quoting Murray Brown, deputy district
director of the U.S. INS in Honolulu, as saying that he knew of "no
plans to bring refugees to Hawaii," and that "planes bringing orphans to
the United States will go to Travis Air Force Base in California," adding
that, "anyone who is taken ill in transit will be hospitalized in Hawaii if
necessary—we have made plans for that."

Even at Honolulu's Tripler Military Hospital, a spokesman said
that they had "received no orders to move or to prepare to move any
medical personnel now stationed (in Hawaii) to Vietnam or other bases
closer to Vietnam." Such orders, the spokesman said, "would come
from Washington."[22] Apparently, only the on-base military at Clark and
Hickam expected to be involved in Operation Babylift.

It seemed that Washington was too far away to see the nature and
the intensity of the emergency. Medical personnel would be needed at
Hickam, for there was no way to care for the orphans in Vietnam, even
if doctors from Tripler had been sent there. The military commanders
on bases and their personnel seemed to be the only ones who understood
what was actually going to happen—and that hundreds of children could
not be loaded onto planes in Saigon and flown directly the nearly 7,000
miles to Travis Air Force Base. There had to be stops, and at every stop
there had to be care of all kinds given by hundreds of volunteers—not
simply hospitalization for the children who might become ill en route.
Many of the orphans were ill when they boarded and becoming more
critical by the hour. Certainly both Clark and Hickam were preparing

for the influx even as the INS was unable to recognize the severity of the problem or the enormity of the operation or the desperate need.

Ed Daly had provided an awakening to the need; President Ford had provided a promise. Now, faced with tragedy and loss unimagined by anyone, the disaster provided an impetus to honor those who were lost by finishing the job they had started with that first heartbreaking flight. Not even a pause in the effort changed the purpose of Operation Babylift; indeed the heartbreak increased the determination, dedication, and compassion of the military and civilian participants at all the bases and in all the countries. Babylift would fly again.

8

Carrying On:
The Morning After

A t Clark, the morning after the crash dawned bright and hot
as the saddened volunteers prepared again for an influx of
orphans, and wept with joy and tenderness when the children, many of
them survivors of the previous day's tragedy, arrived on a C-141 military
aircraft. The children were met with a warmth and affection that would
carry through to the end of Babylift. As later flights came through Clark,
the volunteers would experience tiny children clinging to them, attaching
themselves, but it was not just the children who did not want to let go. The
caregivers themselves would find difficult the necessity of bonding with
them, and then passing them on to an unknown future, trusting them to
the collective greatness of heart that would take them on their way.

Considerably smaller than the C-5, the C-141 was used for most
of the succeeding Babylift flights. With a wing span of 160 feet and a
fuselage length of 168 feet, the aircraft had a smaller cargo deck, but
a troop compartment with the same number of seats as the C-5. For
twenty years the C-141 had been the primary aircraft used to re-supply
McMurdo Research Station on the Pegasus Glacier in Antarctica.[1]
Dependable and consistent, it would serve the military well for decades,
with no mission more urgent than Operation Babylift.

Holland reveals how well the care plan worked and how efficiently the children were offloaded and stabilized by feeding, bathing, and medical care. Most important, perhaps, is her tender revealing of the kindness and love that wrapped each child, the fears that were soothed, the security that was offered as children were held and cuddled and as, at last, they slept.

Saturday, April 5, 1975, Clark Air Base, P.I.
I may never stop crying.
Yesterday we prayed for baby-bottles.
In the greater, sadder wisdom of today, we pray for BABIES to give the bottles to, whether we have enough bottles or not.

Please, God, send the babies.
We'll feed them. Send them on.
Please, God, send the babies.
Safely from Saigon.

Again our prayers are answered.
The first flight of Vietnamese War Orphans is landing at Clark Air Base.
Some are survivors of yesterday's tragedy.

My blurred vision clears as, two by two, the double row of Volunteers march out to meet the plane.
I stand and wait. I behold a miracle.
In one door with empty arms; out the other door each Volunteer comes, cuddling a precious fragment of humanity. A remnant has been spared. Love is tangible.

A tidal wave of emotion sweeps through the hangar carrying us all on its crest. No man can keep back his tears. No woman even tries.
These are the most thrilling moments of my life.

BABIES! BABIES! BABIES! BABIES ALIVE!

I hope they will never stop coming.
But of course, they do. Only 31. Not even one-third as many as died on the C-5 Galaxy yesterday.
No one really knows how many died.
No one will ever know.

Heartbroken though they were, with the situation increasingly desperate and with Saigon imminently falling, frantic workers in the orphanages and at Tan Son Nhut had no time for tears, though, like the volunteers at Clark and Hickam, they must have carried on with grieving hearts. Their focus remained on transporting children to the airport and loading them onto any possible flight. The first to leave, within hours after the crash, were 31 children aboard a C-141 that had brought military equipment into Saigon and returned to Clark with the children. A Pan American Airways Boeing 747 that same day carried 409 children and 60 escorts safely to Seattle via Tokyo, a flight that was independent of the U.S. government program, having been chartered by Holt International. And there were others. A second 747 carried 40 orphans from the Friends for All Children (FFAC) agency, children who had survived the horror of the C-5A Galaxy crash, and a C-141 carried 100 children and 10 escorts for Catholic Relief Services.

A Canadian Royal Air Force C-130 took 63 children from Cambodia and Vietnam out of Saigon to Hong Kong and ultimately to adoption in Canada. The Australian Air Force took another 200 children to safety in Australia. In addition, on that day, a Boeing 707 jetliner, chartered by the London Daily Mail newspaper, left England for Saigon to bring back 150 orphans for adoption in Britain. During the 24 hours following the crash of the C5-A, the whole world had stepped up to the plate for the children.[2]

Of all those who stepped up, no group surpassed the 1st Test Squadron at Clark Air Base in compassion or dedication. Flight after flight, bus after bus saw untiring volunteers returning to fulfill the needs of the orphans, and equally the needs of their own hearts. Holland's diary continues with vivid, lyrical prose that reveals how much the operation affected the many volunteers, and how intensely caring for the children became a project for her family, the Folts parents and children:

> *There are some infants so tiny that they are carried off the plane in CARDBOARD BOXES, sometimes three in one box. Precious buds of human life. Yes! BUDS! FLOWERS! The Volunteers look like florists delivering boxes of flowers.*
>
> *I may never stop crying.*
> *But I must!*
> *Another flight is on the ground! This time there are 110 babies!*

Hallelujah! Hallelujah!

I never believed in the stork before.
But there the big bird is—on the runway.
An interpreter, who leaves the plane carrying a child, is needed at the
reception center. I offer to take his charge and he hands him over. A tired
little head pillows itself on my shoulder. Two little arms hold on to me for
dear life.

VIP buses are waiting.
I board one with some difficulty, being admittedly, a grandmother-type
with irresolute ankles and wobbly knees. As soon as thirty Volunteers
are seated holding our respective Vietnamese children, two Taggers come
aboard and the bus follows a police escort to the gym-nursery-in-waiting.
Someone comes to tag my baby boy, explaining this important procedure.
This is F-U-N-N-Y, because my Patte is Captain of the Tagger Teams
and is setting up the Color Code. So guess who is working many, many,
many, many hours—with the help of Wagner High School students and
other unwary souls?
RIGHT!
My Patte's MOTHER!
I listen politely.

Each flight is color coded. To identify which group comes on which flight,
each child is tagged with a numbered card in its flight color.
So we must make:
200 Red Tags with Red Happy Faces on both sides!
200 Blue Tags with Blue Happy Faces on both sides!
200 Orange Tags with Orange Happy Faces on both sides!
200 Green Tags with Green Happy Faces on both sides!
200 Purple Tags with Purple Happy Faces on both sides!
200 Black Tags with Black Happy Faces on both sides!

Print the name of the color on each tag so there can be no mistake.
Number each tag with the same number on both sides.
Tie each tag with yarn. Measure enough yarn so it can circle a baby's
ankle or wrist or an older child's neck. (Who would have thought that our
beautiful afghan would serve such a beautiful purpose?)
Make 50 special Hospital Tags of each color.
Check for errors in numbering.
Double check.
And NOW, we may begin all over again!

HAPPINESS IS HELPING TO DRAW
HAPPY FACES ON 2,000 NUMBER TAGS
FOR 2,000 VIETNAMESE ORPHANS.
And our second-grader adds, "ME, TOO. SU-SU."

But now we are at the gym door.
An arrogantly young Volunteer whisks my little one away.
Feeling bereft and incompetent and at least 99 years old, I call after him in
a quavering voice, "God Bless you, Baby Boy."

Babylift had barely begun, with one load of 31 children and another of 100, when the media began to publish estimates of the enormity of the need. "At this point," according to the *Honolulu Star-Bulletin*, "adoption officials estimated there were 18,000 to 25,000 orphaned children in the Saigon area, most of them not eligible for foreign adoption," since they had to be under 7 years old and without any parents.[3] Apparently, Amerasian children, who had Vietnamese mothers, did not qualify under Vietnam's rules, even though it was widely believed that having American fathers placed them more at risk than other children. In the orphanages, these children were often the ones whose rescues were deemed most urgent.

At Clark and at Hickam, preparations were more than complete, for after the heartbreak of the crash, volunteers yearned to be able to do something—anything—for the "wretched refuse"[4] described on the American Statue of Liberty, the homeless of a collapsing nation. Members of 1st Test Squadron at Clark answered the call eagerly. The first flights to Clark that day were met with orderly enthusiasm at the runway, where Gen Manor and the many volunteers were ready for them. After a two and a half hour flight, the children's enormous needs were met by volunteers that included Patte and her mother, as well as the other women—and some of the men—of the squadron, working among the hundreds of other volunteers. Surviving couples tell touching stories of the days and nights of Babylift:

Captain Fred Aldrian was a 1st Test Squadron pilot stationed at Clark whose wife Kathy recalls, "They were airlifting people into Clark and they let us know, the officers' wives group, that they needed help. I had four young children myself at the time, but I spent one night there. It seemed like there was a lot of illness, and I remember seeing sores on their faces and bodies, a lot of babies in cribs."[5]

At Clark, the facility was set up for the babies and children first; later the staff set up a tent city for the rest of the refugees, the families who must be accommodated until they could be moved on to Guam. When the flights started coming in, one after another, everyone involved felt the urgency of managing planeload after planeload of children, followed later by whole families of "boat people" and other refugees as Saigon fell to the Communists.[6]

Of the operations at Clark, Gen Manor remembers, "There was a really wonderful turnout of help in addition to the medical people that I brought in for that purpose. The families, the wives club, the NCO activity, all were absolutely outstanding; I was very proud of them. They worked long hours and made sure that everything was done to enhance the survival of these very small babies."[7]

Maj McAtee, who had been so impressed with the organization when Gen Manor got the word to prepare, concurs. "We signed up to care for the children that arrived via C-141s in rapid order. It seemed the whole base responded, since there was at least one care giver for each child and sometimes two or three. My wife, Ann, and I cared for one who was in very bad shape. We were concerned he wouldn't live. Evidently, he and many of the children with him came from an orphanage where very little food and care were available. His skin was badly marred by rash and a number of sores and he was clearly malnourished. He slept a lot and was disoriented when awake. All he wanted to do was eat, but couldn't digest much. The doctors were phenomenal. Most of them worked the entire time the children were there, taking an occasional power nap when they could."[8]

"It was a heartbreaking event for all of us involved," remembers Carolyn McReynolds, wife of Lt Col Frank (Mac) McReynolds. "My charge was two brothers from Cambodia, one about 10-12 years old and his brother, who was maybe one year or a year and a half. Of course, they were in a state of shock and couldn't speak or understand a word of English. The older brother was older than most of the other children. He was very protective of his younger brother and hugged him and held hands the whole time—never letting him go."[9]

At Honolulu Airport, where one of the first flights after the crash stopped for refueling before going on to Seattle, the children were met again by a massive volunteer effort, this time giving assistance mostly on board the plane. "Many are dehydrated and undernourished," reported Janice Wolf, a staff writer for the *Sunday Star-Bulletin and Advertiser*. "Several have measles, chicken pox, pneumonia, or colds," added a volunteer stewardess. "Some of the children are very frightened. Some of them were in foster homes and very attached to their Vietnamese foster parents."[10]

The children were fed on board during the flight. At mealtime the older children had omelets and sausages, though one stewardess remarked, "I don't think they knew what it was, but they ate it anyway." For the 290 babies below the age of two, there were formula and commercial baby food, as well as 300 cardboard "bassinettes," 400 bottles, and a "seemingly inexhaustible supply of diapers." Escorts included volunteers, doctors, nurses, nutritionists, and social workers, all to see the children on to Seattle en route to the adoptive homes that were waiting for them.[11]

Involved from the beginning, Dr. McKinny boarded the jumbo jet to check the medical situation, and found among the little passengers a number of colds, runny noses, and diarrhea. The doctor was startled by the scene in the plane, saying, "My God, there were 10,000 babies from one end of the plane to the other. And 100 teeny, teeny, teeny, wee ones and I mean small ones. There were bottles stuck in mouths everywhere."[12]

The upstairs lounge was a makeshift hospital, where the children with measles, chicken pox and pneumonia were housed, some receiving intravenous medication. The doctor seemed particularly touched by a four-month-old infant weighing about seven and a half pounds who was dehydrated and suffering from pneumonia. "But he has a spark of life in there that is kicking," McKinney said. "He's going to make it to Seattle."[13]

Like Clark, Hickam had volunteers, many military, some FCVN, some other civilians, available to assist the escorts by boarding the plane to help with feeding and changing chores. Having been kept at Clark long enough for feeding, bathing, and sleeping, the children were perhaps somewhat more stable on arriving at Honolulu.

Pan American cleaning crews boarded the plane to assist by tidying up, though only after they were reassured by Health Department physician Dr. David Pratt that it was medically safe to do so. McKinny recalls details of this flight well. Hawaii's Governor Arioshi had objected publicly to the landing in Hawaii because he feared tropical diseases being brought to the children of the state. McKinny's comment was, "Since when are poverty, malnutrition and neglect catching?" Newspapers and TV picked up this comment, and Arioshi was furious. The difficulty caused by Arioshi's expression of fears was that the cleaning crews, because the children were not being offloaded, had to go on board with them to clean the plane, and they refused to do so because of the governor's comments.

McKinny, like Pratt, went with an immigration officer to talk to the crew and "tell them the reality, that it was no danger…to them." The workers were still afraid of contagion, but they agreed to board if they could wear masks. "So they went on that plane," McKinny recalls, "and I don't think they had those masks on more than thirty seconds. They pulled those masks off, and they were weeping and they were picking up those little orphans. It was a glorious moment for mankind!"[14]

Major Anthony P. (Tony) Callanan and Ginny, volunteering at Clark, felt strongly about getting the innocent children out of the war zone. "I felt badly for them," Ginny says. "I felt badly for them, but at the same time, (my) heart just went out to all those little ones, so darling…They were less than a year old, the group that I saw. They were nine months maybe. They were healthy and just beautiful babies. It was a strange thing. Why?"[15]

Why, indeed? Ginny wonders even now why this group of infants seemed so healthy, while so many others were malnourished and ill. The explanation lies, perhaps, in the fact that different groups came from different situations in Vietnam, with differing degrees of stability. In pure speculation, it is possible that this group of relatively healthy babies was made up largely of those who had been foster children in private homes, and therefore their environment, while not luxurious, could have been more stable. In any case, Ginny was deeply touched just by "being a part of that whole thing."[16]

Col Albert M. Navas, Commander of the 374th Tactical Air Wing, and his wife Barbara were part of the effort, and Barbara speaks of the routine of the volunteers who boarded the planes: "When a plane came in, each baby had a sponsor. We went down the aisle and picked up a baby and talked sweetly to them and took them off the plane. When we came down out of the airplane, we were met by doctors and nurses who checked each child. If there were dire circumstances, they took them to the hospital, or if not, to the refugee center set up for them. They had a system of red tags for the hospital and green tags for the refugee center. There were about 20,000 people at Clark at that time," she recalled, "so there were more than enough volunteers."[17]

While the officers' wives volunteered daily and nightly, whenever a flight came in, the men carried on their normal duties, also working with the orphans almost as a second shift. Captain Parker (Rocket) Rakocy and his wife Rose Marie were part of Clark at the time. Like several of the other officers, Captain Rakocy was in the 1st Test Squadron, code name "Combat Sage," which had specific duties that of course could not be set aside entirely during Babylift. Like the other pilots, he flew his regular missions and sandwiched between them the time to help with the orphans.[18]

Though Tony, Tuck and Rocket had playful nicknames typical of the group, they did not play at their work (although Tony did consider it "fun"). As members of the 1st Test Squadron, they, and others in their group, "tested F-4 air-to-air weapons systems such as the AN/APG-109 radar, AIM-7 (Sparrow) missiles and AIM-9 (Sidewinder) missiles for the aircraft flying combat in North and South Vietnam."[19]

The squadron consisted of approximately 30 members with a variety of functions: Pilots, Navigators, Weapons System Officers, Engineers, Analysts, Controllers, and Maintainers. Most missions were flown against the BQM-34 drones.[20] The men flew F-4 Phantoms and also trained aircrews and maintainers to operate and care for the weapons system and to deploy the missiles in combat.[21] Life, and the war, certainly went on during Babylift, especially for the pilots, yet virtually everyone at Clark understood the importance of the Operation and participated when they could.

The story of the crash of the C-5A is compelling and unforgettable, but it is not the only story. It was the morning after that opened a larger narrative of truth involving thousands of stories—one, in fact, for every orphan, every service member, every volunteer. The tragedy influenced all that followed - all the flights, all the people who worked so hard to give new hope to the tiny victims, all the victims themselves. Such an event is never really over; it lives in the hearts of all who experienced it and who felt the many kinds of pain brought by loss and, finally, the healing brought by time, perspective, and hope. Always, there is a morning after.

9

Moment by Moment, Day by Day

Despite the conflicting feelings around the world about anything related to the war, feelings that would intensify as the days played out, participants in the massive humanitarian effort were uniformly diligent and consistent in their eagerness to help with Operation Babylift. "It really was gratifying to see people turn out," General Manor said, "to set aside their own interests and help out without any complaint."[1] This dedication was reflected in Holland's diary as she recorded her further efforts and her feelings through the experience. Somehow, she seemed to know that, in spite of worldwide press coverage of the operation, it was not possible for people to understand the moment-to-moment drama of the days and nights of hands-on care.

Sunday, April 6, 1975, Clark Air Base, P. I.
Does ANYONE, ANYWHERE know what is happening here?
Would a cynical world believe in totally unselfish commitment?
No matter how the story may be garbled and distorted or even profaned,
surely some of its lucent magnificence will filter through.

I wish everyone I love could be here to share this experience.

The Babies are coming!
99 on the Orange Flight.
The Babies are coming!
79 on the Blue Flight.
Hallelujah! Hallelujah! You won't believe this, but we have 1200
Volunteers to take care of the 300 children who are sheltered in the Base
Gym tonight. Some babies go directly to the hospital. Some must be
isolated. But these 300 must be loved and cared for around the clock, 24
hours, 4 shifts. Figure it out for yourself. This is a SUPER SET-UP
dedicated to the proposition that it is important for each orphan to have
individual love and lots of it during this stop-over with us at Clark. And
it WORKS! Look around you! Listen!
Can you believe that no one is crying?
No one except me, that is.

The diary confirms what Gen Manor and Maj McAtee described as preparations for the anticipated influx of unknown numbers of children, but the logistics of care seemed less essential than the need of the children to be cared for with tenderness and love. "Children were scared," relates Pearson. "They didn't understand the bathing, cleaning, and disinfecting process and some were hard to hold, so an additional escort was assigned. It was a painful process for most of the older children. However, after they were clean and had seen the doctor, food became first with them; suckers were a big success. The diet had to be set for each child and some had to be separated from others so they would not see the food others were getting. Each one got a well-nourished diet and high-protein, well-balanced food provided by the Services Squadron Chow Hall."[2] Through this whole process, each child had a personal caregiver offering love and support.

From the very first flight, the emphasis was on this personal care, having a volunteer for every child. The tendency of many of the frightened, confused orphans to form immediate attachments to the caregivers made difficult the task of caring for them and then letting them go. Each child went through this abandonment many times before arriving at the adoptive home. Though their conditions were more critical and their care more palliative at Clark, the consecutive wrenching away from caregivers at all the locations touched the hearts of everyone involved. Only Holland, an observant and dedicated historian, could record the condition of the children who arrived at Clark and Hickam that month, and withstand the sorrow of letting them go: "I shall not see my young friend again," she writes, "but I cannot forget the questions in his eyes."

Some of these youngsters have runny noses and croupy coughs.
Some of them have broken, split, dirty fingernails that apparently have never been trimmed or cleaned.
Some have impetigo.
Some have diarrhea.
Some are nauseated.
Some have pneumonia.
Too many are polio victims completely helpless without their braces—
BUT THEY DO HAVE BRACES!
Some have measles.
Some have chicken pox.
Some are covered with boils.
Too many are disfigured by cleft palates or harelips that need corrective surgery.
Thank God, only two or three are terribly emaciated, with bones threatening to break through the skin.
Some are filthy.
Some have lice.
Some have bloated bellies, the supreme irony of starvation.
Many are dehydrated.
Some are feverish.
Most are frightened.
Nearly all are slow to smile.
All will hold a friendly hand.
Many will put their arms around you.
Incredibly only one or two are ever crying.
Understandably only one or two are ever laughing.
Most of them are too quiet, too still, too withdrawn.
This sounds grim, I know, but as a whole, the children are in good condition. Surprisingly good condition.

Some of the wee ones are too tiny to believe. After they are bathed and dressed in soft little baby things donated by Clarkites, they are adorable. But then, they are just as sweet or sweeter without ANY clothing. And that is how some of them arrive.
The walking children undergo even more remarkable transformations.

*The Cinderella story comes true again each night the Baby Flights come
through. Water, food, baths, and clean clothing—in that order, work just
as well as waving a magic wand.*

Holland, after giving this litany of specific problems, illnesses,
physical conditions, and behaviors, leads us through her hours with one
older child, "her" child, hours that held similar experiences for other
children and other volunteers throughout the night. Older children would
likely remember their experience, their caregivers, even the loading, the
flight, the unloading. They were more cognizant of their situation, and
they were the ones who needed the harried, overworked interpreters, who
did not normally attach to one child but moved to wherever they were
needed at any given moment. The poet sees these things happening, and
in fact sees one of 'her' children turn to an interpreter for the comfort of
his own language:

This exodus is harder on the older children.
My child tonight is nine years old. He is very thin, very tense, very serious,
and apparently speaks no English. He just looks at me and looks at me
and looks at me. However, he is vastly more relaxed now, since I asked for
help from one of our interpreters. (Vietnamese wives of American Airmen
are giving invaluable help as Volunteers.) After a few words with him, she
reports that he needs to go to the bathroom.

How dumb can I be? Imagine his desperation.
Well, watch me break a few records running with him across the gym floor.
Some of the children do not understand indoor plumbing, but this boy is
different. As soon as I open the door, he dives in.

He is also terribly thirsty. I figure this one out on my own. After draining
a tall paper cup of water, he opens a small zipper bag and unwraps—you
won't believe this—a TWINKIE! I can hardly trust my own bifocals.
Wouldn't you like to know the story behind or before that Twinkie? I am
sure he doesn't need this sweet-treat, because he will soon have dinner. But
how can I tell this solemn hungry child that he can't eat food that is his
very own? Devouring half, he saves half. (Tissue anyone?)
When the chow call comes, he is reluctant to go, and I again appeal to
my interpreter. After a brief talk, he exchanges his frustrated American
grandmother for a charming Vietnamese grandmother who, overhearing the
conversation, offers to stay with him through the night.

Exhausted though she may have been, Holland had the strength and
the presence of mind to fulfill an obligation—to record the historic events
in which she was participating, the "lucent magnificence" of the story,
probably never realizing that her simple, lyrical, emotional report may
be the only personal written record of the days and nights of Babylift at
Clark. Intuitive and generous, she saw the "big picture" and the purpose
and the hand behind it. Daughter Patte expressed well the feeling: "It was
so completely obvious that God had a hand in it all…losing that plane,
and then the next day, here they came!"[3] Before Babylift was over, many
others would feel the same powerful emotion: that the hand of God was
directing the lives of the children and of the caregivers who were so
passionate about their mission, people who included active duty military,
retirees, military dependents, civilians, government employees, and others
who were with local Filipino organizations operating on the base.

Volunteers caring for the children were not the only ones working day
and night to keep the process moving. Mavis Pearson's husband, SMSgt
Tom Pearson, worked in the Aerial Port Squadron where all aircraft are
processed for flight. "Any passenger for the aircraft transited through
the Passenger Service Terminal. All in-coming and out-going military
members, their spouses and all Temporary Duty assigned personnel
transited the terminal, so all flights from Vietnam were received and
processed there." SMSgt Pearson and the staff at the terminal worked
tirelessly for long hours meeting the aircraft at all times of the day and
night to process the passengers, as the children were off-loaded from the
aircraft by a 'sponsor' volunteer and on-loaded to the buses that took
them to the Gym.[4]

Like Holland and others at Clark, the volunteers at Hickam carry vivid memories of the April flights and the urgency of care. Of rescue planes that went through Honolulu, Ann Say recalls, "The first flights that came through were big planes, the ones that were ten seats wide, 747s, the big stretch ones. They would line these cardboard bassinettes up and strap them all down with the seat belts, and they'd get maybe six or seven kids in the middle five seats, so you'd open the door and there would be four or five hundred kids on this airplane, and the stench, because they were all sick, was terrible the first time we boarded. Later, we knew to expect it. In the first class section, they had the steps that went up to the overhead bar, a small area. On the first flight that came through, some of the kids had gotten chicken pox, and the ones with chicken pox were up in the bar, isolated. By the last flight that came through, the ones that didn't have chicken pox were in the bar, there were so few of them. I mean, the chicken pox just swept through the orphanages." (This recollection may account for the number of Clark volunteers who mention rashes and sores on the bodies of the children.)

The next day, after the long night of April 6, Clarkites again stepped up willingly for two more flights:

Monday, April 7, 1975, Clark Air Base, P.I.
Green Flight—96 babies
Purple Flight—104 babies

This is a night to remember. Instead of one, suddenly there are two planes on the ground, both full of Vietnamese children, a total of 200 salvaged lives.
Buses speed away from the hangar with the expected 96, leaving only a small number of Volunteers to welcome the 104 surprises.

Once the emergency is recognized, people materialize from the pulsing air. Almost as many men as women queue up to enter the plane.

I stand in the Baby Line with two high school teachers shanghaied from a Tagger Team.
"I have never changed a baby's diaper in my life," one of these excited women admits. But she marches gallantly forward to instant parenthood.

I am next in line when a male flight attendant hands a tiny new infant to this diffident Volunteer.

"You have just become a mother," is his inspired announcement, and she smiles a radiant smile as she accepts his gift. Like all Volunteers before and after her, she leaves the plane in a state of euphoria, holding her precious baby as tenderly as any experienced Mom.

So many volunteers and so great a need must have inspired in many of them the same thoughts that Holland recorded about her nine-year-old "young friend." There were so many questions and so few answers about the individual children, the only certainty being the need for care. Her words reflect the sensitivity of a compassionate woman and the response to the emergency that must have been felt by hundreds of her compatriots of all ages as they gathered children in their arms and cared for them:

*There are no more teeny-tiny ones so I look around for a special child.
I see her.
Poor little tyke. One year, maybe slightly more. She is obviously too miserable to bear her misery any longer without rebelling. Her eyes accuse me, accuse the whole world.
Her disposable diaper has proved unequal to her need and should have been disposed of hours ago. Every inch of her is filthy. The odor is unspeakable.*

*The bus c-r-a-w-l-s to the gym.
Thank God, I have supplies in my grandmother bag for just such a calamity.
In the gym, I strip off her dreadful clothing and clean her bony little body as best I can. How I would love to let her sit in a tub of warm bubbles. Baby oil is soothing, but she needs to soak her bottom. This must wait until after a doctor sees her.
She is still whimpering when I offer her a bottle of prepared formula and a jar of rice and chicken. She eats but does not like her milk. She devours several crackers and drinks water thirstily. She sprawls out on her bed, still unable to respond.
She smiles for the first time when I make a Raggedy Ann puppet perform for her, but even this is a fleeting reaction. Her behavior is that of a desperately tired child so I let her alone. She flops about on her mattress, turning from side to side.
She listens when I sing a lullaby. It may be the only lullaby she has ever heard. Babies usually fall asleep promptly when I sing to them, probably to escape my totally unmusical voice. But not even this works now. She*

takes an ounce or two more of her bottle and whimpers again.
A sudden inspiration comes from nowhere. I put a cracker in each small
hand for her to keep for tomorrow. Only then does she settle down and let
me pat and talk her to sleep.

Bye-O, Bye-O,
Little Stranger,
Bye-O, Bye-O,
Baby-bye,
You are safe now—
Out of danger—
Bye-O, Bye-O,
Baby-bye...

Sleepy? Um-m-m-m-m-m----

Quiet moments such as these were few on both bases; too much was
happening for one volunteer even to be aware of it all. For Holland,
Babylift was reduced, for a few hours, to one baby, one purpose, while
other volunteers settled in with theirs. Each day, each flight brought more
children, and each volunteer's experience was a story of its own, lived
over and over through the days and weeks of child care. Through the
intervening years, each child's experience has become a story as well,
the story of a life, of an inauspicious beginning in a military gymnasium
and a continuing biography of a new family, of hope and health and
education, of a new generation and a life that goes on, even now.

10

The Orphans

In Honolulu, with so many events tumbling upon one another, the Says simply tried to stay focused and to do all that they could. "Our role was to raise as much money to support this effort as we could. We were a gathering point because everything had to go through Honolulu to go on to the mainland, so they were touching down and picking up supplies. Bill and I were working very hard to get supplies over (to Hickam), at that point figuring we probably wouldn't get a child, because it was all happening so fast."

In Saigon, in addition to other difficult decisions, the staff were forced by circumstances to leave the tiniest babies behind. The flights to Clark were short, about two and a half hours, but they were having to regroup and reload for the longer flights to Honolulu or Yakota and on to San Francisco or Seattle. "Sometimes the layover was 24 to 48 hours," Ann says, "and the babies were so sick and undernourished that some of them weren't surviving. So by the last flights, (the escorts) were trying to triage, and they were trying not to bring out children that were smaller than ten pounds because they were afraid they weren't going to make it. There were just decisions that had to be made to save as many as possible."

In addition to raising money, FCVN volunteers continued to meet the orphan flights, children now arriving in large numbers with massive needs. Ann describes the mounting needs and the rising intensity of Babylift as the days in April brought more and larger groups of children to Honolulu. "The Honolulu airport had built a new wing." she recalls, "They hadn't opened this part of the airport yet, and so they were pulling the planes that had refugees and orphans on them into the new area, because so many of them were so terribly sick and it was accessible to Tripler Hospital. They could get ambulances for transport to the hospital, and use military services to support what we were trying to do."

At times, in the midst of the planeloads of orphans, there were still some groups coming in on regular commercial flights, small groups with a few sponsors. "I was getting calls," Ann says, "saying, 'We've got a group of missionaries who are coming through Honolulu tonight. Can you get some people down there to give them some relief while they're on the ground, to be able to assess the babies?' So we'd get whoever we could," she says, "neighbors, friends, anybody, to get down to the airport to care for those babies."

At Clark too, the efforts continued. McAtee recalls, "Squadron members volunteered to take care of the sick babies in the gym, but what we saw in the process was overwhelmingly sad. There were so many sick and malnourished children. It made you sick to the heart. Skin diseases were rampant and many children were in severe pain. There were a number of deaths, although I don't know the exact number. So many were just barely holding onto life. At the same time, there were also many miracles with the children who made it. So often, they surprised us by their rapid recovery from conditions we thought were unrecoverable."[1]

Despite the discouraging and uncooperative remarks by Governor Arioshi at the outset, there were opportunities for adoption in Hawaii, initially only among the military, and later, among civilians as well. The family of Capt Richard Kurth, of Kaneohe, Hawaii, was able to adopt little Nguyen Thi Lan at nine months. Abandoned at the age of three days, cared for in a Saigon orphanage called Newhaven Nursery, little Lan, whose new name was Carly, began her journey to freedom on the C-5A Galaxy, surviving the flight that had ended so tragically. Ultimately, she arrived at San Francisco, where her father was able to pick her up at the Presidio and return with her to Hawaii. Bruised from the crash, but healthy, Carly was one of the children whose adoption was arranged by Friends for All Children.[2]

Other stories abounded in newspapers and personal memories, as the flights came through. At Hickam on April 7, the Military Airlift Command terminal lounge filled with 55 infants and 11 children "old enough to walk." One of them, identified by a tag tied to her ankle with yarn as "No. 38," arrived on one of several MAC flights April 7 "stopping off at Hickam Air Base for a clean diaper and some love." Only a few months old, No. 38 was carried by a Red Cross volunteer from the plane to the MAC terminal lounge, where cribs, diapers, baths and baby oil waited to be used following medical checkups. The little girl, with mucous on her nostrils and eyes and a wracking cough, was examined and treated by a medic and a nurse, then cleaned and given a bottle.[3]

Volunteer Audrey Sprague was meeting her third flight of orphans, commenting, "They reach out for your love. They respond immediately." The volunteers, wrote *Star-Bulletin* staff writer Pierre Bowman, "exuded love" as they carried the orphans from the plane. These children were flown on to California that night, and then to Denver, the central location from which they were escorted to the approved families who were waiting for them, while Cherie Clark, of FCVN, planned to return to Saigon for another load.[4]

Early on the morning of the 8th, another flight carrying children went through Hickam with 300 babies and 79 adult escorts. Sixteen children, suffering from diarrhea, dehydration, and pneumonia, were admitted to Tripler Army Medical Center, while the others flew on to the mainland.[5]

UPI reported that this flight, reduced to 284 children by the necessary hospitalizations at Tripler, arrived in the United States, brought in by an Overseas National Airways DC-10 chartered by USAID, which was also paying hospital bills. Like others, these children were transferred to the Presidio from Travis Air Force Base and cared for by "Orphans Airlift," a San Francisco-based agency formed to help in the evacuation. One physician assisting at the Presidio's orphan reception center said of them, "They are sad and depressed and they form intense attachments to individuals who casually come by. If the person walks away, they are just destroyed. When they are consoled by someone they are very tender. They are the most responsive and loving kids in the world. They need to be cuddled and held."[6]

It was this tenderness and responsiveness that touched the hearts of volunteers from Saigon to San Francisco and all points in between. At Tripler, the same kinds of stories surfaced. Nelson Kim Phong, 2, arrived unconscious, malnourished, and dehydrated. "He was comatose and lethargic," said Tripler pediatrician Dr. James W. Bass. A few days later, he played with a small flashlight "ignoring the intravenous tube feeding his tiny right arm." He was one of the sixteen orphans taken to Tripler from Hickam, having arrived on the Overseas National Airways jet that had stopped en route to Travis.

Dr. Bass remarked that the children were receiving "not only medical care, but tender, loving medical care," which he believed might be as important as the antibiotics. Nurses and attendants rocked and cuddled the little ones. "The children really seem to respond to any emotional stimulus they get," said head nurse Maj Marilee Tollefson. Many of the nurses grew quite attached to the tiny orphans, as they saw fretful, unresponsive children change to children with "social, happy responses," noted by Dr. Bass, who said, "The long-range outlook for these children is good."

Nelson and several other small patients appeared at a Tripler news conference with their nurses and doctors, who reported that only two children remained in serious condition, "suffering from long-term deficiencies, neglect, and malnutrition, complicated by secondary infections." Dr. Bass said that tropical diseases had been "ruled out" in all the children,[7] a reference perhaps to the health objections of Mayor Arioshi.

It is worth noting that as the situation deteriorated in Vietnam and desperate children with all kinds of physical problems were taken to hospitals at Clark and in Honolulu, health institutions unrelated to the mission or the orphanages rose to the occasion. Jack M. Streight, Imperial Potentate of the Shriners of North America, who was in Honolulu to visit the local Shriners' Hospital, held a news conference at which he stated, "We are interested in every crippled child in North America or who is brought to North America." He expected that the U.S. military would transport some crippled war orphans among the many children who were arriving daily. Shriners care for all children without cost to their parents, and orphans of war would not be exceptions— outstanding news for those who were arriving in braces, or with other disabling problems.[8]

Meanwhile, half a world away, the same compassion and generosity of spirit revealed itself in the U.S., where the president of the National Association of Blue Shield Plans (NABSP) issued a message to "All Blue Cross and Blue Shield Plan Executives." In it, he stated that the NABSP board had met on April 6 in Chicago and had "approved a proposal that all Blue Shield plans be urged to take steps to ensure that Vietnamese orphans—even though they are not yet legally adopted—be covered as soon as they are placed in the home of a Blue Shield subscriber having family coverage." The board noted that there was "no need for a special effort by plans to identify and add the Vietnamese orphans' names to the membership files. Plans can simply provide benefits as soon as the infant or child is identified as a Vietnamese orphan living with a subscriber family."

The Blue Shield statement was to be a joint action with Blue Cross and was endorsed by the president of the National Association of Blue Cross Plans. Though the Blue Cross board had not yet met, he felt that "the humane cause involved is overriding and he would urge Blue Cross Plans to follow the same procedure," and placed his signature on the joint communication.

This simple circumstance, a decision both professional and personal, gave needed assistance not only to the orphans but also to the families who assumed responsibility for them. In the midst of the ongoing transport, these actions by the Shriners' Hospitals and "the Blues" represented yet another heartening example of kindness and of the willingness of good people to do good things.[9]

11

Hiatus and Criticism

Confusion abounded about Babylift and whether it would continue. Political considerations affected the operation even as the transports were ongoing, the volunteers were focused on children, and organizations such as the Shriners and the Blue Cross and Blue Shield plans were stepping up to help. On more than one occasion, the quixotic South Vietnamese government gave and rescinded permission to evacuate orphans—sometimes for hours, once for days. This is reflected, of course, in Jean Fox Holland's meticulously dated diary, where there are no entries for April 8, 9, or 10.

Although as the month played out, the Babylift would end only when the month-long final evacuation of Saigon ended, the *Honolulu Star-Bulletin* reported on April 7 (April 8 in Saigon), "The large-scale evacuation of Vietnamese orphans from Saigon officially ended today as the last of more than 1,700 children flew to new homes under Operation Babylift." Dr. Phan Quang Dan, deputy premier for social welfare in Vietnam, commented, "From now on the orphans will leave on a reduced scale." The 'last' 205 orphans departed in two U.S. Air Force planes headed for Clark Air Base as Dan watched.[1]

Though the reason for the ending was purportedly that the number of allowed children had been transported, the announcement followed the April 5 bombing of the Presidential Palace in Saigon by a Viet Cong sympathizer in the South Vietnamese Air Force and the resulting 24-hour curfew and sealing off of Tan Son Nhut Airport.[2] Dan's statement may have reflected the difficulty of continuing to transport, load, and fly out the children in increasingly dangerous conditions.

Later the same day, pressure from the United States, Canada, and Australia resulted in resumption of the program, the Government of Vietnam saying that it would permit more of the orphans to leave if they were "assured adoption."[3]

Whether USAID was able to continue their large-scale evacuation of orphans or not, "smaller groups indicated they will continue to evacuate others."[4] Cherie Clark, of FCVN, told Associated Press correspondent Steve Wilson, "We have been flooded with mixed-blood children because of all the reports of killings of Amerasian children." Though she personally had not seen such atrocities, many refugees coming from the north had reported seeing them. Asked how many more children there were in Vietnam who need adoptive homes, Clark replied, "A million. Seriously."[5]

In Saigon, Dan described the airlift as an "emergency program" to handle the backlog of orphans that were already in the process, and said that 1,400 had been cleared to leave, expanding to 1,700 as paperwork was processed. By this time, Operation Babylift flights had arrived in San Francisco, Seattle, Travis AFB in California, and Vancouver, B.C., Canada, in addition to the first flight taken to Oakland, California by Ed Daly. The response to the need in all those locations, as it was at Clark in the Philippines and at Hickam in Hawaii, was "overwhelming," as doctors, nurses, and civilians "volunteered to tend the children at the makeshift nursery and reception center" at the Presidio and the other destinations.[6]

In the United States, the "official end" of Babylift brought a gearing down of some relief efforts, but New Canaan, Conn. businessman Robert C. Macauley, who had already put up a quarter million dollars, planned to bring 1,000 more orphans to the U.S. "There are a thousand children over there with exit visas and we've got a thousand parents lined up," he said. "We'll get another plane. We're going ahead on the premise we can get more out. You could get 100,000 adopted the way the American sentiment is now."

Sentiment was governing reactions to Babylift in Vietnam as well. Criticism was arising from non-Communist political opponents of President Nguyen Van Thieu in Saigon, and also from the North Vietnamese and the Viet Cong, who accused the U.S. and Vietnamese governments of "stealing and killing thousands of our children."[7]

South Vietnamese politicians, headed by neutralist Tran Ngoc Lieng, went even further, calling the orphan airlift an "inhumane" propaganda campaign to obtain more war aid from the U.S. Congress, and demanding that it stop. His group published a letter from Dan, in which Ambassador Graham Martin is quoted as saying that the evacuation "will help create a shift in American public opinion" in favor of South Vietnam—a publication that may have been a gaffe on the part of Dan, whether Martin made such a statement or not, given the political hotbed of the time.[8]

On the same day, April 7, the news also reported, "Appalling refugee problems continued to plague authorities," and that at Phnom Penh, Cambodia, "rebel gunners blasted an ammunition and fuel storage area at Phnom Penh Airport, sending a giant column of black smoke skyward," but that "the U.S. Airlift and evacuation of American Embassy personnel (in Cambodia) continued."[9] The entire region was exploding people, with refugees streaming into Saigon from North Vietnam, from Cambodia, and from the beleaguered Republic of Vietnam itself. Removal of these desperate people was ongoing and frenzied. Clearly, the more-or-less controlled evacuation of both orphans and other refugees may have been over in only a few days, but more desperate, harried, and chaotic escapes lay ahead.

Major 'Bud' Johnson and Betsy had gone to Thailand on a trip with Major Tony and Ginny Callanan when the evacuation of personnel from Vietnam was ongoing. They had no trouble "catching a hop" to U Tapao to spend a week on Pattaya Beach. Attempting to catch a hop back to Clark Air Base was another matter altogether. By that time, every incoming MAC flight was full, with Vietnamese women and children evacuating from Vietnam via Thailand.

The young couples found that the evacuation process throughout Southeast Asia had escalated to the point that "every plane that came in was filled with evacuees. We didn't know if we'd be able to get back home." Ginny says. "An airman kept playing 'Take Me Home Country Roads,' by John Denver, on the juke box in the cafeteria, over and over again!"[10] The sentiment of 'take me home' seemed to be the theme of the day, with nostalgia playing a part in that musical choice. They waited and waited, and finally did get a ride, only because Tony knew the pilot of one of the planes leaving for the base. They boarded a plane filled with Vietnamese families. Arriving back at the base, the wives went to the gymnasium to assist with the ongoing refugee effort.[11]

The newspapers were filled with all kinds of information, and perhaps misinformation, about Babylift and the events surrounding it. Reports of President Gerald Ford's involvement in San Francisco were published widely, with a touching photograph of Ford carrying an infant off "a Pan-American Airways 747 onto American soil in a driving rain."[12] Such reports may have encouraged support of Operation Babylift, but they did little to encourage support of the war.

Other reports detailed Viet Cong shelling of Saigon's suburbs and South Vietnam's largest oil storage facility—the first major shelling barrage anywhere in the Saigon area since December.[13] Viet Cong use of the extremely accurate Soviet-made 130mm field gun, with its range of 17 miles, was bringing the war ever closer to Saigon and to Tan Son Nhut, the only exit accessible to the refugees.[14]

So the war and the flights went on, until Dr. Dan's announcement that marked the "official end" of the "authorized Babylift" on April 7, though the "rough agreement" itself, between the adoption agencies and the South Vietnamese government, had actually allowed several days more—a deadline of April 10—for getting all the children out.[15]

While the military worked so efficiently and the volunteers so tirelessly, there was opposition early on and continually to Operation Babylift, both within Vietnam and around the world. Any process or event involving thousands of people in actions unprecedented in the history of war and peace will inevitably draw criticism. In the case of Operation Babylift, emotions ran high, and opposition came sometimes from the heart of a well-meaning critic. It seemed to emanate from politics, from social positions, from one philosophical stance or another, even from personal experience. In free societies such as those participating in Babylift, critics of all stripes can and do speak out, and that is as it should be, though some of the criticism was barely relevant to what was actually happening.

What was described as "political use of orphans" was "deplored" by Jack Adams, executive director of the Holt Adoption Program, who realized that the transport of orphans to the United States was becoming a political issue. After nineteen years of serving children and parents through the civilian Holt agency, Adams understandably regretted "any events which seem to tie together American military assistance and the serving of these children." The Holt program had indeed leased a commercial jet and had taken their hundreds of children to safety in Seattle, an action independent of the military and certainly successful and commendable. Yet it was only through American military assistance that the massive job of moving thousands of the children was possible.[16]

In the U.S., peace groups were charging that the airlifts were "tantamount to stealing Vietnamese children," but Adams and Robert Chamness, Holt director in South Vietnam, did not respond to the accusation, Adams saying only that the Holt airlift of 385 children to Seattle was done "with the full cooperation of the South Vietnamese government." Any action such as the evacuation is "likely to become politicized just because of the close association with any government that is required to carry it off," he added.[17]

The hiatus continued with the cancellation of a mercy flight funded by Save the Vietnamese Orphans, a local group in Virginia that had raised nearly $300,000. The group was told that there were no more visas available for children to be taken to the United States. The planned flight would have left Dulles International Airport for Saigon on the 10th, to return in a few days to deliver 250 orphans to the Norfolk, Virginia area.[18] Although this flight did not happen, others were almost inevitable, given the desperate circumstances in South Vietnam.

Among all these reactions and responses to the actions of organizations, nations, and individuals, the volunteers in all the Babylift locations simply continued to do what they could do in the circumstance—wait for flights, and then care for children and send them on. None of them were doing what they did to affect the relationship between the United States and Vietnam, or to help a particular family get a child, or to whisk out of the war-torn country the children of important people. They were simply responding to the needs of the innocents when it was possible to do so. For some, the simple act of caring provided a form of relief from the frustration of years in the South Pacific country with no real way to improve the conditions there.

"I learned in my first tour in the Philippines," Pearson says in response to the political issues, "that we could not feed, clothe, and medically take care of every young Filipino child, who was dirty and nasty, and whose parents didn't work. The kids begged, but I learned quickly that I couldn't take care of all of them. But these Babylift orphans were children who didn't have a choice to begin with. They didn't have a chance at birth. Anything that was done for them was better than what they had, and we could make a difference."[19]

The difference, of course, was made in the lives of the children, not in the history of the countries or in the orphanages or in the charities and organizations that were doing their part in removing orphans from dangerous circumstances. The difference was in the life of that one helpless child for each volunteer, in one meal, one bath, one doctor visit, one night of rest. The effort would soon go on in spite of the interruption, and the volunteers would be ready.

12

Resumption of Flights

By April 11, responding to the individual needs of those innocents again became possible. Ed Daly, ever the dynamic escape artist, flew again on that day, as did two other flights into Clark. Responding with joy for the chance to help, Jean Fox Holland recorded what is surely the most vivid description we have of that day of three flights:

Friday, April 11, 1975, Clark Air Base, P.I.

Red Flight, World Airways, Daly – 33 Babies
Orange Flight – 133 Babies
Blue Flight – 120 Babies

One plane from Saigon arrives unexpectedly at 3 a.m. and my Patte (Remember her?) who went to bed exactly when I did at 1:30 a.m., and who mistakenly believes she is a better woman than her mother, DOES NOT WAKE ME.
But the two of us together meet every Baby Flight—with this one exception. And let me exclaim again that this is the most thrilling sight I have ever seen.
At this point always, the drama is of the highest intensity, even though the

The continuing diary of Babylift offers touching examples of
transported children and of the heroes who cared for them in their
journey. Holland's detailed description of all that she saw, heard and
felt revealed clearly the ongoing, daily efforts to rejuvenate the orphans
and send them on their way. These are the real stories of Babylift, the
moments with lives barely tolerable, and the warm, gentle, willing spirit
of humanity that brings relief to small, weary travelers who accept, but
cannot understand, what is happening to them. Reading these details
without tears is an exercise in self-discipline:

I see a starving Vietnamese boy eat his chicken bones and all. And I watch a pretty young Volunteer cope when this same boy has a b.m. on the floor.

I hear a slightly built Wagner High School student carrying a girl polio victim in cumbersome braces, refuse help, eloquently misquoting, "She ain't heavy. I'm her brother."

I hear an airman Volunteer, who came on duty after eight hours at his regular job to which he will return come morning, spend most of the night working out a method of man-to-man communication with a troubled Vietnamese boy.

I kiss the tear-wet cheek of a little girl whose hero-father put her on an over-crowded plane and stayed behind to die.

I hear two high school boys, monitored by Mom on the next mattress, comparing notes. One is amazed when his baby burps a baby-burp after a bottle. The other brags, "You should hear MINE!"

I see a Volunteer give a package of cookies to a child who, after eating hungrily, tries to save something for tomorrow by stuffing food in his cheeks and refusing to swallow.

I see the same wonderful women night after day after night after day after night, smiling and functioning; valiant Volunteers who don't have time to think about being tired.

I see and hear the reluctant goodbyes of a 5-year-old lad, shaking hands with his overnight Dad, saying the only word of English he knows, "Hello. Hello. Hello."

I smile at a six-foot-six airman Volunteer from the Afro Culture Workshop, trying to secure a tiny newborn in an oversize garment, one sleeve of which is big enough to hold the whole baby. Mission accomplished, he stands tall, cradling the infant in his hands, grinning back at me with the proudly possessive look typical of all new fathers.

I listen incredulously to a busy group of teenagers including my Number 3 grandson Kelly, singing a song appropriate to their work.

"We've been scrubbing on these toilets
Half the live long night.
We'll keep scrubbing on these toilets
Till we get the dumb things right."

And endlessly on…

I see an unsmiling boy eating chicken and rice with his hands. Abruptly, he stops eating and offers a handful of his precious food to his lovely young Volunteer. When she accepts his gift, eating very messily, he actually chuckles.

I see a big man, a real, red-blooded American hero, who has the means, the will, and the guts to get people out of Vietnam, come hell or Red Tape. I thank God for letting me see such a man.

I smell the nauseous odor of dirty diapers that follows in the wake of the long processions leaving the planes, a stench that heroic effort soon changes to fragrance of soap and baby powder in the gym-nursery.

I watch a lonely little boy sit for hours strumming a two-string toy ukulele and staring into space. I watch that little boy's face light up like a Christmas tree when his Lt. Col. Volunteer brings an electric guitar from home and helps him play it.

I see a Volunteer start to unclench a sleeping tot's hand to remove a chicken leg—and then think better of it.

I hear high school students whistle and cheer and applaud when told that any who want to stay, may work another shift with their babies.

I see an under-sized eleven-year-old Vietnamese girl fighting like a tiger when someone tries to help her carry her baby brother, almost as big as she is. The story is that they are the only survivors of a slaughtered family. This little girl walked over 100 miles, carrying her brother. Let no one dare try to take her baby! She bites! She kicks!

A big American exuding tenderness from every pore walks protectively beside her into the gym, warning away well-meaning people who are running forward to help. Every time I think of this amazing little girl, I weep. Memory of this diminutive War-Time Madonna will haunt me as long as I live.

I watch tearful temporary parents carrying their babies aboard planes bound for America. I know that all of these babies could have good homes without leaving Clark Air Base, but no adoptions are permitted here for some heart-breaking reason.

I see a sobbing Volunteer lay her infant gently down in a cardboard flight box, and I hear her choked words, "This is one more time you are being abandoned, Baby. I hope it's the last time."

Oh, Lord, What an April!
I may never stop crying.

While their grandmother worked at caring for the orphans and maintaining her unique diary of the events, grandsons Mike and Kelly Folts, sons of Col Doug and Patte, were attending Wagner High School, the American dependents' school at Clark. As the transports became more frequent and the job more demanding, "Wagner students by the hundreds actively shared in 'Operation Babylift.' One hour and 15 minutes after [a school official] was called and asked for volunteers, 250 students had signed up."[1]

Mike Folts went out to the flight line near the hangars and lined up with other students. Children were brought off the aircraft and handed to the students, who were told to attach themselves to that one child and stay with him or her until the next day, when they were to go on to the mainland. Mike and the other students helped with delousing of the children, and showers (which, he says, must have been traumatic for them), followed by food and cots and bedding. Each student stayed all night with the child, then boarded a bus that took them to the flight line the next morning. This happened several times, and the school supported the effort by allowing students who had been up all night to miss their morning classes.[2]

Kelly Folts remembers the layout of the gym as being efficient, though crowded. The area for each child and sponsor butted up against areas on either side, so "the bonding achieved between sponsor and baby was achieved amid chaos. The ambient noise was intense and the overhead lighting stark. It wasn't very conducive to 'calming' or 'welcoming' a child, yet somehow it seemed to work." Shift changes were orderly and efficient. "The sponsors were lined up and marched down an aisle, and when there was a sponsor at every pad, the procession stopped. The old sponsor took a few minutes to 'welcome' and hand off the child to the new sponsor."[3]

High school students were also uniquely visible in the refugee center. Whole families of refugees were being processed at the same time as the orphans, but in a different location. In a personal letter to a friend, Col Folts describes the students' contribution with clarity and pride:

"Every adult refugee was processed through a facility known as the 'Wind Tunnel.' It was a large open hanger with two restrooms. Most of the time there were several hundred people in the hanger, either processing or being processed. Needless to say, the restrooms were much overloaded and in constant need of cleaning. The military personnel did what they were able to do, but it was impossible for them to keep up. A group of students from Wagner High School took the job on and made it a fun thing. They would come marching into the hanger with mops and toilet paper and buckets about every hour singing 'HI HO, HI HO, IT'S OFF TO WORK WE GO!' Walt Disney would have been proud of them. I know I was."[4] Like the students in the Babylift gym, these young people knew how to make the best of a bad situation. At 14 to 18 years of age, they were imbued with what we all find rewarding—the sense of urgency, the satisfaction, the knowledge that what they were doing, however menial, had meaning and importance in the grand scheme, that they contributed to the success of the mission, and that their work mattered.

Other students did other jobs assigned to them. Elementary students collected clothes for the children. One high school student, who had lived in Vietnam, was able to serve as interpreter, and other "unsung heroes" worked overtime in the mess halls, the electric plant, the latrines, and other essential locations to help make the orphan and refugee projects succeed.

Patte Folts, head of the Taggers, who organized the number, medical condition, and location of the babies, remarked that all workers were "ready to do whatever was necessary, and do it with a smile. It was a love project," she said, "and everyone wanted to be part of it."[5]

In the Wagner High School newspaper, the *Falcon Crier*, one anonymous student wrote movingly of her personal experience with the orphans:

A Tenderhearted Teenager

When I got to the chapel along with numerous other seniors, they had changed shifts early for "orange flight," so I was on stand-by for "pink flight."

Chaplain Wragg and Mrs. Barth gave us a briefing after everyone was signed in and given a badge.

Later, at the flight line, we lined up double files as the plane landed, excited in the expectation of getting the babies.

One of the last three on the plane, I found that all but one of the tiny children had been taken care of, and the older ones were getting off on their own. As I hurried through the plane, someone got the last tiny child and the last two people on got older children on the way down, leaving two of us "childless."

Feeling slightly forlorn in the midst of the bright lights, I heard a man shout, "Hurry! I need two women who are not interpreters." Then he set off in a run, followed by the last two of us. He led me to the bus, where I took a tiny girl from the arms of a Vietnamese interpreter.

She didn't look at me, she just dug her tiny fingers into my arms as if her life depended on me. During the whole bus ride to the gym, even though

I talked and sang to her, she never looked at me.

We weren't at the gym much longer than it took to get bed numbers, names, etc., recorded, and short physical examinations for the babies, before we were hustled off to the mess hall. I guess it's the first and last time I'll ever get to ride in a VIP bus with a police escort.

The sight of those children clapping their hands and laughing at the thought of food, and the way they gobbled it down, was the most heartwarming experience I've ever had.

At first they ate whatever was put in front of them. Later, however, after their tummies were full, some refused to eat their cabbage.

The first time my charge ever looked at me was when she was sitting in my lap in the mess hall. For all that delicious food, especially the red jello, she gave me a look that told me I'd be her friend forever.

She usually ate whatever I gave her, occasionally stroking the bread or reaching for the orange drink. When I stopped feeding her the jello, though, she grabbed the bowl and looked amazed that it was all gone. She looked so unhappy that I asked someone to bring her another serving. It was then that I heard the first sound to come from her. On seeing the jello, her face lit up and she shrieked with delight.

For the rest of the shift, even though I gave her a bath, which she hated, she remained my friend. We played, and when I tickled her, I heard her laugh for the first time.

At about 10:30 she settled down to rest but insisted that I hold her hand or keep my arm around her.

When the replacements started coming in at about 11 p.m., she sat bolt upright, frightened by the rush of new people. Then, when a lady knelt down beside her mattress ready to take my place, she began to scream and grab at me. It was all I could do to keep from crying as I left her in the charge of a stranger to both of us.[6]

Other volunteers remembered similar heartbreaking experiences: small children would attach to their caregivers, only to cling desperately to them when the time came to go. After the many hours of flight, deplaning, rest, and food, the loss of the one person who had come to represent safety and comfort must have been a frightening experience for the bewildered children too young to understand any of it, and it happened to them over and over.

Mike Folts recalls the announcement that the entire senior class would be allowed to stay another shift if they wanted. Knowing that a friend's father had died in the C-5 crash, the whole group must have felt a gamut of emotions as intense as those of the children, but they worked at their various jobs with a diligence that reflected understanding of the need.

Mavis Pearson, whose heart was touched by her work as a volunteer, saw two little girls she has never forgotten:

Reunited: Two Little Girls

During the arrival of two aircraft within thirty minutes of each other, the volunteers met the second aircraft and arrived on buses at the Gym. As children were unloaded and brought into the area to begin in-processing, I noticed one young girl (who had not yet been processed) tear loose from her escort and sprint across three rows of mattresses to get to a young girl who looked to be about the same age (four or five years old was my guess), and they locked arms and cried. The two escorts were overcome by emotion and just let them hug and cling to each other for a long time (mainly because they could not pry them apart). Of course, the one who had arrived first was clean, while the other was still dirty, with torn clothes, flip flops that were larger than her feet, her hair long and matted, but that did not seem to matter to them. I noticed that they each had something in their hand and would not open it; in fact, the one who had been processed would not open her fist, and the doctor had told the volunteer to let her hold it closed. As they sat on the clean bed, they opened their hands, and we learned they were holding each other's picture. They had been friends in the orphanage. We found out from a translator that an airman had gone to an orphanage picnic and taken Polaroid pictures of small groups of orphans and then cut out each little face. He gave these to the children and the two girls had exchanged them and had them crushed in their hands. We never knew who he was, but he had the old Polaroid camera that instantly made the children's pictures. We thought the girls might have been sisters or family members, but not so; they were just friends.

Once the girls had been together for quite some time, the clean little girl held her friend's hand while she was bathed and cleaned up to continue to the in-processing line. We laughed as we watched the clean girl splash water all over both the volunteer and her new-found friend. She kept showing her a sucker she had and apparently knew if her friend got through the line, she, too, would get one; in fact, they got the same color.

This became a case of one volunteer getting two girls rather than one.

A Vietnamese spouse came to the gym when she heard about the girls and spent some time with them, finding out who they were and how they knew each other. She cried with them as they told her their story, which the Nuns had shared with them. Apparently, the girls were left at the orphanage when their mothers were unable to care for them because of the shame; the fathers were never known. The mothers were driven from their village because they had had children by black Army Sergeants, so they took the girls when they were very young to the orphanage to be cared for by the Nuns, and the girls did not remember their mothers. They were friends from the time they were placed in the orphanage until they were chosen by the Nuns to send to the States.

Touched by the story, the volunteers made sure that the two children left Clark on the same flight, though there was no way of knowing whether they remained together after that.[7]

Indeed, all of the volunteers worked through an emotional roller coaster as they fed, burped, changed and calmed one child after another. It was a soul-satisfying experience to improve the condition of each little charge, yet so difficult to let each one go to yet another caregiver, another flight. Then, in mid-month, the flights virtually stopped bringing orphans, though other refugees were flowing through Clark at an amazing and accelerating rate.

The enormity of the number of refugees had origins in events during the years preceding the 1975 evacuation. When the fighting stopped after the 1973 Paris Peace Accords, there was an influx of people into South Vietnam for all kinds of employment opportunities. Swelling the number of civilians already there, these people, as well as many Vietnamese who worked specifically for the Americans, now had to come out—were told to come out. Clark was flooded with people who were allowed to be there for only three days, after which they were expected to go on to the mainland. This was necessary because Clark was actually set up to accommodate a maximum of 5,000 refugees at any one time. As April progressed, however, the number grew to a total of 12,000 souls, mostly Vietnamese with no home to go to. A tent city was set up, but the food, medical system and supply stores were severely taxed, and the engineers were kept busy setting up sewer systems.[8] Everything was accomplished, but nothing was easy.

The flow of these refugees was unremitting, but for some days there were no Babylift flights at all. Finally, on April 15, after 3 days with no flights, Holland noted that another load of babies had arrived. The flight would be followed by more, through most of the month.

Saturday, April 12, 1975, Clark Air Base, P.I.
NO BABIES

Sunday, April 13, 1975, Clark Air Base, P.I.
ONE BABY!

Monday, April 14, 1975, Clark Air Base, P.I.
NO BABIES

Tuesday, April 15, 1975, Clark Air Base, P.I.
44 BABIES!

Suddenly, it stops.
Apparently, Operation Babylift is over.
Halfway through April, Clark's score stands: 882 Vietnamese War
Orphans safely in the United States of America, nine babies still
hospitalized, one wee cherub returned to heaven.

My arms feel very empty; my heart feels very full.
But this is only the calm in the eye of the hurricane.
Now comes the deluge of refugees…

Thousands and thousands of despairing PEOPLE; HUMAN BEINGS,
desperately afraid, running for their lives, offering the strongest possible
evidence against Communism's rule of terror…
Watching planeload after planeload of these exhausted men, women, and
children walking into the hangar for in-processing, I am more than ever
convinced of the tremendous importance of our Babylift, prompted and
interrupted by cataclysmic events. The small pitiful bags of belongings, all
that remain of former lives, plead poignantly for "this wretched refuse from
Vietnam's teeming shores."
I ask myself one question again and again.
What horror could possibly be horrifying enough to cause these hordes of people to
leave everything behind and run, any unknown being preferable to the known?
Tragedy, not a word but a grim reality, is the theme of each succeeding interview.
But that's another Operation…

I am on an emotional seesaw. Up and down. Up and down.

So the Holland Diary goes on, halfway through the month of April, revealing the unfolding of events in Vietnam, where "another Operation" has begun. Operation Frequent Wind, the name describing flight after flight departing Saigon to extract all refugees possible from the country, began even as the rescue of orphans continued amid increasing chaos in the city and at the airport. At Clark, and at Guam and Wake Islands, Operation New Life, the building of tent cities to house the thousands now processing through the base, was continuing. News media around the world detailed through print, photographs, and film the exodus of desperate refugees, who fled by boat or by air, many of whom became known as "boat people." The fortunate ones were picked up from the sea by ships to fill the rapidly rising tent cities.[9] The less fortunate were never picked up, and many perished at sea, sinking in makeshift boats that were actually not sea-worthy.

At one point near the end of April, as the Midway lay at anchor off Thailand onloading refugees brought out by aircraft, a small, overloaded motor launch approached. With no authority to take these "pathetic souls" on board, the admiral in command of the task force requested instructions from Pearl Harbor. In the desperate moments of waiting, Captain Lawrence Chambers simply took action: "He twisted his ship on its anchor chain so that it was in 'international waters.' He sent his Executive Officer, Captain Larry Grimes to the scene so that he would be able to provide a firsthand report of the boat's condition." Grimes reported the vessel to be in terrible shape. Since the boat would not be permitted to land in Thailand and "sending the boat back out to sea would likely be a death sentence," Grimes did not wait for permission. "He sent one of his officers into the flimsy craft with a fire ax and directed him to chop a hole in the hull. As the boat began to fill with water, the frightened refugees were brought on board the aircraft carrier. Grimes says, 'we purposely scuttled' the boat, saved eighty-four lives, and rejoiced because 'it was the correct thing to do.' The official ship's log is a little more discreet; it records, 'Forty-foot fishing boat approached Midway with eighty-four Vietnamese refugees aboard. Indicating boat was damaged and sinking—repairs attempted. Repair attempts in Vietnamese fishing boat unsuccessful. Vessel sank alongside Midway. Refugees taken aboard Midway."[10]

Throughout the days and weeks of April, such scenes of dramatic rescue were repeated over and over, some according to regulations, and some according to the heat of the moment. No one could have anticipated the kinds of unorthodox decisions, methods, and actions that would be necessary as time carried the long war to its conclusion.

13

Getting Around the Red Tape

During the ongoing chaos of Babylift, other evacuations from Saigon were fraught with delay, bureaucratic red tape, communications inefficiencies all amid the bottleneck at Tan Son Nhut Airport. The massive evacuation of refugees dubbed Operation New Life accelerated to the point where the airport saw flight after flight intended to take out American dependents and other adults and families. The problem was that the planes, which had arrived loaded with cargo, were only partially filled on departure, sometimes carrying only a few people. In fact, "…many of the USAF aircraft left Tan Son Nhut empty because of personnel processing difficulties…The primary reason was the refusal of nonessential persons, such as Defense Attache Office personnel on reduction-in-force or nonessential lists, terminated contractors, and retired Americans to leave until they had the paperwork needed to take their Vietnamese dependents with them."[1] And paperwork was almost impossible to acquire.

Major Dale Hensley, a member of the supervisor of Airlift Unit working on the Tan Son Nhut flight line, described in retrospect his perception of the processing problems: "None of the evacuation plans considered the amount of red tape that would be encountered and generated by the various government departments and nonofficial agencies. Bribes, threats, and covert operations were necessary to evacuate even a few dozen people per day. Even when proper clearance was finally obtained, the official plan did not provide for the personnel necessary in the early part of the operation for processing people aboard USAF aircraft. Baggage inspections, aircraft security, and personal searches required a tremendous workload and a great amount of time."[2]

The evacuation was bogged down also by the requirement of the Government of Vietnam that Vietnamese dependents of Americans must have passports and exit visas to leave the country; these were almost impossible to obtain, and American civilians refused to leave without their dependents, who needed them. In addition, "the bureaucracy of the U.S. Civil Service System, with all its built-in procedures and safeguards, posed a substantial obstacle to forcing U.S. employees to leave the country."[3] Defense Attache Office employees who were willing to go were actually flown out under the cover of being orphan escorts with Babylift flights.[4]

At one point in late April, a plan called "Project Alamo" was set up at the airport to facilitate processing up to 5,000 people per day. The plan called for the Evacuation Processing Center to be moved to the Defense Attache Office Annex for full-time operation on the morning of April 20 to handle the large influx of evacuees expected as a result of the new sponsorship paper produced the day before. This simple document allowed those evacuees who had been told to leave to sign an affidavit attesting that the people with them were their dependents.[5]

The problem with Project Alamo was that it did not work. It did not allow enough personnel for the slow processing of refugees, and there were unforeseen bottlenecks in the system at the gymnasium. There, the flood of people from the Annex underwent processing of paperwork and manifesting, as well as baggage checking, handling, and loading. Lines that had been a mile to a mile and a half long were not visibly shortened with the new plan. There were simply too many people and too many cumbersome processing procedures.[6]

One stunning example of determined ingenuity is a story that must be told, because one officer at Clark was able to do so much to save so many. Col Doug Folts, father of Mike and Kelly, son-in-law of writer Jean Fox Holland, and husband of Patte, played his own part in the desperate removal of Americans and their dependents and allies from Saigon. His story, here in his own words, is one of many that could be told about those harrowing weeks, and it is a part of Babylift, as much as Babylift is a part of the entire frantic evacuation. It reveals the kind of determination, creative thinking, and sidestepping of formalities that were necessary in order to get people onto an aircraft and out of the country while escape was still possible. As events unfolded, frustration led Folts to travel from Clark Air Base to Saigon to unravel the crippling tangle of regulations.

Vietnam Evacuation

My involvement in the Vietnam Airlift began the first part of April 1975, when the evacuation of Vietnam first began. At the time I was Director of Logistics at Clark Air Base, and the problem of receiving, billeting, and feeding the evacuees fell on my people and me. April 1975 was probably the longest month of my life. I am sure that I slept some during these 26 days but I have no memory of doing so. If I did I was sitting in my chair. The same goes for everyone who worked with me. Their loyalty and dedication to the task were phenomenal.

In the first couple or three days, we were sending several C-141s into Saigon each day to bring out Americans. Very few people returned on these flights. I knew we were on a short fuse, probably less than thirty days, to get the job done. So I decided to go into Saigon to see what the problem was and to see if it could be solved. The third TAC Fighter Wing's Chief of Police elected to go with me.

We found that the evacuation was being managed by USAID, and though it was efficient, it was bogged down in regulations. The selection process for evacuees was clumsy to say the least. We spent time interviewing and questioning those people who were being considered for evacuation, and found several things that needed to be changed: Evacuation required a current passport and Vietnam exit visa. This would have been fine for a vacation trip to Disney World, but it didn't cut it for an evacuation. It should be stated at this point that the Vietcong were just outside Saigon at this time, so exit visas were not being handed out indiscriminately, as the Vietnamese felt that they needed someone to help them fight for their country.

The most common problem was that those Americans who had married Vietnamese and had families, but had not obtained the proper exit paperwork (passports and visas) had a real problem. If they chose to leave, they had to desert their families, a choice many, if not most, would not make. There were also no provisions for those people who had worked for Americans for many years to evacuate. There were secretaries, telephone operators, fork-lift operators, drivers, and executives who would otherwise be abandoned and left behind—a death sentence, or a long sentence to a re-education camp.

The first day, I met with the USAID director and told him that I intended to change most of what I had observed, and asked for his cooperation and assistance. Since his secretary was one of the Vietnamese who should be evacuated, I found total cooperation with money, vehicles, and personnel. I spent the rest of that day smoothing the procedures in the processing center and shuttling personnel to the awaiting aircraft in vehicles with heavily tinted windows. The people who worked for me were more concerned with the human side of the operation than with documentation. By the time the first airplane took off to return to Clark, it was full.

When I returned later that evening to Clark Air Base, I found what I had dreaded, State Department personnel complaining loudly about the undocumented evacuees getting off the planes. We just kept our mouths shut and joined them in speculating what in the world had happened. We hoped that by the time they figured it out we would have so many "undocumented" people in the pipeline that they wouldn't be able to turn it off, particularly since there were some very innovative and courageous people working the other end of the pipeline at Tan Son Nhut.

The next morning at dawn, I went back into Saigon. By then I had a list of many people loyal to the United States, living in Saigon, who my CIA friends felt needed to be evacuated. One of the people who worked for me at Clark was a USAID employee, who had come out with the first group of people and had contact with an operator (probably a CIA agent) in Saigon. For the rest of the time, I was able simply to give her a name and address of someone who should be evacuated, and they were at the processing center the next morning ready to travel.

The biggest problem on day two was exit visas, which I was able to circumvent by filling the cockpit with evacuees, since the South Vietnamese immigration officials were not allowed to enter the cockpit. We managed to fill the airplanes that evening, but there was no question in my mind that the cat was out of the bag, and we needed something more original. I had noticed that the CIA had large shipping containers in their fenced-in area on the flight line (at Clark), and it occurred to me that with proper preparation, we would be able to fill these containers with people. When I returned home that evening, I talked to the Master Sergeant who worked for me and was capable of doing anything required. I told him I needed three containers fitted for occupancy and positioned on the runway ready for loading the next morning. I also asked him for a Vietnam exit visa stamp and gave him a copy to take back to his source.

My job depended heavily on communications. I simply had to be able to communicate with those on the other end of this human pipeline. Two people made this possible. One was the Vietnamese lady who had come out on one of the first planes. She simply observed the need and said she thought she could help. She was so effective that I had a phone installed outside my command post and she was there every time I needed her for the next twenty or so days and nights. I would tell her whom I needed to contact and she did the rest—I never asked how.

The other person was a U.S. citizen who was an operator in Saigon. Although I never met her, I talked to her almost hourly for all of April. Nothing I ever asked her to do, including locating and evacuating someone who lived in the bowels of Saigon, was impossible. She just did it (or had it done). Never a question. Never a complaint. I don't know how she did what she did, but she will forever be my hero. I talked to her when she was on a ship off the coast of Vietnam the night Saigon fell. I finally had an opportunity to tell her how important she had been.

On day three, I left Clark with three unloaded personnel containers and a Vietnam exit visa stamp (self-inking, no less). Day three went very smoothly. The containers went directly to the CIA compound, where personnel had been accumulating people since the day before. Those in the containers brought out to the airplane just before takeoff did not require exit visas. All others did. We managed to keep the processing center empty most of that day.

There was one instance I wish to mention because it moved me considerably. There was a gentleman on the flight line who had been helping me load containers and marshal people. He was a middle-aged forklift driver, and toward the end of day three he came to me with tears in his eyes and asked me if there was any way he could be evacuated. He told me that he had worked fifteen years for the American government, and he knew it would mean his death if the Viet Cong were able to capture him. He did not have a passport, so the exit visa stamp was out, but I instructed him to wait quietly outside. With forklift running, at the last moment before the entry ramp was raised, he was to come inside and up to the flight deck, which he did. One other couple who were brought out to the airplane by the USAID director, just before takeoff, were the owners of the "Buffy" factory that made large ceramic elephants, which were common to all Vietnam vets.

At the end of day three, there were 17-18,000 evacuees at Clark. Some were documented. It was the next morning that my boss received a wire from the State Department directing that I get out of the refugee system. I immediately contacted my friends in Saigon, and they told me that there would not be any problem. The system was set up, operating satisfactorily, and they saw no reason why all subsequent airplanes could not be filled.

There were so many heroes involved in the evacuation and so many acts of human kindness that it would be impossible to share them all. Thousands of orphans came out during the evacuation. Their reception and care fell primarily to the wives of U.S. military, virtually every woman at Clark. When an airplane landed, it was met by these women, who each became responsible for the care and feeding of one child until it left Clark or until the lady was relieved because of total exhaustion. Every one of these ladies gave of herself until there was nothing left to give.

There were also many human interest stories from this period in time. One was a man who had run a U.S. civilian company in Vietnam, who came to me with a large check and asked that I use it to feed the evacuees. There is no provision in the service to accept such a gift, so I simply wrote a receipt signed "received by the U.S. government, $2000 dollars for the purpose of feeding the evacuees," and signed it. It bought a ton of food. After the evacuation, I wrote a letter of appreciation to the donor.

Another great story is when some of the CIA agents I had met in Saigon came to the house for dinner one night early in the evacuation and asked if they could leave their three briefcases at our home for safe keeping. My wife said, "Yes," and put the briefcases under our bed. Some 20 days later the agents returned and asked for their briefcases. Right before they left with them, with the contents intact, they said, "Mrs. Folts, you might be interested in looking in one of these." They were jammed full with gold.

On the last day of the evacuation as I sat in the command post, our last C-130 landed. I had to smile, because it was jammed with Vietnamese. Incidentally, I received a pair of "Buffies" on this flight, a gift of someone in Saigon. I treasure them as the last two "Buffies" out of Vietnam.[7]

Asked about his removal by the State Department, Folts replied simply, "The State Department was in charge of being sure that everyone entering the Philippines was American or had a passport and visa. It was their job. My job was to get as many people out of there as I possibly could. Were they compatible? I think not.

"It was my decision. I could care less if they had a visa or passport. I talked to them. If they were married to an American or worked for Americans, I sent them to the States, and let them sort it out there. They were good people we brought out. They have been nothing but an asset to our country."[8]

T.T. Hong, a young girl of 17 when Col Folts' shipping containers were daily rescuing several hundred refugees, describes her journey as a frantic dash on a moment's notice, with only the clothes she could grab as she ran from her grandmother's house to the home of a friend. There, with tearful goodbyes and no time for questions, she and her aunt and a few others were put on a bus to the airport. She relates that it was dark when they got there, and she was crying as she was led into a warehouse with benches. Told to be very quiet, they were later loaded onto a C-130. "I was half-American." She explained. "They would have killed me. We didn't know."

"All of us just got so scared, so panicked," she said, remembering. "I was sick the whole time. My aunt had to make room for me to lie down. I was crying, heartbroken. I did not want to leave my grandmother. Everybody was so scared, so nervous; we didn't know what was in the future, what we were going to do. It was just scary. Two days after we left Vietnam, we heard that the north was taking over the south."

T.T. had a rather difficult life, even after leaving Vietnam to live with her mother in Honolulu. "But you know what?" she says now, "It made me strong. Taught me to stand on my own two feet." After high school in Hawaii, she joined the National Guard and then the U.S. Army, in gratitude to the country that took her in. After a 20-year career in the regular army, and a subsequent life in the United States, T.T. still feels great respect and affection for her adopted land.[9] Multiply her story by thousands, and the ongoing effect of Col Folts' plan is apparent.

Folts wasn't the only one with creative ways to get around the entanglement of regulations and restrictions. Dr. McKinny had used his own methods for years to move children along in the adoption process, and increased his efforts in the emergency.

Like the other orphanages, An Lac was experiencing difficulty in getting permission from the Vietnamese to take the older children out, especially the boys, who were expected to remain and to serve in the Army of the Republic of Vietnam. Even boys who were approved to go were sometimes pulled off the aircraft at the last moment. In attempting to establish some sort of guideline, McKinny inquired of the Minister of Social Welfare, "What about the physically handicapped and the mentally challenged?" The response was, "Oh, you can take them." So the doctor and other caregivers taught the children nine and older how to act and walk as if they had cerebral palsy, and got them on the plane. "That was my finest moment," the doctor said, "my very finest moment."

McKinny's other means of handling the bottlenecks that held up adoptions had been used for years and were continued, indeed expanded, when Babylift made bypassing the adoption formalities critical. McKinny had been able for years to get around regulations that could take "a year or more of, you know, just crap," by getting everything done in a few weeks. "I learned quickly to go over to the Minister of Social Welfare," he said. "If you had any child in Vietnam at that time, you could not adopt without getting the President's consent, which he would do only about every six months. I had a friend in the foreign minister's office, and I'd take him four wash-and-wear shirts and tell him whose paper it was on Thieu's desk and he would move my paper to the top."

Another ploy used by McKinny was done in the passport office. The passport official's wife was an obstetrician who was unable to get anesthetic locally and needed it for her patients when they delivered. "I would have my hometown physician get me bottles of Trilene," he said, "So I would put two bottles on the [official's] desk and he would take me down through the many stops for signatures." At every stop, McKinny would leave vitamins. "I would go out at the end of the day with my kids' passports and visas," he said, "and I would go back and put two more bottles of Trilene on the passport desk."[10]

In some ways, the doctor may have done more good by using medication for bribing his way around the regulations than he could possibly have done by following them. The anesthetic and vitamins were invaluable in the circumstance and may have helped the Vietnamese more than money, which is not always used as it should be.

Bill and Ann Say family, Fall 1975. Left to right are Bill David, Bill with Marcie (the baby in the flight bag, ultimately adopted from Operation Babylift), Susan, and Ann with Matt.

Bill and Ann Say, August 2011.

Marcie Say, 2014.

Lt Gen LeRoy Manor, pictured in 1976 when he was Chief of Staff of Pacific Command (PACOM), based at Hickam Air Force Base, Hawaii. Previously, as a Maj Gen, he had been Commanding General of the 13th Air Force at Clark Air Base, Philippines, in charge of 10 bases in the region. He and the base commanders fully prepared Clark for the influx of orphans and refugees.

Col Doug Folts, Air Force photograph, 1977.

Col Doug and Patte Folts in 1977. They were based at Clark Air Base in the Philippines, and their entire family volunteered for Operation Babylift.

Jean Fox Holland, Patte Folts' mother, and author of the Babylift diary, which documented daily events at Clark Air Base, pictured with children's toys from her grandmother bag, taken in the Philippines in the mid-1970s.

Patte and Col Doug Folts, with T.T. Hong, who escaped as a teenager by hiding in one of Col Folts' shipping containers, Sept. 5, 2013.

Capt Dennis "Bud" Traynor, who piloted the first authorized Operation Babylift plane, which crashed outside Saigon on April 4, 1975. Traynor was able to control the crash landing, and more than half of the passengers survived. Air Force photograph, 1976.

Regina Aune, Ray Snedegar, and Aryn Lock-hart preparing for their return trip to Vietnam in November 2014. This was their first journey back since all three survived the Operation Babylift flight that crashed in April 1975.

Col Regina Aune, who was the Chief Medical Officer on the flight that crashed, and who helped to save many babies and children. Air Force photograph, 1999.

SMSgt Robert Thomas Pearson and wife Mavis in 1976. Mavis worked at Clark Air Base for the 374th Wing Commander. She responded to the phone call with news of the plane crash, and assisted in the setup of communications between the U.S. Embassy in Saigon and the command post at Clark.

Parker Lee "Rocket" Rakocy, November 1974, in the cockpit of his plane. Rocket and his wife Rosie both volunteered in Babylift at Clark Air Base.

Rocket and Rosie Rakocy family, 1980. Back row left to right are Rocket, Rosie, Parklyn and Jason. Front row are Thomas, Rosalyn, Timothy and Elisalynn. The four younger children were adopted from the Philippines.

Tuck McAtee upon arrival in Vietnam in February 1966, being greeted by the Wing Commander (on the left) and a Vietnamese lady in traditional dress. The plane is the F-100 that he flew to Vietnam. He landed at Bien Hoa Air Base, about 30 miles north of Saigon. Tuck recalls, "It was an exciting time for me and the Vietnamese people for they truly believed that, with our help, they could resist the Communist oppression from the north."

Tuck and Ann McAtee, returning home to the U.S. from Clark Air Base in the Philippines, 1975.

Bud and Betsy Johnson, Volunteers at Clark Air Base, on their 50th Wedding Anniversary, Dec. 2014.

Older orphans eating at the Go Vap Orphanage. Photo courtesy of Bill Kurtis.

Infants in the Go Vap Orphanage in Saigon, whose fate is unknown. Photo courtesy of Bill Kurtis.

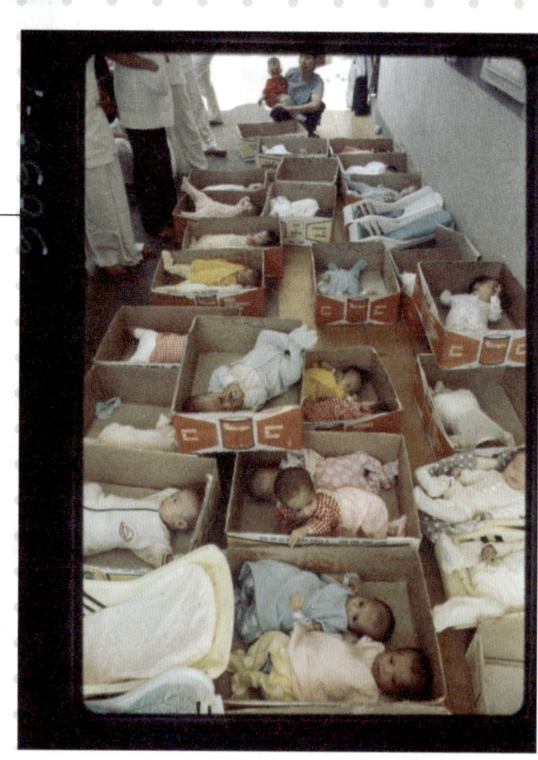

Infants from Go Vap Orphanage, awaiting loading on the plane, and adoption. Photo taken by Bill Kurtis, who was on assignment for CBS to cover the Fall of Saigon in April 1975.

14

Angry Opposition

The challenge of confronting—or bypassing—the tangled red tape of two bureaucracies was exacerbated by publicity revealing the anger over Babylift that was building worldwide in parallel with the growing support system that enabled the transport of the children. Though opposition of various kinds had begun arising early on, after the first few flights, now it seemed the resumption of activity after hiatus brought out a flurry of renewed complaints from many sides, from opposition groups to government bodies, from Americans to Vietnamese.

Though the airlift had begun "with a sense of urgency and compassion," it continued amid "bitter argument over whether taking children from their homeland" was an appropriate way to deal with the ongoing crisis. It angered those who had always opposed foreign adoption because they saw it as taking away a nation's children. On the other hand, those who may have defended the adoption system became "saddened and perplexed" by the haste and disorganization of Babylift.[1] Indeed, the haste and chaos were both causes and results of the need for evacuation, but it must have been difficult for those not on the scene in Saigon to understand fully what was happening.

One woman who had worked with refugees in Hong Kong in the early 1960s had also made a study tour of refugees throughout South Vietnam, Cambodia, Thailand, and other countries for the University of Hong Kong. Sita Byrne, a Hawaii resident, spoke unemotionally of keeping families together so there could be real communications among family members. "Most of the refugees are peasants. They don't know much about politics." She said the Hong Kong pavement dwellers lived in appalling conditions, "but they adjusted to the situation." In the end, she suggested rather simplistically, "I think it would be far better for us to send our money over there to sponsor a needy child. Then he could remain in his own country with his own people."[2] In reality, though her statement may have been valid in ordinary circumstances, Vietnam was long past the stability that would have enabled the sponsorship that Byrne envisioned.

Indeed, even 3 years earlier, money for the orphanages wasn't saving very many of the children of war. Those who were not in the facilities had to have a way to be taken there, or die, and many did. In 1972, Bao Tran was a young soldier in the South Vietnamese Army fighting with the Americans when he was approached by an old man who carried a tiny baby tucked into a straw hat. Saying that the baby had been found trying to nurse on its dead mother, he implored the soldier to carry her to safety. Tran carried her 60 miles to an orphanage, gave her a name meaning "Precious Pearl," and left her there. She survived and thrived, but he spent 7 years as a prisoner of war, and was unable to find her when the war ended. Miraculously, they were reunited in the U.S. many years later. Precious Pearl was saved, but money alone did not give her a life.[3]

Like Sita Byrne, the Quaker service group American Friends Service Committee (AFSC), which opposed the orphan flights, felt that the airlifts violated the cultural traditions of the country. An AFSC spokesperson said, "Putting massive funds into feeding these kids and keeping them with their friends and relatives is a better solution than bringing them here." The children needed an extended family, she said, and they were themselves needed on the farms of Vietnam.[4] The idea of these small, malnourished, abandoned children being needed on the war-torn farms, many of which no longer existed, seems as ludicrous now as it must have seemed then to the people who knew what was happening in the crumbling country, but judgment is easy from a distance and from a stance requiring no involvement.

The concept that money would solve the problems of the thousands of children in the orphanages raised the ire of numerous people, including Lt Cmdr John Krall, who had assisted the nuns at Minh Tri Orphanage in Saigon for two years. By April of 1975, when he heard of the Babylift, he was determined that the children of Minh Tri, "the poorest orphanage in the country" would have a chance.

"Don't talk to me about 'stealing children'," he said. "I've read a lot of criticism about Babylift, saying that the children are perfectly safe and happy there, and that it would be better to leave them in the orphanages and send money. How many of those people who are writing that stuff have ever been in a Vietnamese orphanage? It's pretty naïve to think that you can send money there and it will all go straight to the orphans. There'll be a lot of hands into it first."

Krall went on to say, "Those kids are starved for affection. They clung to my clothes the first time I ever went there…they need homes, families. And it's just crap that they aren't in danger. The Viet Cong is creating more orphans every day. The half-Vietnamese, half-American children will not be tolerated."[5]

Unfortunately, such opinions as those of Byrne and AFSC merely reinforced the ideas of other opponents to the evacuation. Byrne spoke as if a toddler left by the side of the road would be picked up and cared for by fleeing refugees who could barely take care of themselves; as if orphanages that had lost access to money and supplies to continue their mission (and were operating in the midst of gunfire and explosive rocket damage) could provide food and comfort as the city was falling; as if there were time for philosophical discussions about the cultural impact of removing infants and toddlers to the safety of adoptive homes. There was no care; there was no food; there was no time. There was only hope of survival, and that only by airlift.

Some Vietnamese in the United States were equally opposed to the operation. One Vietnamese high school student in Berkley, California, said, "Vietnamese love their children, and will take care of them no matter who is in power next." The student, insulted by the evacuation and believing that it was "robbing" his country, had been brought to the United States himself after being wounded and was healed and safely receiving an education in his adoptive country as he spoke.[6] What would have been his fate if he had not been evacuated to the United States? What would have been the fate of his much younger countrymen if they were not being taken to safety, as he had been?

George W. Weber, head of the New York Theological Seminary and an antiwar activist, was "infuriated" by the airlift. "The idea that it's to save children's lives angers me," he said. "It's the desire of families in this country who want children badly that has led to the airlift, not the likely death of the children, because that's unlikely." He felt that children in orphanages were actually safer than homeless refugees.[7] In earlier days in Vietnam, this may have been true; certainly it makes sense that shelter beats homelessness. But those earlier days were over in Saigon. Again, being on the ground as the city fell while thousands fled and children died might have changed his perspective.

As it happened, the Viet Cong, had they spoken to Weber, would have agreed with him. In mid-April, Radio Hanoi and the "Liberation Radio" of the Viet Cong denounced the removal of the orphans as the "criminal act" of kidnapping. One broadcast claimed that the children "would be brought up to be spies, commandos, or call girls."[8]

In Saigon itself, the operation seemed not to be a big issue, though some non-Communist Vietnamese felt that removing the children was wrong. To some, the photo of President Ford carrying a Vietnamese infant symbolized the "shallow and hypocritical" American character, and raised the question of whether Babylift was simply a political ploy. A Saigon university professor sadly expressed feelings of shame.[9]

Regardless of the condemnations or approbations about the process of evacuation, it was inevitable that accusation of fraud would rear its ugly head. In San Francisco, reports surfaced that some of the "orphans" were actually children of political and military officials. Maria Eitz, of Friends for All Children, which had sponsored some of the flights, suggested that bribes may have been involved, since some of the children's papers indicated that they may have had relatives in Vietnam. In addition, a spokesperson for the AFSC said, "There are unquestionably children in the airlift who are true orphans. But I talked to a number of children who said they are not."

The organization's Jane Barton claimed to have spoken to three children of a South Vietnamese Colonel and their young cousin who were on a flight.[10] Another child turned out to be the daughter of the director of FFAC's Saigon orphanage. Why the presence of the child of an orphanage director would be objectionable is difficult to imagine, since most parents would sensibly save their own children, knowing that the parents themselves would inevitably leave Saigon.

Certainly it was true that some children were not orphans. Two children adopted by Dr. and Mrs. Patrick A. Reardon of Colonial Heights, Virginia, arrived with a letter from their parents in Vietnam, entreating the Reardons to care for and educate their two children. The two fathers had become friends when Reardon was serving at a hospital in Vietnam where Nguyen Duc Huy was a chief medical technician. "If Saigon is attacked, the terrible spectacle will look like in Hell, and people who can escape from the state of torture and suffering will be lucky and happy," wrote Nguyen, the children's father. Nguyen said that the happiest moment of his life was watching his children get on the plane, a moment he describes as one of his successes. In the letter, he expresses heartfelt thanks, and asks for prayers for "our poor Vietnam."[11]

Nguyen's two children, who had parents but were flown out with the orphan flights, were technically part of Babylift. Certainly the same sentiments expressed by Nguyen guided unknown numbers of mothers and other relatives to attempt to save their children by getting them to an orphanage and out of the country. The amazing thing is not that the adults would try to save their children in this way. The amazing thing is that anyone would expect them not to do so.

As the days flew by, countless mothers must have done as Ha Thi Cam Huong did for her 9-year-old son: She stood outside An Lac Orphanage for hours, hoping for a last glimpse of him as he boarded a bus for the airport, where two U.S. Air Force C-141 cargo jets waited. The son of an American father killed in Vietnam, the boy was given up by his mother in order to have a chance to travel to safety in America, to escape the life she feared for him.[12]

Officials of Orphans Airlift, a non-profit agency established in San Francisco to receive the orphans, said they relied on U.S. adoption agencies based in Saigon to authenticate the children's status.[13] Spokesman Bernard Powell said of the many charges of fraud that none had been proved correct. He said it was possible that some of the children being flown into the U.S. were "not orphans in the real sense of the term." They may have been abandoned by parents who were unable to care for them, or they may have told interviewers what the children thought they wanted to hear.[14]

In fact, the abandonment by that time was probably beyond what anyone in the U.S. could imagine; the truth was that hundreds were being abandoned daily, with others, like the son of Ha Thi Cam Huong, taken through miles of impossible traffic to orphanages or to the airport by family or friends in an effort to get them to safety. Only those working with the children on the ground in Saigon could even begin to comprehend the immensity of the problem and the impossibility of knowing everything there was to know about every child—indeed, even of knowing much of anything about some of them.

A case in point is a group of Cambodian children "rounded up by an assortment of 'adoption agents' that included a monk, a barber, and a free-lance photographer" brought to the U.S. by USAID without immigration papers necessary for adoption. Ineligible for adoption, they were allowed to land, but were "not legally here," a spokesman for the Immigration Department said. This inexplicable issue between USAID and immigration officials created a group of 28 orphans who were "children without a country."[15] In Leesburg Virginia, a spokesperson for a relief organization indicated that there had not been time for obtaining immigration paperwork for these children. The children themselves had told her that there were four mortar attacks at the airport before they could reach the plane and one more as they were taking off, so their departure was chaotic. In addition, the embassy in Phenom Penh was abandoned, so if there was documentation for the children, it was in the empty building. The children were taken to foster homes, but their legal adoption was in doubt.[16]

On Thursday, April 10, an interesting series of articles appeared in the *Honolulu Star-Bulletin*, all on one page together, offering disparate viewpoints but no solutions. Originating in Phnom Penh, the first article, entitled "It's 'Phony Issue,' Say Diplomats," states that plans to fly hundreds of Cambodian children to the U.S. and Australia were criticized by American diplomats in Cambodia, who said that the rescues were a "phony emotional issue" to take people's minds off what was happening in Indochina. One U.S. diplomat said, "The American people have to get some phony emotional issue. That was the same with the POWs and now they have manufactured the orphan issue."[17] One would think that this would have been a career-ending statement, coming as it did only two years after the release of the POWs, an issue that could hardly have been considered 'phony,' and in the midst of an evacuation effort that was essential and ongoing.

Directly beside this article is one originating in Saigon entitled "Most Are Actually Half-Orphans," explaining that under South Vietnamese law, a child with only one parent was legally an orphan, a fact that may explain in part the uproar over whether the children were actually orphans or not. In the U.S., they would not have been. In Vietnam, they were. Officials estimated that there were between 300,000 and a million such children in the country, with perhaps 15,000 of them bi-racial and with possibly 18,000 living in 110 registered orphanages before Babylift began.[18]

A third article on the same page raises another issue: "U.S. Has Thousands of Its Own." Coming from Washington, this article begins with one statement and ends by contradicting itself. In the beginning, it states, "As people scramble to adopt Vietnamese war waifs, thousands of American children remain orphaned and ignored." One social worker felt that "…the reaction to the Vietnamese children is an emotional response in a crisis. Many people haven't thought through what it will mean to them if they adopt one of these children." This person did not realize, probably, that most of the prospective parents had waited for months, if not years, for the visas to obtain the children they had been approved to adopt and were well aware of the possible problems. Yet, after describing the problems with adopting American children, the article ends with, "Social workers express delight that the recent focus on the Vietnamese orphans has sparked a general public interest in adoption."[19] Were the American children "orphaned and ignored," or was there renewed "general public interest in adoption" as a result of the "recent focus on the Vietnamese orphans"?

Finally, beside the other three articles is one that gets back to Babylift: "300 More Set to Leave Tomorrow." Coming out of Saigon, this article details the efforts of American Betty Tisdale and others to remove the nearly 400 children in FCVN's An Lac orphanage to the United States. Having received permission from Deputy Premier Phan Quang Dan to airlift two planeloads of children to the U.S., Tisdale described him as "one of the most compassionate men I have ever met in such a high position." She was able to arrange for two U.S. Air Force C-141 Starlifters to take the children to Clark Air Base, where commercial jets arrived to take them to Honolulu and then on to the mainland. She added that she would return, as more babies would fill the orphanage. A U.S. Embassy spokesman reported that about 50 orphans would leave Cambodia the next day, and that 104 had already been taken out in the past few days.[20] Clearly, the hiatus following the announcement of termination was not complete, as some flights from both Vietnam and Cambodia were getting through.

Taken together, the four stories on the same page pretty much summarize what was being said and done about the orphans: It was a phony issue; some weren't really orphans; the U.S. had plenty of its own; 300 more were set to leave the next day. Nothing was making much sense in April of 1975, yet those on the ground in Saigon, at Clark, at Hickam, and on the west coast of the mainland proceeded as best they could to do as much as possible of the work in which they believed.

Ann and Bill Say, Dr. McKinny, the 1st Test Squadron volunteers at Clark, the pilots and escorts and other dedicated personnel had little time for arguments in the press, and in cases when they heard of criticism, they simply ignored those complaints, responding with more caring, more work, more love. Gen Manor had to say about criticism, "We didn't have any of that at Clark. The Philippine government of course were always concerned about people coming through Clark who were immigrants, but they pretty much went along with it and were very supportive."[21] Apparently, the focus there was on saving children, not on doubting origins of orphans or on questioning motives of caregivers. Years later, Manor summed up his feelings: "Were they orphans? Who makes these rules? There were people who had backbone and gumption to do things, and they did them!"[22]

As a volunteer with "backbone and gumption" in Honolulu, Ann Say experienced the negative publicity and the generalized anger in a very personal way. The memory of one flight from Cambodia, in particular, has stayed with her through the years, ending, as it did, in controversy that exemplified the whole irrational response to the evacuation and to the war itself. Ann received a call requesting assistance for a group of missionaries who had evacuated an orphanage in Cambodia and had arrived at Honolulu International Airport by commercial air with 20 children. The sponsors needed someone to go to the airport and relieve them, because they were traveling alone with all the children, some of whom were very, very sick. Ann called FCVN volunteers and went with them to the airport, where she called an ambulance for the sickest among the babies. Naturally, the media were present in large numbers, both reporters and photographers, and contact with them seemed unavoidable.

"I was holding one baby that had such severe diarrhea that he was dehydrating and couldn't eat or drink, and Tripler had sent me some suppositories to give this baby. So I was holding a naked baby, because he had messed all of his clothes, holding the suppository in, and this

reporter came over and got in my face with his microphone, and said,
'What do you think you're doing, helping these people? Don't you know
that they could be Communists?' and just attacked me. And I'm holding
this baby, and I'm feeling this pressure comin', this pressure comin',
this pressure comin', and finally I just took my finger out of the baby,
and he just shot stool all over the camera, all over the reporter, all over
everything. I never had any more trouble with reporters. There were
people who were very positive about what we were trying to do, and
there were people who were very, very, very angry…the whole country
was that way. Nobody knew how to deal with Vietnam."

Media attention to the Babylift aspect of Vietnam was much like
media attention to all other aspects of the war: both a boon and a bane.
While negative, enraging publicity through print, radio, and television
sources abounded around the country and in the world press, still there
was much being published that was needed and helpful. Truth be told,
in the free societies in which the reporting occurred, media attention
to events was essential regardless of the slant of the message. People
were reporting the truth as they saw it, from a stance of normal human
and personal inclination. In fact, it would be impossible to measure
the influence of the media, both helpful and harmful, on decisions and
actions of involved people worldwide. While news of the ongoing flights
out of Saigon angered some, at the same time, the media blitz brought
news that was welcome to others, who needed information.

A case in point is an adoptive family in Massachusetts, where
Geraldine Bartoloni, a young mother who had had one successful
pregnancy out of four, "saw on the evening news that babies were being
airlifted from Vietnam." With the Catholic charities home study already
accomplished, she said, "I called and asked to be considered for a child.
Time went by, and the phone rang late one afternoon, and we were asked
to come to the agency that same night. It was so exciting. Jennifer came
into our arms wrapped in an airline blanket weighing 13 pounds at 15
months old. Off we went to begin our journey as a family. It was meant to
be. I will love her forever."[23]

This scenario was repeated hundreds of times because of the
communication of information made possible by the media of the
day. Actually, an effort was made by the Blue Cross and Blue Shield
organization, in the instruction to the local health care plans, to avoid
sensationalizing the publicity: "It has been determined that contact with
the media on this matter should be undertaken on a plan-by-plan basis as
soon as local decisions are made. Care should be taken to ensure that the

primary purpose for publicity is to get the media's help in making these benefits known to the families involved."[24]

Jennifer herself, the lucky baby who became a beloved Bartoloni, says now, "As I grow into a middle-aged woman who has been blessed from day one, all I can think of is how grateful I am for the opportunities to grow, develop, love, and learn. So many connections have been made and so much love has been shared between me, my family, my friends, and this world!"[25]

Though the volunteers at the bases and orphanages, and the missionaries both in Vietnam and in transit, were unaware of these heartening events on the mainland, they must have held in their hearts a vision of children wrapped in airline blankets carried into loving homes at the end of their journeys.

15

Volunteers and Adoption Policies

For some of the missionary flights, Honolulu was their destination; they simply got out of Saigon and went as far as they could, and some of them couldn't take the children any farther. For those children, FCVN volunteers were looking for ways, working with the social services agencies, to place them with people who had home studies completed.[1]

Time and circumstances had begun, unofficially, to change the adoption policy in Hawaii. There were appropriate homes in the state, homes where the parents had prepared by fulfilling their application and other obligations. "In Honolulu," Ann recalls, "we were looking for homes for some of the (missionaries') children through the social services agencies. I'm not a social worker, so I was directing the interested parents to resources that could help. Nobody was going to get a child that didn't have a completed home study, because we weren't just going to hand them to people…and so one of the things we were doing was calling people who had good legitimate home studies and saying, 'We have this missionary who got here from Cambodia with ten kids; can you take one of them? Do you want an American child, or will you take one of these?' We were trying to place them that way, because some of them couldn't go on to the mainland, and the missionaries didn't have any way to care for them on the mainland, so we were trying to place them in Hawaii."

Everything about Viet Nam was news, and Ann had gotten on TV with one of the national news broadcasts. A news crew had gone to her home to interview her, because they knew she was working to raise funds and had pleaded publicly for more assistance. She shared what FCVN was doing to greet the refugees and the many children, whose needs were so great, asking for medications and supplies. Since their family name was uncommon in Honolulu, and since their phone was a listed number, it was an easy task for anyone with questions about the adoptions simply to look up the number and call Ann.

At one point, a reporter on the island called Ann and said, in desperation, "My wife and I are childless, and we want one of those babies…" believing that Ann was in control, "…and if you don't see to it that we get one of those babies, we will kidnap your children." From that point on, Ann and Bill realized that they could not leave their children unattended for a moment, not in the yard, not in the house. "Those kinds of threats were coming into our home," Ann said, "and it was frightening, because we were trying to do something good, and people were frantic to get these children, or angry because people were helping these children… All kinds of emotions were unpredictable and unexpected."

"My phone got to where it never rang," she added, "you just picked it up, and there was somebody on the other end, and the phone company got upset because it was not a business line. I had to have somebody come stay in my house with me…so I could get some rest, and care for my own children. It just turned out to be crazy, and, because (the interview) got broadcast nationally, the callers were people from the mainland who had completed their home studies and were on the waiting list, had been assigned a child, and they were calling and saying, 'Did you see little Le or baby Dang?' Of course, I didn't know who I was seeing."

News reports verify Ann's experience. The *Honolulu Star-Bulletin* reported on April 4, "In Hawaii, telephones of those affiliated with agencies that aid in adoptions have been ringing off the hook, night and day. The orphans of Vietnam have touched the hearts of all, and people have responded by expressing their willingness to open their homes to these children of war." Local chapters of adoption agencies were taking names of those who wanted to adopt so home studies could begin. There was even a coupon in the paper that day that could be clipped, filled in, and mailed to the *Star-Bulletin*, who would direct it to the appropriate agency—an incredible offer, considering that, until Babylift, according to Ann and Bill, there had been no placements of Vietnamese children in Hawaii and none intended even then.[2]

Ann remembers that, in the midst of all the effort, the publicity, and the intense urgency, the appearance of Hawaii's Governor Arioshi on the local news had gained a great deal of attention. The governor had taken a very negative stand on the issue of Southeast Asian adoptions, and he appeared on the night immediately following her appearance on the news, saying, as Ann remembers it, "We aren't going to let any of these kids stay here in Honolulu. Don't even think about wanting these orphans; we don't want them in our state." He took, she said, a very "negative, nasty posture on it." In addition, *The Honolulu Advertiser* reported on April 4 that Arioshi claimed, "The State has received no word on any plans to process Vietnamese orphans through Hawaii. The only Federal contact with Hawaii has been a query on the State's attitude toward health and immigration standards for the processing of the refugees. It is the State's position that routine Federal immigration standards should be maintained," the Governor said.[3]

The information given to the news media seemed to support the Governor's position, for in *The Honolulu Advertiser* of April 5, in an article entitled "Stopovers Scheduled in Isles," there appeared this specific statement: "A special Pan Am charter with 400 children from Saigon will arrive in Honolulu this afternoon on a re-fueling stop. The plane will then continue on to Seattle, Wash. Because of Federal public health regulations, no one will be allowed off the plane here." However, McKinny reports that some children were taken off every flight as necessary, and volunteers were allowed on to assist escorts.[4] Ann remembers that on nearly every flight, both children and sponsors deplaned at Hickam, where children were checked by doctors, changed, and fed, as they had been at Clark. It simply was not possible to fly from Saigon to the mainland with hundreds of children, many of them sick, without stopping for care, food, and medicine. Certainly, there were concerns by some observers about public health, but all the children were cared for at every stop without incidence of public health issues, according to the people who cared for them at Clark and at Hickam.

Unlike Arioshi, Frank Fasi, the Mayor of Honolulu, was exceptionally cooperative with the refugee effort, even offering to VIVA his campaign headquarters in downtown Honolulu for their use as an office,[5] a fact that, conflicting as it does with the governor's attitude, reflects two circumstances that influenced political decisions of the day in the state: the massively overlapping constituencies of the Mayor of Honolulu and the Governor of Hawaii, and the deep divisions that permeated all levels of American experience as the war wound down.

Resuming Babylift after the lapse of three days, the flights on April 11 were the first to carry out of Vietnam children who had not already been assigned to adoptive parents, a feat made possible by President Ford's willingness to cut through the bureaucratic red tape. All these children were small, since the government of Vietnam would release only those under 10 (on some days), or 12 (on other days), turning down requests for the older boys and for the Vietnamese staff members of the orphanages.[6] Later, of course, McKinny's ploy of feigning illness saved some of the older ones.

The first allowed to leave since Operation Babylift was halted a few days earlier, nearly 300 orphans were flown out of Saigon on the 11th aboard a series of flights, the first going to Clark aboard a DC-8 jet, and continuing to Tokyo. The Air Force flew two C-141 Starlifter transports carrying 267 more children and arriving at Clark later in the day.[7]

By the 13th of April, Arioshi's intention to allow no adoptions in Hawaii was beginning to fall quietly by the wayside. Following the earlier adoption by the Kurth family of Kaneohe Marine Corps Air Station, six more children from An Lac Orphanage arrived at Honolulu Airport after a journey with a larger group from Saigon to Clark, Honolulu, and Los Angeles, and finally, the six of them together, back to Honolulu. The six had flown with one of the largest groups in the Babylift flights, consisting of 219 from An Lac orphanage, 38 from FCVN, and 22 sponsored by a Norwegian organization. Among the orphans was a group of Cambodian children who had fled the Khmer Rouge takeover. Dr. McKinny flew with the load of orphans from Saigon to Clark and then on a World Airways jet to Los Angeles, returning to Honolulu with the six adoptees. Deeply affected by the experience, the doctor began to weep when he described his and the orphans' chaotic departure from Saigon aboard a C-141 Starlifter, and the beating (by ARVN soldiers) of the bus driver who had transported them to the airport and attempted to board the plane.[8] It seemed that the longer Babylift continued, the more difficult it was, and the boarding at Saigon was the most dangerous and heartbreaking of all the actions that had to be taken to save the children.

Three of these six children were adopted into military families: three-month-old baby boy Vu Tien Huan became the son of TSgt and Mrs. David Manges; five-month-old Vu Thi Lien was met at the airport by SSgt and Mrs. Herbert Wagoner; and two-year-old Vu Thi Kim Ngan went home with MSgt and Mrs. Ronald Landback.[9]

The other three of the six were among the first allowed to be adopted into civilian families on Oahu and on the Big Island: Melvin and Audrey Ah Sing received their baby boy, Vu Thien Vuong; Mr. and Mrs. Adolph Nussbaum adopted three-year-old Nguyen Chu Son; and Mr. and Mrs. Tony Locricchio, in a roundabout series of fortuitous events, welcomed their seven-year-old son, Vu Tien Hoa. Locricchio, a legal aid attorney, was in Los Angeles on business when he was notified that his assigned child was at the airport there. He located Vu at a hangar sheltering Operation Babylift children and took him along to Honolulu. On arrival there, Vu was clutching his American father, refusing to leave him at all, an action typical of the desperation of these small refugees who had been through so much and were so alone.

Tears were common at Honolulu International Airport that day. Mrs. Manges, crying, said of her new infant, "He's great. I'm so ecstatic, and I just want to get him home," adding, "I'm so glad it's over with, and I'm very happy."

Other adoptions were allowed in Hawaii as time carried the effort to more and more families. By April 24, among the many who passed through the base, seventeen more children had arrived at Hickam with adoptive parents ready and waiting. Clearly the "no adoptions in Hawaii" intention had broken down completely, as both military and civilian parents met the children, having been through the steps of the adoption process with Catholic Social Services to adopt the children. This group ranged in age from eight days to eight years.[10]

At Clark, the focus of the operation remained on caring for the children, feeding them, checking their health issues, and preparing them, strengthening them actually, for the long journey yet to come. "The gym was very large," recalled Betsy Johnson, whose husband, Maj Franklyn R. Johnson, was Range Safety Officer for the 1st Test Squadron at Clark. "It seemed that the whole room was filled with all ages of children. My first baby couldn't have been more than a few weeks old. Each volunteer was assigned to one child…It was surreal, especially at night, when it was so quiet in the gym with all those people there,"[11] she said. "They only stayed until another flight could whisk them all off to the U.S.; it was only about a day for each group. All I do remember is how tiny and helpless those little babies were."[12]

Kathy Aldrian remembers getting phone calls: "Can you come? We don't know how long you'll be here…you might have to stay overnight… we're working on a shift to relieve you…" Sometimes it was difficult to say no, but the couples all had young children, and the husbands were flying and were gone a lot. Kathy spent a few nights and days helping hold babies who were being checked over and taken care of by the medical staff. One very comforting thing, Kathy feels, is the realization of "how lucky we were to be protected. Even when we were overseas we were always protected by our government, always taken care of well, and you don't think about there being orphans. But there are very poor countries and very unstable governments. We are always sympathetic with that." And of Babylift: "I felt that if the government decided to do it, and we were military, of course we supported it."[13]

"I remember some of the children died, and it was very sad," wrote Maj McAtee. "To see so many children in such dire straits broke our hearts. We could only hope that they would make it and someday look back to realize how lucky they were to get on those planes. I fought two tours in Vietnam and wanted badly for those wonderful people to find their freedom and independence."[14]

Through all of this working and caring for children, there was little worldwide publicity about Clark's part in Babylift, because President Marcos gave conditional permission for all those planes to land in the Philippines, and the condition was that there was to be no publicity.[15] So there were few photographers or reporters save those who went on to publish in Hawaii or on the mainland, and there are today very few daily records of this vital humanitarian effort at Clark, except in military publications such as *The Stars and Stripes*. Soon after the events the *USAF Southeast Asia Monograph Series* documented important aspects of the war there. The seven studies in the series were written by airmen who fought in Vietnam and were published by the Airpower Research Institute at Maxwell AFB in Alabama. However, the hands-on, daily and nightly experiences of the Babylift effort at Clark, followed by, indeed overlapped by, Operation Frequent Wind and Operation New Life, with whole families of refugees in tent cities, are lost in the caverns of unrecorded history. Those experiences live only in the memories of the heroic groups and individuals who carried them out…and those people are fewer each year.

At Hickam, there was no such restriction on publicity; in fact, much of the information available on Operation Babylift in Hawaii is found in the free press—*Honolulu Star-Bulletin* and *The Honolulu Advertiser*; both of these covered the stories of the orphans almost daily. At Hickam, too, several chaplains were assigned two-week rotations from Hickam to Wake Island, where a tent city was set up for "boat people" and other refugees taken there by the American military. These chaplains kept written records of their time there, detailing the duties fulfilled during eighteen- to twenty-hour days of their two-week rotations.

In the history office at Hickam is a notebook containing the chaplain records, including the diary of an Air Force Chaplain, The Vietnamese Minister's Report on activities on Wake, the Wake Island Daily Newsletters from May 16 to July 31, a photographic essay of Wake events, several editions of the *Hawaiian Falcon*, and some letters of appreciation. These remain the only history of the evacuation of South Vietnam kept at Hickam Air Force Base.[16] All this information is available to Americans without restriction, but no such records seem to have been kept of Babylift, which happened so fast and in so many locations. Any records that may have been kept at Clark, in the various offices, would have been moved to Andersen Air Force Base on Guam when Clark closed in 1991.

Publicity in the free press may be a good thing in general, but another flurry of negative publicity plagued the operation by the middle of April. *The Washington Post Service* reported that orphans brought to the U.S. in 1972 had spread hepatitis to volunteers and to adoptive families, a statement disclosed by Ralph Nader's health research group. In a letter to Health and Welfare Secretary Caspar W. Weinberger, the group charged that the government had failed to check properly for health problems in the Vietnamese orphans flown as part of the Babylift. Officials at the Centers for Disease Control in Atlanta simply denied the charges. Nader's watchdog group made statements about hepatitis and bacterial diseases, but the only cases they could actually point to were those of diarrhea; volunteers were being checked for bacterial causes of that illness.[17]

At the same time, the INS began to investigate possible bribery in the airlifting by USAID of the 28 Cambodian children, the "children without a country" who had arrived in Leesburg, Virginia, via Bangkok, Manila, and Los Angeles without adoption paperwork. INS Commissioner Leonard F. Chapman, Jr., seemed to be interested less in facilitating the eventual adoption of the children than in whether bribes were involved in transporting the children and whether "parents could surface in Cambodia, another country, or in this country and claim these children."[18]

In point of fact, the origins of those children and others could reasonably be questioned, given the fact that the Khmer Rouge had taken Cambodia in early April, emptying the capital city of Phenom Penh and sending an enormous stream of refugees into the jungles of Cambodia, Vietnam, and Thailand. Children were coming from everywhere in the region.

As late as April 25, *The Honolulu Advertiser* reported that Bishop Mark J. Hurley, after a 10-day fact-finding visit to Saigon "assessing the refugees-orphans-Catholic Church situation in the wake of North Vietnam's military sweep through the south," reported that church leaders in Saigon were "opposed to the United States indiscriminately airlifting Vietnamese orphans out of South Vietnam." He spoke of the need for a cease-fire to give relief organizations time to assess the situation, of "on-the-spot practical judgments" needed by such agencies, and of evacuation priorities to be established—all recommendations for which the time was past, the report too late. Tellingly, however, he ended with a realistic statement that overall, it was difficult to make any quick judgments on what was or wasn't right about the recent Vietnam airlifting because "it's now a desperate situation" in South Vietnam "and these people are literally frightened to death..." Given this desperation, he said that it was unfair of the American press to criticize the airlifting of non-orphan children, reporting that served only to "cloud" important humanitarian issues. Thus, ultimately, Hurley offered a realistic, common-sense view that had surfaced in very few news reports.[19]

Asked about negative reports and accusations in the media, General Manor replied simply, "We didn't get involved in any of that. These were sponsored mostly by church organizations, and I was confident that those organizations would take care of those details."[20] Indeed, the people on the ground at Clark when the planes landed could hardly have set aside care of any given child because he or she may not have been an orphan. The process was ongoing, the children were arriving in droves, and the questions would have to be asked and answered after the evacuation was over.

Clearly, by mid-April, it did not matter what the South Vietnamese government announced, or what political motivations were suspected, or what the Viet Cong demanded or the U.S. State Department said. The press was full of cautions and halts and suspicions, but Babylift had taken on a life of its own. The only thing that mattered was loading and flying another jet, and another and another.

By April 12, all of Saigon was in chaos, and Tan Son Nhut Airport was deluged with desperate people trying in any way they could to board a plane. For the next two weeks, until the very end, newspaper and television reports around the world revealed their heartrending attempts to board, to cling to a wheel, to force themselves into or onto any airplane that was preparing to lift off, even attempting to throw their children into the loading planes.

The 23rd through the 26th of April saw flights leaving Saigon as often as the military planes could come in and the orphans and other refugees could be loaded (mostly illicitly), amid violence and bloodshed. "Most went out directly from the flight line, with the Supervisor of Airlift Unit handling arrangements, either at Air America or on the main ramp. Mr. Ed Daly, with his World Airways 727, made two of the later orphan flights on 21 and 25 April, carrying out 470 orphans and their escorts."[21] By April 25, "the crowds were starting to peak in the Annex area and there just were not enough military or civilian processing and security people to provide necessary checks to stop unauthorized personnel from entering. Once in, it was impossible to find or sort them from the masses, unless they tried to crash the gates or board buses while not on manifests."[22]

To add to the logistical problems, April 23 brought a "tremendous roadblock" when President Marcos "decreed that no more than 200 evacuees could be in the Philippines at any one time." With 5,000 evacuees already at Clark when the announcement was made, Military Airlift Command and the Pacific Air Forces suddenly had to move at least 5,000 evacuees out of Clark to Guam, Wake Island, and Yakota Air Base, Japan, while simultaneously expanding the evacuation from Siagon.[23] "It wasn't so much a specific limit," Gen. Manor recalls. "But we were bringing a tremendous number of people into his country, and he was concerned about that. We had a good relationship with the Philippine government. We assured him that we would respect the immigration rules of the country."[24] Thus, moving massive numbers of people out of Clark became a priority equal to that of moving them in.

On the 26th, in the face of ever-increasing security and control problems, the Commander-in-Chief of the Pacific region "requested an additional C-130 squadron from the continental United States to help clear the congestion at Tan Son Nhut and among the islands." At that point, a Little Rock AFB, Arkansas, Air Reserve unit deployed along with an en route support team from Dyess AFB, Texas.[25] This added to the effort two teams that were well trained but inexperienced in the matters at hand. Still, availability was key in the situation that demanded growing numbers of personnel to process the evacuation.

Babylift was deeply entangled in the larger, ongoing refugee evacuation that was barely controlled and would sweep the orphans along with it. At the outset of Operation Frequent Wind, passenger loads had been limited to 94 for the C-141s and 75 for the C-130s. By now, the peacetime rules had been dropped, and standard loads of 180 were being prepared for both aircraft. The Supervisor of Airlift reported loads as high as 316 on a C-141 and 243 on the C-130. Aircrews reported C-130 loads of more than 260.[26] Rules were gone for both Frequent Wind and Babylift. Clark remained the first care center for the children, with unknown numbers there at any one time. The volunteers simply cared for all that arrived and sent them on when they could.

Holland writes from the heart of flights coming in "all day, all night," of the building excitement and the Babylift flights among the Freedom Flights, of the inevitable end, of "restored faith, renewed hope."

On Wednesday, April 23, 1975, the evacuation of War Orphans from Vietnam miraculously resumes; with 26 babies coming in on two flights, 10 on one, 16 on the other. Far too few… Rumors reach us of how many are waiting…

Momentum builds up on Friday, April 25, with two flights bringing 194 babies.

And NOW, it is Saturday, April 26!

The flights do not stop all day, all night.

The noise of the planes is never quiet.

Some people cover their ears.
Not I.

With respect approaching reverence, I listen to the deafening, awe-inspiring sound of angels' wings.

Sandwiched somewhere, somehow in among forty Freedom Flights for refugees are two Baby Flights, one aircraft bringing 248; another delivering 116. A record total of 364 BABIES! Hallelujah! Hallelujah!

And there are more…
On Sunday, April 27, twenty-five babies.
On Monday, April 28, sixty-four babies…

The very last… The very, very last…

I may never stop crying.

The official total is 1,565 toward the promised 2,000. But this does not include large numbers of walking children on a special Daly Flight, that we do not tag-count because they only stay with us a few hours, just long enough to win our hearts.

And now, and now, this incredible month is April-ing into May.

This is the one remaining day.

The final flights are taking off for America with 117 babies, leaving only 43 to fly out later by Med Evac.

But before writing amen, I must make my confession of restored faith, renewed hope.

"The flights do not stop, all day, all night," Holland wrote, and it was true. The evacuation of the children was overlapping with Operation New Life and Operation Frequent Wind, with the Thirteenth Air Force helping to coordinate Air Force airlift efforts under a single theater airlift manager, Brig Gen Richard T. Drury. "Air Force cargo planes airlifted more than 50,000 passengers from Saigon in 375 Operation New Life flights. Between April 4 and 28, C-141 Starlifters from the 60th, 62nd, 63rd, 437th, and 438th Military Airlift Wings airlifted refugees out by day, while C-130s from the 374th and 314th Tactical Airlift Wings evacuated Vietnamese by night. There were 161 New Life C-130 missions, which transported 20,834 passengers from Saigon to the Philippines the last week in April."[27] All day, all night, indeed.

16

The Last Flights

In Saigon that April, the many and continual day-and-night flights were exceeded only by the many and ubiquitous journalists who descended on the city in the last weeks, adding to the multinational groups who were already there. There were no problems of permission for publicity (or lack of it) in Saigon. Media people from all over the world wanted to cover the fall of Vietnam, which no one doubted was both inevitable and imminent. Among these people, most of whom knew each other, many of whom had daily contact in lodgings at the Caravelle Hotel, was Bill Kurtis, on assignment for CBS to write a series of news stories on the unfolding drama before the fall. One of the stories he wanted to write and to photograph was the Babylift, and one iconic photograph turned out to be so revealing of the overwhelming need that it was indeed worth "a thousand words." Boxes and boxes of babies were lined up on the floor, waiting to be loaded onto a USAF cargo aircraft headed for Clark Air Base in the Philippines.

"The Catholic Archdiocese is particularly strong in Chicago (my home base in 1975) so I connected with a Father McVey, in charge of their orphan program," Kurtis relates. "I shot the photograph in a half-way house near Tan Son Nhut airbase where the babies could be kept cool. A C-130 was waiting on the tarmac to take them to the Philippines and then directly to Chicago." Kurtis had become interested in an infant that he describes as "a baby in pink" at Catholic Relief Services' Go Vap Orphanage, because he had discovered that she was going to a home near Chicago. He took a photograph that included her, tucked into a box in a long row of boxes.*

"The little six-month-old girl, Phan Thi My Hoa, was headed for a family in South Bend, Indiana," Kurtis recalls. "They had adopted two Chinese babies…and were a wonderful and loving Catholic family. Vietnamese helpers and nuns were tending to the children, and soon after the photo was taken, they gathered the boxes into their arms and got on a bus for a short ride to the airstrip. I lost them when they walked up the ramp, but I was shooting the process. I also had a film crew in Chicago to get a picture of the 'delivery' of Phan Thi My Hoa when she got off the American Airlines flight and was carried directly to Dr. Harris and family waiting at the gate." Thus, Kurtis photographed the last flight sent out by Catholic Relief Services. Years later, he was instrumental in helping the baby in pink, all grown up, to find her birth parents in Vietnam.[1]

Kurtis' fascination with the children, the process, and the ongoing tragedy of Saigon's fate, entangled as it was with the mass of humanity and the uncertain future, was matched many times over in the hearts of reporters and photographers from all over the world. Throughout the hot, humid days of mid-April, and on to the impending conclusion, flights were more numerous and landings and take-offs more dangerous, not only because of the attacks on the airport, but also because there were so many flights, both day and night, that there were sometimes only 20 to 25 minutes between take-offs, a situation unacceptable in normal times. The press from the entire free world documented transporting, loading, and flying out of not only orphans, but thousands of fleeing Americans and their Vietnamese allies. Clearly, Bill Kurtis and his colleagues were seeing the death of a free Vietnam.

Ed Daly, too, knew he was seeing the end. In the *Honolulu Star-Bulletin* of April 26, he expressed that both orphan and refugee flights from Saigon would probably be over within three days. "The flights will be ended in 48 to 72 hours, and that's about how long Saigon is going to last," he said.[2] Daly had just arrived in Honolulu on a Babylift flight that stayed overnight at Hickam, where the base gymnasium's makeshift

---

The baby in pink appears in the photo on the front cover. In the front row, she is the 2nd baby from the left.

dormitory held 256 cots set up side by side.[3] As the time played out, Daly's prediction proved accurate; several flights the next day were the last to leave Saigon.

The passengers on the Daly flight included 207 orphans, 43 other refugees, and 6 adults, all of them aboriginal Montagnards, the mountain people of Vietnam.[4] The Montagnards, well-known for fighting so fiercely with the Americans during the war and well-respected by the American troops, were sponsored by the Children's Protective and Security Society International, a Danish organization preparing the children to be adopted in Denmark.[5] The World Airways 727 jet landed at Hickam for a rest stop at 5:45 p.m. after a 16-hour journey from Saigon that included stops at Clark Air Base, Andersen Air Base on Guam, and Wake Island.[6] Charles Patterson, a World Airways official, said, "The Montagnards were most severely discriminated against by the Vietnamese people. These children have left a lot behind them."[7]

Mike Heninger, Air Force spokesman, said that more than 650 volunteers, wives of officials and non-commissioned officers, came from military bases on Oahu; in addition, many others came from the Red Cross. Like the volunteers at Clark, these had worked out a plan to have enough volunteers to be with the orphans on a one-to-one basis during their 24-hour stay.[8]

Two more flights carrying about 65 orphans each and the last planeload of 185 would arrive at Hickam the next day, all on their way to Denver. With those loads, UPI reported the end of evacuation flights of Vietnamese orphans from Saigon.[9]

The heroic and historic Operation Babylift was over. "So many volunteers spent so many emotional hours trying to take care of their child," Mavis Pearson recalls. "When we took our child to the airplane to continue their trip to the states, we spoke of how this experience would be with us always. Although we knew they had been through a devastating experience, we told them we loved them, hoping they would know and remember that we cared for them with pride and looked forward to their freedom. A part of us wanted to know where they were, who gave them a home and gave them, hopefully, a wonderful life."[10] The end had come, and for the most part, the volunteers would never know the fate of the children they sent on their way.

Upon this ending, unknown thousands of orphans, caregivers, and other refugees with ties to the Americans were left behind in a closed society to a fate that would be unknown for many years. A decade later, Kien Nguyen, eight-year-old child of an American father at the time of Babylift, was able to leave Vietnam through the United Nations' Orderly Departure Program at the age of eighteen. After spending time in a refugee camp in the Philippines, he arrived in the United States, where he set to work obtaining an education and securing his future. Today, Nguyen is a dentist in New York City. In 2000, he wrote *The Unwanted*, his memoir of the ten years he spent in Vietnam after being left behind at the age of eight. In his Epilogue, he writes of the many Amerasians he knew in Vietnam as he grew to eighteen, and of the reasons behind his writing.

Nguyen remembered not only the Amerasians he had known in Vietnam, but also their sad and desperate lives, which he himself had endured, witnessed and heard described for the ten years after he was left behind. Thousands of Amerasian children lived lives of "...terror and repression, abuse and neglect, strength, and ultimately—for the lucky ones—survival." He writes, from the heart, about and for those estimated 50,000 Amerasians in an effort to mourn the lost childhoods of the victims and to reveal "their buried secrets."[11]

About the last flights, the Holland diary reports hope and inspiration, as well as significant change. With the end comes introspection—the poet sees life differently because of the events of this remarkable April, and it is not beyond imagining that hundreds of escorts and caring volunteers felt themselves changed as well:

Wednesday, April 30, 1975, Clark Air Base, P.I.

Dear America,
Dear Earth,
Dear everyone I love,
I WISH you were here
So you could understand.
Something beautiful is happening.
I KNOW it is happening.
It is happening to me.
I am growing up.
And I am only sixty-one.
But then I've always been precocious.
...I must be tireder than I thought...
But I do not FEEL tired.
I feel re-born. I feel all new.

Old priorities are changing.
Old values are being re-evaluated.
This is important.
This is significant.
This is true.

I look on old treasures, old activities, old routines, old attitudes, old satisfactions, even old contributions to my small world community, and I see that April has transcended the important things of March.

(Even our daily pilgrimage to the Post Office for mail from the States now comes last instead of first!)

All things are changed.
I am changed.
I am learning how splendid life can be.
I am discovering that above and beyond time is timelessness.
In moments of crisis I find my adequate self.
I am strong with unexplainable strength.
I am intensely alive.
I step out of life into Life with a capital L.

I know I can work 24 hours and still thrill to the announcement that a plane is on its way with 200 more babies who will need my help.

It is wonderful to realize that thousands of others are part of this high drama; this sweat-starting, breath-stopping, throat-contracting, heart-swelling, mind-expanding adventure.

The most unlikely people are working as partners with God and each other.

If this miracle can happen here—and there is no IF; it is happening—then there is hope for the future despite worldwide evidence to the contrary.

I see, hear, taste, smell, touch — and give LOVE with no expectation of return.

This is agape.
I experience God.
This is the Ultimate Thrill!
Oh, Lord, what an April!

As the Babylift was ending, the situation in Saigon and at Tan Son Nhut was grim. Maj Gen Homer D. Smith and Col William E. Legro conferred with other commanders via telephone about the frightening general atmosphere. From April 22 through early the 29th, the impression in the city was one of "relative calmness" complicated by the lack of hard intelligence data. Though the Tan Son Nhut flight line was still open, the airport was under fire. The city itself, surrounded by 14 NVA well-armed and well-supplied divisions, was eerily quiet, leading to two uneasy questions: "What are they waiting for?" and "Are we being given some time to get our people out of Vietnam?"

In the end, the calm was an illusion, too brief to become an opening. When the C-130s were on the ground loading, the rockets and mortars began to hit the airfield with extreme accuracy—the control tower, a fuel truck, an airplane on the runway. Lt Col Arthur Laehr recorded his impression of the attack: "Intelligence had warned us that we would be hit by rockets and artillery on the 29th. I firmly believe the NVA were ready earlier. I think they waited until we got our numbers down to the point where we could make the helicopter evacuation work." Thousands of people were concentrated at the airport when the shelling there began. The Defense Attache Office located at the airport held at least 1,500 in the gym alone. That day saw the last USAF fixed-wing aircraft to leave Tan Son Nhut.[12]

Tan Son Nhut, under attack for weeks by then, was closed to travel. Subjected to relentless rocket fire, exodus from the base was halted when the signal that was dubbed "White Christmas in April" played over Armed Forces Radio. This signal was part of the 365-page plan that had been prepared for the evacuation of American Embassy personnel, their families, and all other employees who worked for the U.S. Government in an Embassy-assigned position. Mavis Pearson, who worked for the 374th Wing Commander at Clark when the Vietnam Embassy evacuation was planned, got the job of typing the large document and remembers that it was to be Bing Crosby who called a halt to the flights, when everyone tuned in heard the signal: "I'm Dreaming of a White Christmas." It was to be the ending of the airplane evacuation, and the beginning of the helicopter extractions.[13] The original plan was for "White Christmas" to signal "an orderly exodus of Americans and South Vietnamese. Buses were to pick up the evacuees and transport them to designated helicopter pads, but as the communists descended upon Saigon, mobs of hysterical citizens wrecked the plans. What occurred was an every-man-for-himself surge whirling in an atmosphere of pandemonium."[14]

On April 29 and 30, helicopter flights removed, dramatically, the remaining staff from the roof of the embassy and from buildings housing the CIA, and the DOD. The event left indelible images in the minds of Americans as film crews and photographers sent out their records of the harrowing event. Many years later, a Broadway production, *Miss Saigon*, took the country back to the spring of 1975. Its drama and music rang through theaters across the country as the helicopter extraction was replayed on the stage with a smaller version of an actual helicopter lifting the screaming, desperate people upward into the fly tower of the theater. One musical number in the show is called 'Bui-Doi,' and during its performance, photographs of the mixed-race children in orphanages are flashed up on the screens throughout the theater. The sights are horrible, but they document the plight of the children in Vietnam and their unspeakable misery at the time that the production depicts.

In the reality that inspired the theatrical production—a reality more than dramatic, more than desperate, more than heartbreaking—the leader of a USAF fighter flight escorting the helicopters from the roof of the American Embassy reported: "The next burst of antiaircraft fire came from the heart of the city. More reason to be sad, but no time for it then; the helicopters were already loaded and launching from the roof of the embassy building, back down the river toward the beach and waiting ships. The shuttle continued, but soon our A-7s were low on fuel and it was time to go home…I looked back one last time, just a bit overwhelmed at having witnessed history in the making. After 20-plus years of war, a city was falling, a government toppling, a country changing. Twenty years of bloody fighting with hundreds of thousands killed."[15] Saigon, and Vietnam, were lost.

Holland feels this ending like a death. The end of any war brings a stunning moment of disorientation to the combatants and no less to the patriots—and protesters—at home, because in that moment, everything changes. Everything.

Too soon it is ending.
Saigon is dying.
The priest is come and the candles burn…
Saigon, Saigon, Saigon, Saigon!
Beloved City of Sorrows….
City of ravished tomorrows…
Hundreds of babies still are waiting with escorts
In hiding near Tan Son Nhut Airport.
But, alas, it is too late.
Too soon it is ended.
Saigon is dying… Saigon is dead.
Pray for Saigon's people now—on this day of their city's death.

Thursday, May 1, 1975, Clark Air Base, P.I.

IT'S OVER!

Newspaper headlines keep screaming at me.

IT'S OVER!

In my grandmother-bag, there are many numbered Baby-Tags, tags with
Happy Faces that will never be tied on a tiny wrist or ankle.

In my grandmother-bag, there is a sock-doll intended for any unhappy
little Vietnamese girl who might need a sock-doll.
Where are you now, little girl?
Where are you now?

It probably was Solomon who spoke of appointed times—
a time to weep
and a time to laugh…
But extraordinary times like these run the emotional gamut.
So I do both.
I laugh with hysterical sorrow.
I weep with hysterical joy.
There will not be another April like this April.
I may never stop crying.

The telephone rings.

Someone else will answer it.

I'm busy—eating bonbons.

But they do not taste the same.

I hope they never will.

Thus, Jean Fox Holland closes her journal, knowing that her life, like the bonbons, will never be the same. Those who were involved in Operation Babylift, in whatever capacity, wherever they were, would carry the experience with them always.

17

A Year of Miracles

That stunning moment of disorientation affected Ann and Bill Say as it did everyone else in the country. At this point, they just needed to step back and regroup. "I was exhausted, absolutely wiped-out exhausted," Ann said, "and Bill had to go to the mainland for a convention, so I let the (adoption) agency know where we were going and how to get hold of us." Ann's family lived in California, and she needed to visit her parents and get some rest. In addition to physical exhaustion, Ann had been dealing with pneumonia, and a stay on the mainland seemed the best way to recoup and regroup. The trauma was over, and life had to return to normal. "We had just worked night and day, I mean, we had the orphan flights, but we also had the missionary flights and commercial flights from Cambodia, from Laos, we had flights coming in from all over, and kids coming in, so I went to California to get some rest, sure that we weren't going to get a child. The kids that came out from FCVN and FFAC were already assigned and they would go to those families, and they weren't able to get out any more than what was assigned." So Bill and Ann prepared the family to leave for the meeting in San Diego, where Ann and the children would find respite from April's unremitting activity. Operation Babylift had ended, and they had not received a child.

The last night the Says were at the convention, they were in the hotel room when the phone rang. Someone from the FCVN facility in Denver said, "Ann, we've got all the children placed, and there is still this one little girl here. We don't know if she…she's very malnourished. She may be retarded because of the malnourishment…I think she's about 2 ½ years old, and we wondered if you and Bill wanted to take her." The months of waiting, the weeks to obtain a home study, the efforts to acquire exemptions from the South Vietnamese, all finally had paid off in the most unexpected way, at the very end of the frantic transport of children. A child would be theirs at last.

"So I said, 'Sure!'" Ann replied, "I'm in California, so send her here; don't send her to Hawaii. I'll just wait in California for her. My family can meet her that way, and she can rest a bit before we go back to the islands." So the Says went to Ann's parents' home and waited. And waited. And waited. When Bill had to go back to work, he booked a flight to Honolulu.

Finally, after two days, Ann called FCVN and asked, "Folks, what's happening with this child?" The answer was, "Well, we were going to call you. We know that Matt's just barely walking; she's not 2½ years old. She's closer to 2½ months old. We mistranslated the documents." The FCVN people knew each other well and were aware of one another's family situations, so the volunteers in Denver knew Ann and Bill had three young children, with the youngest barely more than a year old. Caring for an additional infant would be difficult.

Ann knew that one of the big challenges for the volunteers had been sorting through boxes of documents from the orphanages to match up the children with the right papers, so the error was certainly understandable. The children, and the boxes, had been transported from Vietnam to Clark or Guam, to Hawaii, to the Presidio in San Francisco, to Denver, and from there to their new homes around the country, and the children were not always present when the translations were done. "We're ready to send her," the volunteer said, "but she's younger than we thought. Will you still take her?" Ann said, "Sure," and called the airport.

Bill relates, "I was literally on an airplane to go back to Honolulu. I had to go back to work, and Ann was staying on for a few days with her family to visit with them. The steward on the airplane came back and asked me if I was who I am, and I said I was, and he said 'We've got a telephone call for you at the gate.' And I said, 'Now if I get off the plane to get this telephone call, am I going to be able to get back aboard?' He said, 'Oh, yeah, no problem.' So I got off the plane—my luggage of course was still in the hold. I had nothing but what I was wearing. I got off the plane, picked up the phone, and it was Ann—and she was excited. She said, 'They've got a baby for us and they're going to bring it in tomorrow,' and I said, 'Oh boy, ok, I'll stay,' and of course turned around to say, 'Ok, you can let the plane go,' and it was already gone."

The next morning, May 6, the entire Say family waited at Los Angeles International Airport where they had been told to wait, and one person came off the Hawaii-bound jet with a baby in her arms, asking, "Are you Ann Say?" Ann replied, "Yes, I am," and was told, "Here's your daughter. I hope you know where there's a drug store close, because she has no more formula and no diapers. This is all you have, this baby," and she placed in Ann's arms a tiny five-pound baby, a survivor of triage and a journey of thousands of miles on the one of the last flights to escape.

"She handed me this child, didn't ask for any ID, didn't ask for anything, just handed me the child. We were the only people standing there. She got back on the plane and took off. So my kids for years thought that the reason airplanes circle airports is that they have babies in their tummies and they're waiting for moms to come to the airport and get them. We had a hard time talking them out of that one."

In the car, Ann removed the baby's bonnet and unwrapped her. She was dressed in a little pink dress, and five-year-old Susan looked at her and said, with the wisdom of childhood, "Maybe someday she'll be pretty, Mommy." Marcie was not a pretty baby at that point. She was very tiny, and "one ear was completely smashed into her head, you couldn't see it…and this side of her head was an inch taller than the other side, so it was very pointed, and flat on the back," Ann said, "They had always propped her bottle for her, nobody had held her. She had big eyes and was very skinny, scrawny, with diaper rash head to foot, and open sores."

From this inauspicious beginning, Ann and Bill would nurture a happy, healthy child who grew to become an educated, confident young woman. Marcie later destroyed early photographs of herself as an infant, wanting no one ever to see them. And indeed, no one needed to. They did not represent who she really was, nor who she is today.

Bill went back to the islands and Ann stayed on for a week. The other children played at Grandma's house, and Ann tried to feed the malnourished baby, who never cried, would sleep only on the floor, and fought to get away from being fed, being touched. "When I'd hold her to feed her, she would fight so hard to get away from me, from being touched, that her little head and feet would touch, she'd make a circle, fighting to get away." She would not eat when being held, couldn't keep formula down when Ann finally got her to eat by placing her in an infant seat, and fought hard to get away whenever she was held for any reason.

Back home in Hawaii, Bill and Ann settled their family in as best they could, with 14-month-old Matt and the new tiny Marcie both needing frequent, direct care. "Matt had croup as a baby, he had terrible croup, and so he would go to bed with a glass bottle of ice water, because it relieved his throat for him. It was something we could do to bring the swelling down from the croup, and so that was what he wanted, that icy cold bottle in bed with him."

Marcie on the other hand wanted nothing more than to be let alone and untouched. The Says took her to a pediatrician who gave her diluted soy formula, which was her main food until she was 18 months old. She didn't want to be held, didn't want to be fed, and the pediatrician said, "You have to hold her when you feed her, because she'll never get over this orphan syndrome if you don't." She needed to be fed every 45 minutes because of her malnourishment, and she wouldn't wake up on her own.

Those days and nights have stayed with Ann in very clear memories: "I'd set the clock, get up, go in and wake her, and she would cry and fight because she didn't want to be touched. I would change her, feed her, and then Matt would see the bottle, and he'd want one. I'd get him fed, get both babies back to sleep, and in 45 minutes it was going to start all over again. And so I was only sleeping in these 45-minute intervals. In all of my waking hours, I wore Marcie in one of those little pocket packs, like you see mothers wear strapped to the front of them, to get her used to being held in motion." Time and consistency seemed to be the keys to easing Marcie into the family.

In what Ann calls "a year of miracles," Susan had her own explanation for Marcie. "I was just overwhelmed with having her," Ann said, "and Susan was almost five, and she said one night when I was listening to her prayers, 'I don't know, Mom, why you're so surprised that we have this little girl. I go to Sunday School every Sunday and they teach us to believe that God hears our prayers. I'm not surprised

that she's a baby.' So I asked her, 'Why is that?' And Susan said, 'I was
praying to God that there was a good mommy here, and if there was a
little girl that needed that mommy, that God should send that little girl to
us. And so here she came, and you and Dad kept saying she was going
to be 2 ½ years old, and I knew she wasn't going to be 2 ½ years old,
because I was the one that was praying, and I was praying for a *baby*.'"
To Ann's amazement, she went on with irrefutable logic: "And God
answered those prayers. See? He did, and I got just what I prayed for."
"So," Ann reflected, "she said that's why we got a baby, and I have to say,
it probably is."

In time, the difficult life of adjustment for the Says and Marcie
returned to some semblance of normalcy. Their friends in the FCVN
Honolulu chapter gave Marcie a baby shower, and the room was full of
volunteers recalling the Babylift, remembering the events in Honolulu
and the chaos in Saigon, when Doris Witt, the flight attendant who had
gone in Ann's place on the last flight to land in Honolulu approached
Ann and Marcie. Stunned to see this particular baby, Doris said, "Oh, my
goodness! That's my baby! I have a picture of that baby in Vietnam."

"And she did!" Ann remembers, "She wouldn't let me keep the
picture. She said I had the baby; she wanted the picture. It was 'her baby,'
and Doris said, 'They were not letting the teeny tiny babies on the plane
anymore and I had fallen in love with that child, and I wanted to get her
out. I knew that we were the last flight, so,' she said, 'I put her in my flight
bag and I got on the plane and figured, what were they going to do? They
couldn't go back. And this is the baby that I took out.' That is why such
a tiny baby escaped, and why FCVN had one more child than what they
thought they had at the end, and so…Doris did something I couldn't even
have done if I had gone," Ann said. "She put her in her flight bag and got
on the plane. No one knew she was there 'till after the flight took off."

Doris solved another mystery about Marcie as well. She knew that
the baby's tiny size had resulted from severely limited nutrition in her
first few months. Marcie had survived all her brief life on water in which
carrots had been boiled. As a result, the watered-down soy formula was
the only food her tummy would tolerate for months.

So Marcie made her journey from Saigon to Clark and to Honolulu,
from there to Denver, and finally to San Diego and her new family, then
back to Honolulu—a vast distance for a tiny being. One extra baby found
one last set of parents because a volunteer who followed her heart would
not leave her to perish in her war-torn homeland. Thus, the child so

wanted by Ann and Bill (and prayed for by Susan) had been saved in the only possible way—by the action of one compassionate woman who did what no one else could do: secretly rescue one tiny, forlorn baby girl, in the midst of a chaotic mission to save thousands.

So many events in the "year of miracles" seemed to Ann to have been directed by the hand of God. The thousands of orphans who were saved, the arrival of Marcie at the very end of their hope, the involvement of Bill with VIVA while Ann worked with FCVN, and the opportunity that arose that spring to sponsor a whole family of refugees, the Dang family, after the end of Babylift…all of it seemed miraculous.

Even their finances offered a small miracle: "At tax time in April, we'd been through this utter chaos, we didn't know where any resources were coming from any more, because we had no money, we were barely making it," Ann recalled. "We did our taxes and we had spent 2,000 dollars more than we had earned that year, and we were less in debt than we had ever been. There was no accounting for it, but we made it through that year and didn't have any taxes, got Marcie settled, and got the Dangs settled, up and going and on their way. It was a gift from God to care for them. What a year!"

Years later, when Marcie was in high school, she wrote an essay about the Dang family, recalling that the families had kept in touch, and that the Dangs were careful to educate Marcie about her Vietnamese heritage. The two families are friends to this day, with the Dangs living in the United States, and with children and grandchildren of similar ages to those of the Says.

Bill's work with VIVA, and his abiding interest in service to others, led the young couple to another miracle…the possibility and the decision to leave Bill's career in banking and go to seminary to begin training for full-time service. After all they had done in the past few months, Bill realized that working full time so he could afford to volunteer part time was not a fulfilling life. How much better it would be to do the work he loved, full time, in service to others. He felt it was a calling, and Ann supported him. In time, the family moved to the mainland for that purpose, and the ministry became their full-time work.

It has been said that international adoptions should not be allowed because a child should grow up in his or her own culture; certainly this was an issue with Sita Byrne and others like her. That may or may not be true in peace time; who is to judge that philosophy? In time of war, when the children's country is crashing down around them, when death is imminent and certain, a philosophy of cultural purity cannot save them, but the Herculean and desperate efforts of those who are passionate about the children can.

Marcie is a young woman now, back in Honolulu after growing up on the mainland with her minister father, her gentle mother, and her three siblings. Young as she was, still she was affected by the early experience. She was malnourished and very tiny as a baby, and she is small as an adult. And she still has a preference for sleeping on the floor, a need that was instilled even before her memory could tell her why. Even now, at forty, "If she's having a bad dream and you want to wake her, or if she's sound asleep and you need to wake her, like you do with kids, you have to talk her awake, you can't touch her, or she does that same reflex. She's never, ever gotten over that," Ann says. "When she's sick, she will get out of bed and sleep on the floor; that's where she's comfortable, from having slept on the floor as a tiny baby. She doesn't want to be in bed. It's a throwback to that time."

Bill and Ann, upon retiring, moved for a time to a condo on a lake in Missouri. There, at a gathering of neighbors, one man noticed photos of their Asian daughter. "Where did you get this child?" he asked them. "From Vietnam," Ann replied, "She was brought out of Saigon with the Babylift in 1975."

"I know about the Babylift," he said. "I was very involved with that operation."

Stunned by his simple words, Ann realized how small the world is and how all of us are part of one thing, one experience of life. The wide dispersion of the Babylift, through the complex network of people, circumstances, aircraft, locations, and all the events of all the families, encompassed stories that needed to be told, and her story was one of them.

We are a part of all that we have known: the people, the places, the stories, the times we live in. All that has ever moved us to joy or to sorrow—the words and the music; the color and light and shine of our lives—all of it is one powerful, transformative experience. When one of us succeeds, all of us do; when one of us is lost, all of us are diminished. Each unique, discrete individual participates in the making of the world, of what it is, and what it will be. This Ann saw in a moment.

History must be remembered and recorded by those who live it, by people like the Says, the volunteers, the doctors and nurses, the military crews, the medical teams, the children themselves. All told, though the numbers vary, estimates are that about 2,700 children were flown to the United States, with 1,300 more going to Canada, Australia, and Europe. Their stories have been told in books and articles, in letters and photographs and Internet websites and in family legends. In the stories is the inspiration for new effort, new heroic individuals and teams who must respond to new crises. So the story goes on, recording the lives of the littlest victims of war and disaster, both yesterday and today. There is never an end to the needs of the children.

18

The Bases and the Aircraft: What Happened Next

Clark Air Base and the dedicated, caring people who responded so willingly to the need in that hectic spring were commended by the generals in a message that appeared in the *Philippine Flyer* on April 25, 1975:

Generals Note Base Efforts

Kudos continue to come to the Clarkites who opened their hearts and offered their time to orphans during Babylift operations here.

From Gen. Louis L. Wilson, commander in chief of Pacific Air Forces, comes the following message, addressed to Maj. Gen. LeRoy J. Manor, commander of the 13th Air Force:

"Please convey my personal 'Thank You' to all those assisting in the airlift of Vietnamese and Cambodian children to safe havens. My personal observation of the dedication and compassion of your people, despite the sad circumstances, has been gratifying.

"I know the entire Clark AB community volunteered their wholehearted support, and am proud of every one of them. My sincere thanks for their efforts to date. Keep up the good work."

General Manor also extends his personal thanks and appreciation for all the Clarkites involved in Operation Babylift, and added "I am sure it will be a long time before any of us forget the hard work or personal satisfaction of caring for these small charges."[1]

As for the military bases themselves, the inevitability of time
has brought changes to them all. In the Philippines, four years after
the Babylift, the post-WWII Military Bases Agreement between the
Philippines and the United States was revised, transferring command
and security of Clark and other American bases in that country to the
sovereign nation of the Republic of the Philippines under President
Ferdinand Marcos.[2] General Manor was asked to come out of retirement
in Hawaii and return to the Philippines to chair the negotiations that
resulted in the 1979 agreement. He worked very closely with Ambassador
Richard Murphy and was provided an office at the U.S. Embassy. The
project lasted several months, and was successfully completed; the new
agreement was signed by both governments in 1979. The agreement was
revised again in 1983.[3]

Over the next few years, the corruption and lack of stability during
Marcos' regime led to problems with the New People's Army, the terrorist
military arm of the Philippine communist party. When the Military Bases
Agreement expired in September 1991, just months after the disastrous
June eruption of Mount Pinatubo, the United States Air Force moved
the headquarters of the 13th Air Force to Andersen Air Force Base on
Guam (and later to Hickam Air Force Base in Hawaii), and left Clark
Air Base entirely. The following year, the U.S. Navy moved out of their
installation at Subic Bay.[4] For the first time since August 13, 1898, when
Lt Col Henry McCoy, commander of the 1st battalion, First Colorado
Regiment, raised the American Stars and Stripes in Manila, there was no
American military presence in the Philippine Islands.[5]

Today, the location formerly a city of 20,000 people that was Clark
Air Base in 1975 is an industrial area, though there are several thousand
American retirees and their dependents living elsewhere in the islands.
Many of these are natural-born Filipinos who once served in the U.S.
military forces. Now, the only American military in the Philippines are
U.S. Embassy guards and special forces troops who are there for training
purposes.[6]

Hickam Air Force Base in Honolulu, affectionately known to the
crews of the Babylift era as "Hickalulu,"[7] is still a viable and crucial
part of the American military system, home to PACAF Command, the
overarching authority encompassing the entire Pacific region. Changes
arrived there in 2010, when the facility merged with the naval base at
Pearl Harbor to become part of Joint Base Pearl Harbor-Hickam. The
combined base maintains its history and its traditions with care, honoring

its past and its heroes, but it holds little record of the twenty-two frantic days and nights in 1975 at the end of the Vietnam War, when thousands of children passed through to new lives in new lands.

Records kept by the chaplains who were assigned to two-week rotations on Wake Island reveal details of the massive four-month effort of Operation New Life on behalf of whole families of "boat people" and other refugees on Wake, but Operation Babylift is reduced to a notation on a plaque in the lobby at PACAF headquarters at Hickam, listing "Pacific Air Forces Humanitarian Operations." Sadly, Operation Babylift is erroneously dated "1973," which is actually the date of Operation Homecoming, when the Prisoners of War were released and taken from Hanoi to Clark and through Hickam to their homes as a result of the Paris Peace Accords in February, 1973. Operation Babylift in April 1975 was two years later.

Ed Daly's World Airways, which had begun its humanitarian tradition as early as 1956 by flying out Hungarian refugees who were fleeing the Hungarian Revolution from Europe to the United States, continued in that vein throughout its service as a charter airline for the United States military. With the dramatic last flight out of Da Nang came world fame, intensified by the unauthorized rescue of that first flight of orphans and other refugees from Saigon aboard the World Airways DC-8 cargo aircraft. Daly's reputation as both daring and compassionate was sealed by that flight and by his continued participation, at his own expense, in Operation Babylift.

Subsequent years saw humanitarian flights to Bosnia and Somalia, while contract military flights went to Desert Shield and Desert Storm, and later to Afghanistan and Iraq. The spirit and commitment to public service has continued into the twenty-first century with World Airways carrying the U. S. Paralympic Team to and from Athens, Greece, in 2004 and Beijing, China, in 2008. World Airways also provided emergency water supplies to Florida's hurricane victims and emergency equipment to Islamabad, Pakistan when the Kashmir earthquake struck in 2005. In that same year, the airline so crucial in the Babylift effort arranged a return to Vietnam for a group of adult adoptees, taking the former orphans, all desiring to see Vietnam for reasons of their own, back to their homeland. Today, World Airways is a subsidiary of Global Aviation Holdings, which provides charter air transportation for the U. S. Military and commercial global passenger and cargo air transportation.[8]

As for the C-5A Galaxy, the aircraft that has seen so much of history, the fleet is still flying, currently based at five Air Force Bases around the U.S. Like all other aspects of Babylift, the aircraft has undergone many changes in the forty years since the tragic flight. Improvements and system modifications to improve reliability and maintainability resulted in the C-5B, which deployed in 1986.

In 1998, the C-5 Avionics Modernization Program improved communications, navigation, and surveillance/air traffic management compliance, and also added new safety equipment and a new autopilot system. With improved engines and other upgrades, the C-5B became the C-5M Super Galaxy, deployed in 2009, with a service life expected to extend well into the mid-21st century. In fiscal 2004 and 2011, Congress authorized the retirement of 46 C-5As. In fiscal 2013, retirement of the remaining C-5As was authorized, and all will retire by 2016, leaving a fleet of C-5Bs and C-5M Super Galaxies.[9]

In pointing with pride to the enormous cargo aircraft, young pilots flying her now remark that the plane is older than any of her current pilots. For the "well into the 21st century" version, aiming for 2040 and beyond, pilots not yet born will fly the C-5M in mid-century.[10]

The C-141 Starlifter, which replaced the C-5, transported nearly 1000 orphans from Saigon to Clark in 24 Operation Babylift missions beginning immediately after the crash. Following those flights, the aircraft continued flying missions for Operation Deep Freeze (begun in 1955 by earlier aircraft) to re-supply and change crews at McMurdo Research Station in Antarctica. Flights occurred during the Antarctic summer during January through March each year from 1966 through 2005, when the 141 was replaced for that mission by the C-17. In those 39 years of service to McMurdo, the C-141 aircraft and crews created a perfect safety record, with no accidents on any mission and never an aircraft or crew left on the ice. On each aircraft, for each mission, a small image of a penguin was painted near the troop door, with a few boomerangs representing missions when the aircraft was unable to pass the point of safe return because of weather, and therefore had to return to the point of departure at Christchurch, New Zealand.[11] In October 2006, the last USAF C-141 unit, the 445th Airlift Wing, began to replace its Starlifters with the larger C-5M Super Galaxy and the C-17 Globemaster III. The last C-141 was flown to the National Museum of the USAF at Wright-Patterson Air Force Base near Dayton, Ohio.[12] Others were retired to Davis Monthan Air Force Base in Tucson, Arizona. Some were dismantled and recycled; the Starlifter's era was over.

The C-9 Nightingale, dubbed the "Cadillac of Medevac," was the only aircraft specifically designed for movement of patients, with dedicated medical teams assigned to each plane. Considered for decades as the flagship for medical evacuation, the C-9s were easily identifiable as medical units by the red cross symbol emblazoned on the tail of each aircraft. The fleet was retired from active duty in 2003 and from Reserve status in 2005.[13]

Saigon itself, the city where Babylift began, is a different place now. Gone are the bombs, the rockets, the damage of war in the city and the chaos at the airport. Renamed Ho Chi Minh City, Saigon existed for many years in a closed society. The city prospers now and is the scene of returns by some of the orphans, who are looking to the past to find perspective for the present and the future. Babylift will live on in the lives of these people and their descendants, a population set apart by its origins in tragedy and triumph.

19

The People:
Where They Are Now

Now the individual participants in the brief, heroic effort have moved on in life, or in some cases, their lives have ended. Of the key figures in these stories, Ed Daly, Rocket Rakocy, Barbara Navas, Delores Manor, and Jean Fox Holland have passed on. The Clarkites of the 1st Test Squadron served their time in dutiful, distinguished careers in the military. All who were interviewed for this story are in retirement, scattered around the country, mostly near their families. Each contributor has a continuing story of life after Babylift.

Ed Daly, the larger-than-life hero who started it all, died in 1984 after a long illness, much remembered, admired, and loved by those who knew him and his achievements.[1] In his lifetime, he was respected and honored by those who knew of his purposeful, heroic intentions, and at times was reviled with equal fervor by those who disliked his unorthodox methods, but in the matter of Babylift, by the Babylift people, he is universally loved and respected.

Maj Gen LeRoy Manor served at Clark from early 1973 to late 1976, then went to Honolulu, where he retired from his long and illustrious military career as a Lieutenant General. He went back to the Philippines in 1978, after retirement, to chair the committee to renegotiate the Military Bases Agreement with the Philippine government.[2]

Following this service, Manor moved his family to Florida. Sadly, he lost his wife Delores in 2012; he remains today in their Florida home, where he is living a busy, healthy, active life, recently involved in supporting establishment of a museum to preserve an important barrack at Duke Field for the American Special Forces.[3]

It is significant that after so many years and a long and proud career in the military, Manor has recently been honored yet again by the country he served, and by a WWII ally. In April 2014, he was inducted into the United States Special Operations Command's "Commando Hall of Honor" at MacDill Air Force Base near Tampa, Florida.[4]

In March 2015, the French government, in a formal ceremony in Tampa, recognized his role as an American P-47 pilot in liberating France from German occupation, serving from D-Day June 6, 1944, to the end of the war in Europe on May 8, 1945.[5] The French Republic bestowed on Manor their highest award, naming him a Knight in the National Order of the Legion of Honor. He shares the rarified atmosphere of that honor with such historical figures as Thomas Edison, General Douglas MacArthur, and President Dwight Eisenhower.[6] Remembering those years, he says now, "I was just a young Lieutenant and did what I was told. They told me to fly, and I flew."

Col Douglas Folts served three and a half years at Clark Air Base and moved on to other assignments. He and Patte retired in 1985, having served "30 wonderful years" in the Air Force. His duties through the years included service as the Base Commander at Altus Air Force Base, Oklahoma; Chief of Staff of U.S. Forces, Azores; and Vice Wing Commander at Andrews Air Force Base, Maryland. Folts continued volunteer work after his retirement and currently lives with his wife and daughter in Texas. He has written two books and is working on a third.

About his wife, Patte, Folts has this to say: "If you need something done, give it to Patte. I think the Command element at Clark knew this and that's why she was asked to help with Babylift. She helped build a team of volunteers from every walk of life at Clark, including high school kids. Together, the team put together an operation that entwined the heart of every volunteer, helping to relocate roughly 5,000 potential citizens who would contribute so very much to this country."

Jean Fox Holland, Patte's mother and best friend, "was so focused on her work that she was always asking what else needed to be done. She LOVED the orphans with all her heart."

She lived with the Folts family for many years and was proud of her role as the "Base Grandmother" wherever they were stationed, until her death in 1983. "We were stationed in the Azores when she died, and she had become so much a part of the life there that immediately following her death, every Portuguese officer and senior NCO stationed there came by our home to pay their respects."[7] Certainly Holland's heart lives on in her unique journal.

Thirty-eight years after Babylift, Col Folts and Patte, on vacation in his hometown, were introduced at church to one of the container refugees, T.T. Hong, who was 17 at the time she came out in one of his shipping containers.[8] Hearing her story touched him deeply. "This was the high point of my vacation, if not my life," Folts said. "The evacuees from Vietnam have been a credit and contributors to our country."[9] T.T. Hong, long since retired from her own service in the U.S. Army, still lives and works in the country she has come to love.

Capt Dennis (Bud) Traynor, after piloting the crippled C-5 to a muddy rice field in a landing that saved more than half his passengers, then spent one night in Saigon and returned to the crash site the next morning. Along with the other adult survivors, he returned to Clark in the afternoon, where they spent two days in the base hospital for observation and questioning. Most returned to Travis Air Force Base in California on April 15th, and were released to fly again a month later. Traynor proceeded to other assignments in the Air Force.

In subsequent years, Traynor and other members of the C-5 crew were at times required to testify at the multiple lawsuits that grew out of the tragedy and extended over the next 15 years. "At no time," he writes, "were any of the crew criticized, but some of us made several trips to Washington D.C. Federal District Court as Justice Department or plaintiff witnesses, depending on the topic."

Eventually Traynor retired from the Air Force as a Colonel, and he and his wife Pam, well known to members of the Airlift/Tanker Association (A/TA), have since devoted many years of volunteer service to the A/TA and currently manage the Association's information system and the annual convention registration process.[10]

Lt Regina Aune was among the 18 crew members who survived the C-5 crash and were decorated for heroism. Each member of the crew was awarded The Airman's Medal, and Aune, in the office of General David C. Jones, Chief of Staff of the United States Air Force, received the Cheney Award for her acts of valor "in humanitarian interest performed in connection with aircraft," the first woman to receive this honor. It is given in memory of Lt William Cheney, who was killed in an air collision over Italy in 1918. Surely thoughts of Mary Klinker and the ten other crewmembers who perished were in her heart at that moment.[11]

After Operation Babylift, Aune continued to serve her country, earning a Master of Science in Nursing in 1979 and a Doctorate of Philosophy in 1983. Over the years, Aune, like Col Traynor and other crew members, dealt with the difficulties and frustrations of the lawsuits at the same time she was working through the emotional trauma of the C-5 experience. At one point, she left the service and spent a brief time as a civilian nurse, then re-entered the Air Force and served in positions that shaped the future of military medicine, including commander of several medical groups. The last of these was the 386th Expeditionary Medical Group, Kuwait, in support of Operation Iraqi Freedom. In 2007, Aune was inducted into the Airlift/Tanker Association Hall of Fame representing all eras and aspects of the Aeromedical Evacuation Mission. She retired from the Air Force as a Colonel in 2007.[12]

Through all the years after the crash, Aune carried with her the slowly healing psychological and spiritual wounds that are "known only to the heart." She felt "great grief, intense loneliness, and spiritual wandering" for years, finally realizing that pain can be healed through sharing. In an article written for *Military Medicine*, she writes, "As I struggled within myself to heal the psycho-spiritual pain of my participation in Operation Babylift, I experienced a felt need to share in some way the whys and wherefores of my grief and loneliness. Each reaching out, each sharing brought me new insights, new understandings, new ways to view the totality of the experience." Today, Aune recognizes and accepts the changes in herself, and cherishes the knowledge she has gained. "In spite of my darkest moments and most painful memories of that tragic day in April," she says, "hope regarding the ability of the human spirit to endure, to overcome, and to soar always remains."[13]

Like Col Folts, Col Aune eventually was found by one of the orphans who was carried off the C-5 after the crash. Aryn Lockhart was 22 when she called to introduce herself to Aune in 1997, and to thank her for carrying children (possibly herself included) off the airplane. Now Aryn has become a part of the Aune family, a sister to Ellen, Diana, and Elizabeth, the three daughters born to Regina and Bjorne after Babylift. Though Bjorne is gone now, the family of three daughters remains, augmented by the much-beloved Babylift orphan. In the fall of 2014, Aune and Lockhart traveled with two others back to Vietnam, where they took a personal journey through time and began to write the story of their years since 1975.[14]

SMSgt Ray Snedegar, on that fateful April 4, 1975, had served nearly 17 years at that time. "I retired from the USAF as a Chief Master Sergeant on 31 December 1989," he writes, "with over 31 years of honorable service." His military career assignments included Radio Intercept Operator for 3 years, and then Base Operations Dispatcher for 2 years, followed by 26 years as an Aircraft Loadmaster, his position on the Babylift flight. After retiring from USAF, he worked in civilian aviation for another 20 years in an executive position with ABX Air, Inc., an all-cargo airline. He retired from there as Director, Ground Training and Regulatory Compliance.

In retirement, Snedegar stays busy volunteering at the National Museum of United States Air Force, working part time at a funeral home, and spending from April to October each year as the personal driver and assistant to a Baseball Hall Of Fame writer who covers the Cincinnati Reds at all home games.

As for his feeling now about the fatal day so long ago, he has the positive view that many of the adults have developed: "As I have looked back on it over the past 40 years and realize the work that we as an aircrew and medical crew team did that day to save so many of the people on this airplane, I now understand in actuality, a lot of good did derive out of the ashes of this particular Babylift accident. I see it in the lives of the babies we were able to save on that day and how they are leading good, solid, productive lives in the United States and other free world countries. I have met so many at reunions and through correspondence who are adding to society in a positive way."[15]

Capt Parker (Rocket) Rakocy began his military career obtaining degrees in Aerospace Engineering and Engineering Science, becoming a Navigator and Weapons Systems Officer in F-4 Phantoms. After several assignments in the U.S. and 2 tours at Clark, Capt Rakocy and Rose Marie were assigned to Fort Walton Beach, Florida, and to Valdosta, Georgia, before their final move back to Florida. During the 2 tours at Clark, the couple adopted 4 Filipino children, Elisalynn in the first tour and Rosalyn, Thomas, and Timothy in the second, adding 2 boys and 2 girls to their family of 2 biological children.

Rocket spent 22 years on active duty in the U.S. Air Force, and then 23 years as an aircraft/missile analyst with the Air-to-Missile Test Flight at Eglin Air Force Base, Florida. He and Rosie retired there in 2007, and on October 19, 2013, Rocket passed away as this book was being written.[16] Long before his death, he contributed much-needed information to this story.

Rosie remains in the family home in Florida, where she retired following 14 years as a school nurse proudly known as "Ms. Rosie the Boo-Boo Fixer,"[17] a title that became "Nurse Rosie Fuzzy Wuzzy" in later years among friends, as she devoted her time to the care of Rocket.[18]

Maj Thomas (Tuck) McAtee, after leaving the Philippines, moved to Edwards Air Force Base where he taught at the Test Pilot School prior to becoming a test pilot in the newly formed F-16 Full Scale Development test. These were difficult times for the military, and McAtee remembers dealing with the zeitgeist prevailing in the American culture. "While we sensed the public sentiment against our soldiers, we remained optimistic," he writes. "We learned many lessons from Vietnam and, most importantly, we kept our honor. During the next 10 years, we worked with many wonderful people to build the Air Force we have today. Ann and I look upon those years as our best."[19]

McAtee considered the refugees an important addition to the American experience: "Later in life, I worked side by side with one of the older children that processed through Subic Bay (known as the 'boat people'). He was extremely competent and became a great friend. Ultimately, he became an executive in a defense company and contributed a great deal to our nation. All in all, the Babylift and boat people were a gift to America. It was nice to see some good come from all of our sacrifices in such a controversial war."

Capt Franklyn Johnson and his family left the Philippines for a station in Colorado Springs, Colorado, at Peterson Air Force Base, for Air Defense Command in Air Defense Operations. He later transferred to Langley Air Force Base, Virginia, where he worked in Tactical Air Command as Chief, Strategic Defense Division, and then served as Commander of Radar Squadron at King Salmon, Alaska. His last posting was in Colorado Springs at Cheyenne Mountain North American Air Defense (NORAD), where first he was Chief of Command Post Operations Division and Assistant Command Director, and then Chief of Air Defense Division, retiring in 1985 as Lieutenant Colonel. He then worked for 10 years for various military contractors as liaison to Space Command. Betsy taught school in all these places except Alaska, which was a remote assignment for Bud. The couple retired in 1996 and divide their time living in Sun City West, Arizona in the winters, and Show Low, Arizona in the White Mountains during the summers.[20]

Lt Col Frank (Mac) McReynolds and Carolyn left Clark to spend 4 years at McDill Air Force Base in Florida, and then retired in Gresham, Oregon for 18 years. They moved to Tucson in 1996 and lived there until 2012, when they sold their house and moved to a retirement home, where they now reside.[21]

Capt Fred Aldrian and Kathy spent 21 years in the military. On leaving Clark Air Base, Aldrian spent one tour on remote assignment in Korea; then the couple moved to Nellis Air Force Base near Las Vegas. An exchange tour with the Marine Corps took them to El Toro, California, followed by a final posting at Norton Air Force Base near San Bernardino. Retirement from the Air Force found Aldrian working in several civilian positions using the skills he had developed in the military. Today, Fred and Kathy, retired a second time, still live on the west coast enjoying the mild California climate.[22]

Maj Anthony Callanan and Ginny were at Clark in F-4 Operational Training and Evaluation (1st Test Squadron) in Combat Sage from 1973-75. Leaving Clark in 1976, Tony was sent to an F-4 remote tour at Kunsan Air Base, Republic of Korea to 1977, then to HQ Tactical Air Command, Langley Air Force Base, from 1977 to 1982. At Langley, he created the operational and technical baseline for acquisition of commercial computers into TAC Wing and Squadron operations.

From 1982 to 1989, Callanan served as HQ Tactical Air Command Requirements liaison to Space & Missile Systems Center (SMC) at Los Angeles Air Force Base, California for overt and covert space systems. There, he carried the first military man-portable 17-pound Global Positioning System (GPS) receiver at Army & Air Force field evaluations. Callanan retired as Lt Col in 1989 with numerous medals including the Silver Star, of which he is most proud.

Following retirement from the military, Callanan in 1990 began work with Aeronautical Radio, Inc. (ARINC) Engineering Services at the GPS Joint Program Office, Los Angeles Air Force Base, California. He served as Technical Team Manager (TTM) for the first military handheld GPS receiver—the Precision Lightweight GPS Receiver, which revolutionized air-land battlefield operations. While with ARINC, he authored the first computer-based GPS Tutorial for military land, sea & air operations and spent the next 15 years working with GPS receiver training and fielding.

Now Tony and Ginny enjoy living in California, where Ginny is President of the South Bay Republican Women Federated and both are involved in volunteering.[23]

SMSgt Robert (Tom) Pearson and Mavis served two tours at Clark Air Base, 1973-1978 and 1982-1986. They left the Philippines in 1986 and transferred to Osan Air Base, Korea until May 1988, when they returned to the States and settled in Charleston, South Carolina, where Tom retired in 1991. After Tom passed away in 2000, Mavis continued to work in Civil Service until she retired in 2005 and moved to the Washington, D.C. area. Now Mavis remains active working in the medical administration field.[24]

Remembering Babylift nearly 40 years later, Mavis thinks of the volunteers as well as of the children: "We don't realize how devastating it must be to be loaded up and taken to a strange place, how frightening it had to be for them. It was very heartwarming and rewarding for those who participated in taking care of them. The babies were better off because of our effort. We made a difference. How much we wished that people knew more about what actually happened."[25]

Col Albert Navas, the Commander who supported Folts in his successful, if unorthodox, method of removing people from Saigon, moved to Washington, D.C., following the 1975-1977 tour in the Philippines. He served at the Pentagon until he and Barbara retired after a distinguished 26-year career in the military. They resided in McLean, Virginia, until they chose to move closer to their children in Great Falls. Like many others of his age, Albert suffers from memory loss and other health problems; Barbara passed away in 2013, before the completion of this book.[26]

Dr. Wayne McKinny remained in Honolulu, where he served as chief resident in pediatrics at Kapi'olani Children's Hospital and continued to be active in facilitating adoptions after Babylift ended. He recruited assistance from a law firm and from churches in financing the adoption proceedings, believing, "Sometimes you just have to give people the opportunity to do something good, and they will."[27]

Eventually, McKinny and his family returned to the mainland and he now resides in California. Still actively involved and committed in service to others, McKinny founded and today operates a center called "The Well in the Desert" to feed the hungry. His days begin early and pass quickly, and his reward is in the satisfaction of knowing he has helped someone in need.

About Babylift, and about direct service and assistance to others, he has this to say: "You can't do this sort of thing for glory. Dr. Tom Dooley was a good example for me. When he died, he was one of the most admired men in the world. At home he was the inspiration for the Peace Corps, and really famous, but all these years later, (almost) nobody remembers him, so I decided that it's not important what man remembers about your life that counts. It's what God remembers. That's the thing, and so you don't expect anybody to be grateful, you don't look for it, you don't need it, but you take that little pat on the back if it comes."[28]

Joseph Knowland and his wife, Dee, in the years since he wrote the Daly editorial, have carried on their lives in Oakland, becoming civic, cultural, and educational leaders, serving on numerous boards and in advisory capacities and establishing a Knowland family heritage in support of the city. They remain active in their real estate business and in leadership roles in the city of Oakland.[29]

Knowland, who had joined the *Oakland Tribune* in 1954, was given the "Publisher of the Year" Award for 1975 by the California Press Association for his "journalistic leadership" through editorials and news writing as Publisher and Editor of the *Oakland Tribune*. This honor was particularly fitting for a writer who had recognized extraordinary courage and determination and had formed a perspective of them for Americans who were exhausted by too many years of war and loss. Joe Darion's words set the framework; Knowland's revealed the tapestry.

Today, Joseph Knowland says of his accolade to Daly, "It was the right words for the right man at the right time." The editorial appeared in April 1975 just a few days after Daly's flight, and it led to a second tribute to Daly by the business community of Oakland in the form of a celebratory dinner honoring his achievement in bringing out the orphans. Fittingly, the banner at the dinner was emblazoned with the words, "The Impossible Dream."[30]

Journalist Bill Kurtis went on to further his career in journalism, working in Chicago as a news anchor for CBS. In 1982 he re-located to New York, where he co-anchored CBS Morning News with Diane Sawyer. In 1985, he returned to Chicago CBS, where he retired in 1996. At that point, he moved

on to host a series called Cold Case Files for A&E, and then developed Kurtis
Productions, a company that produced documentaries for both A&E and
PBS. Presently, Kurtis is still active in his company in Chicago, traveling
occasionally to his boyhood home in Kansas.

The 'baby in pink,' who was named Pamela by her new family, grew
up in Indiana, where Kurtis was able to visit and do follow-up stories
over the years. Pamela was very bright and active, participating in an
exchange program with the Soviet Union, serving as a leader in her
high school, and participating in vocal music as a soloist. Her college
experience led her to law school in California. Perhaps inevitably, the day
came when she wanted to find her birth parents.

"I had always been the strange 'uncle' in her life," Kurtis recalls. "I'm
sure the myth is that I personally brought her out of war-torn Vietnam to
the safety of America. It wasn't quite like that, but I was the only contact
she had with that 'creation myth' period. So when she started to have
questions, she called me."

At the Indiana home of her childhood, the two talked and
formulated a plan involving an ad and a baby photo in a Ho Chi Minh
City newspaper. This effort elicited a lucky response within two weeks
and prompted DNA tests on both sides of the Pacific.

"Imagine this!" Kurtis remarks, "Probably 30 plus years after the fact,
we make a stab into a forgotten world and get a response. What are the
chances that the first response would be real? So we took Pam's DNA,
just a simple Q-tip against the inside of her mouth, and ran the test. It
was 99% positive." At last, the years circled to the beginning and brought
closure for the journalist and the orphan.[31]

Jennifer Bartoloni, the Massachusetts adoptee now living in Denver,
grew up in a family with parents who subsequently adopted 8 more
children through the foster care program. Jennifer has very positive views
on her life experience as a result of Babylift: "I am inspired by people
who go out of their way to take care of others who can't take care of
themselves. The heroism and heart of all the people who helped the
orphans of Vietnam and those who took the time to tell the story will be
remembered at the most important and sentimental, tender moments
of their lives. I often think, 'I am so lucky. Thank you so, so much.'
Sometimes there is a tear of happiness and sometimes of sorrow." It is
possible that her thoughts and her desire to repay her adoptive country
by serving in the military are shared by hundreds of other adoptees.[32]

Jennifer's mother, from the perspective of forty years, has a view
revealing of what Jennifer's life was like. "We, as a family, were honored

with the opportunity to have Jennifer become a daughter and a sister. It was as if there were a plan that easily fell into place and easily evolved over the years…she is my baby. My thanks to her birthparents for their gift to me, our family, and the world."[33]

Bill and Ann Say lived in Honolulu for 7 years, and then, having decided to go to seminary after Babylift, moved to the mainland. With 4 young children in the family, they went to Ohio for 4 years of seminary, and then, needing a job, they said, "We would like to be in the west, anywhere west of the Mississippi," thinking the church would understand that as a request for a church in the western United States. Bill's first call was in St. Louis, about 15 miles west of the Mississippi. In the end, their entire pastoral career was spent no farther west than Missouri and Kansas.

After the children were grown, Ann embarked upon a career operating Long Term Care facilities for 2 decades, ending as Regional Director of Operations. In this administrative capacity, she oversaw nursing homes in 5 states—Missouri, Kansas, Oklahoma, Colorado, and South Dakota.

Now the Says are retired in the Kansas City area, where their children visit often, some from homes in the Midwest and Marcie from Hawaii. Bill at times fills a pulpit as interim minister when needed; both remain active in their church and family, and enjoy a lifestyle of volunteering and golfing.[34]

Marcie Say, the baby of the flight bag, who had such a doubtful beginning, is now a confident young woman with a career, who feels "… truly blessed to have such great parents who have always supported me, taught me all I know and made me the woman I am today."

"Funny," Marcie adds, "how people always ask if I want to find my real parents, and I always tell them I *have* real parents. They raised me and I would not think of having anyone else raise me. I really have never felt a need to find my biological parents, as I have a wonderful family who loves me and gave me a better life. I knew I was adopted. I could tell I was not like my siblings, but it did not bother me. Since they all had blonde hair, I knew I was different from when I was young. I guess I do not recall asking about my biological parents because I was so loved."

As for the effects of her infancy and her adoption, Marcie says, "I have always slept on the hard floor when I got really sick. For some reason I find it comforting or soothing, a little odd I know. Maybe it was from when I was a baby and no one picked me up to hold me. Thank goodness my mom rolled my head out when I was a baby; otherwise I would have a lopsided head from no one picking me up. At least I don't think I have any pictures showing my head like that!"[35]

Like Marcie, the other Babylift children are grown now, most with families of their own. They are finding one another, meeting and forming organizations and, in some cases, returning to Vietnam for knowledge of their origins. Any search of the Internet reveals sites and communications systems, social media, letters, movies, books…all kinds of contact about and among these Americans.

A few weeks after Babylift ended, while New Life was ongoing, the Commander of the 13th Air Force Maj Gen LeRoy Manor received a letter from J. Tierney in Bangkok, Thailand, which he passed on to the people it so sincerely commended. Tierney had been among the people traveling through Clark's refugee facility. In the letter, he expressed appreciation typical of the thankfulness so many refugees felt in the aftermath of their escape: "My wife and myself passed through the refugee facility at Clark Air Base. I would like to thank, through you, all the very gracious people who were so kind to us at Freedom Hotel. There were so many people who deserve our gratitude but, unfortunately, events were too rapid for us to remember all their names." Tierney goes on to name and to commend one officer, who wishes not to be identified here, saying about him, "I am an American, but if ever America was represented by a generous and good-hearted man, he is it. To put it mildly, he restored my faith in my fellow man. To you…and to all the people who gave so much of themselves, permit me to give a heartfelt thanks."

Those who so many years ago, in their youth and strength, represented America by their generosity and good hearts, causing "good to come from all our sacrifices," are an important part of our heritage, perhaps more than they realize. To see themselves as others see them may be difficult, for they simply did the task that was set before them. As Col Folts remarked, "Everyone involved in any way was only grateful for the opportunity of being there."[36] Babylift was their moment in time, to participate as volunteers, to do the right thing, and to remember; that is as it should be. But to thousands of adoptive parents and children—grown children—around the world, and to other Americans who believed in what they were doing and in the spirit with which they did it, they are more than volunteers, more than heroes…they are national treasures.

Epilogue

The tragedies that ultimately came from the Vietnam War and from the Babylift crash are as vital a part of the memories as are the triumphs of saving so many innocents. All kinds of sorrows can beset the human heart and tear at it in all kinds of ways. The loss of medical teams and crew members, so needed in the effort; of escorts whose only purposes on the ill-fated Galaxy were to care for children and to go home; of the children themselves, who knew so little of life or flight; of fathers whose own teenagers attended Clark's Wagner High School—teenagers who, after the crash, stepped up to care for the blameless children who had survived—all these and more made the country grieve with the families as the news came out of Saigon. The losses effectively set grief next to the anger that was so prevalent at the time, but they gave heart to those who knew they must continue the effort.

No tragedy is greater than another, really, but the loss of nurses was especially painful because of the tremendous need for them. They were not just names, these nurses who were lost. They had been beautiful, vibrant, competent women with a past and a future and with families who loved them. They had a world of comfort and care to offer, and when a nurse's future was cut short, it was a tragedy of major proportions, affecting, as all losses do, her family, friends, and colleagues, but also the wounded, the medical effort, and the nation. These were women whose children were never to be born, whose gifts of care and love were no longer to be given.

Yet, a perspective we must see is the context of the losses. All of the dedicated, compassionate people wanted to be where they were. All of them wanted to do what they did so well, to offer life and hope to the helpless and innocent victims of a war that they had seen become hopeless, that they had watched descend into madness. When they died, our country lost, with each death, a significant part of our own future, our own heritage. Nothing replaces such a loss; yet all were willing participants who knew that, in war, risk flew beside them.

Surely that is small comfort when your father, whose life was devoted to family and service, is gone forever; when your child, for whom you have prayed, is dead; when your daughter, whose dreams you have supported and admired, has died with a planeload of infants. Where is the reason, where the sense? It is seen only in the lives of the children they saved, for those you have loved accomplished their mission…to give a life for many lives, a future for many futures, a love for many loves.

The cost of Babylift was great indeed, too great to bear, for some. For the Willis family, the Klinker family, the Johnson family and so many others like them, the loss was final, heart-wrenching, with ramifications decades into the future, felt heavily even now by grown children who have no father, by their children who have no grandfather and no memory of one. But beyond the dark sorrow is a bright heart. In the wake of the tragedy came triumphant successes and joys that transcended the grief of the beginning and gave life and hope to thousands, creating the ongoing story of Babylift and changing every life that it touched.

Everyone who experienced any aspect of Babylift was changed by the experience, some by a tragic personal loss, others by a transformed perspective that would remain with them throughout their lives. Change unexpected and permanent affected Ann and Bill Say, who were happily living in Honolulu with their small children when Babylift came into their lives. Their decision to leave Bill's career in banking and take the family back to the mainland for seminary stemmed directly from their Babylift experiences. An office was no longer where Bill wanted to be, and did not offer the rewarding hours of his life; volunteering did, so service to others became his full-time calling.

Col Aune, in spite of great grief and a gamut of other emotions, found that what she had gained through change and growth has outweighed even the devastating early losses of close friends, her physical well-being, her flying assignment, her squadron, even her innocence about flight, and, for a time, her Air Force career. "Friendships that began in the tragedy of that day have endured and grown," she wrote. "I have learned much about myself and I have changed in positive ways because of the experience."[1]

Certainly the altered lives of the orphans, the entire purpose of their removal from Vietnam, is the primary and most dramatic result of Babylift. CMSgt Ray Snedegar witnessed the transformations in lives he was able to follow through the years: "I remember the innocence in the eyes of the babies and young children on that day. I see the hope and intelligence in the eyes of those same babies today, who have developed into teachers, principals, deputy sheriffs, nuclear engineers, chefs,

Department of Defense workers, and many other useful Americans. The view I have of those 'children' today when I meet them brings me so much joy, which is far from the chaotic, hot and sweaty, confusing scenes that were happening on that tarmac in Vietnam on April 4, 1975."[2] Reward, like perspective, is sometimes a long time coming. Perhaps the knowledge of the grown children's lives is part of Snedegar's reward.

It is also true that the Amerasian children left behind are not the same. Though they suffered mistreatment in "re-education camps" and other abuses, the United Nations' Orderly Departure Program effort in 1985 enabled some of those children, many of whom were adults by then, to emigrate to the United States and other countries.[3] Of the many others, who remained in Vietnam and remain there still, little is known.

Of all the changes described by the Babylift people, Holland's last diary entry may be the most heartfelt, for it reflects in only five lines the transformation in herself, which she so welcomed:

> *The telephone rings.*
> *Someone else will answer it.*
> *I'm busy—eating bonbons.*
> *But they do not taste the same.*
> *I hope they never will.*

The hearts of all those people were there, in Babylift. Nearly everyone involved with any of the refugees in any way experienced personal satisfaction and growth through their service. Air Force historian Kaye A. Jordan noted this phenomenon in her history of the Operation New Life refugee efforts at Hickam Air Force Base and on Guam and Wake islands: "The experience of writing this history has been particularly gratifying because the vast majority of the new Americans were young, bi-lingual, and had much to offer their new country. Even the oldest, 109-year-old Tran Thi Nam, who arrived with her son Lung Woang, 73; and her step-grandson Nguyen Huu Tam, 38; brought us a lesson in courage, for it was she who told her family to move because she refused to die in a communist-dominated country. Writing about the rescue of people of this quality is uplifting. Running like a theme through these documents is this feeling of gratification felt by the members of the 15th Air Base Wing who participated in Operation BABYLIFT and Operation NEWLIFE."[4]

It is not surprising that all kinds of people responded to Operation

Babylift in all kinds of ways. We are a multifarious species full of belief systems and biases that are a normal part of the human condition. But always and everywhere, there are good people, and as good people, we do what we believe in doing, and sometimes we simply do what we must. The years have confirmed the rightness of what the volunteers and the military stepped up to do so long ago, and through the dark sorrow of loss, we have to see one thing shining: all that they did was done out of goodness, compassion and love.

As winds of time sweep through our lives, they take with them many of our memories, but the days and nights of Babylift are seared into the hearts of those who were there. Their own lives were changed as surely as the lives of the children were saved, but the rest of the world has moved on. Sadly, now almost no one who was not there knows very much about Operation Babylift, an event so desperately chaotic, so riven with danger and urgency, that little was recorded of the events as they happened. It occurred in a time when our nation, wounded in spirit, offered a heroic effort to save the smallest victims of a war that had no victory, and that resulted in no real peace. Babylift stands as a brief, shining light, incandescent in a dark time, exemplary in the annals of war, as America at its best and as Americans open-handed and open-hearted in crisis.

Vitriol and anger followed the American people daily in those days, sometimes generated by themselves, sometimes imposed upon them from afar, sometimes indeed imposed by the American people upon their own military. Yet in Saigon and at Clark, at Hickam in Honolulu and the Presidio in San Francisco, in Seattle and Denver, in Australia and Europe and in other places around the world, the impulse that made one woman place one tiny infant in a flight bag to save her is the same impulse multiplied that made hundreds step forward to save thousands of the children of Vietnam. In that noble, altruistic three-week effort, one transcendent circumstance touched the lives of all the children—they were loved every step of the journey. They have the right and the need to know that. You, the adult children out there in the world, have the right to know that. You were loved.

Operation Babylift:
A Personal Account Based on Human Experience

Originally published in 1995. Reprinted with permission of the author and of Military Medicine: International Journal of the Association of Military Surgeons of the United States, Joanne Manelli, Editorial Coordinator.

By LT COL Regina C. Aune, USAF NC

The ringing of the phone in my room at the Chambers Hall BOQ at Clark Air Base in the Philippines jarred me awake at 6 a.m. I was the flight nurse on alert for C-141 urgent aeromedical evacuation missions. Alert missions were certainly not unexpected in the life of any flight nurse, but the message from our squadron scheduler that morning was not totally anticipated—we (flight nurses and aeromedical technicians) were probably going to be flying missions into Saigon. I was assigned to the 10th Aeromedical Evacuation Squadron (AES) based at Travis AFB, California; our regular mission included C-141 flights between Clark Air Base in the Philippines through Andersen AFB, Guam, Hickam AFB, Hawaii, and Travis AFB.

Early 1975 was a time of transition for aeromedical evacuation because of the Air Force's decision to align it under the Military Airlift Command. Our squadron was in the process of merging with the 9th Aeromedical Evacuation Squadron based at Clark Air Base. Medical crews from both squadrons were flying with each other on the C-141 missions of the 10th AES and the C-9 missions of the 9th AES. The chief nurse of the 9th had briefed members of both squadrons regarding the possibility of flying some missions into Saigon, but the exact nature of these missions and their timing, if they occurred at all, was ambiguous at best. The jangling of the telephone and the alert message made the possibility of Saigon missions a reality but no less ambiguous.

With all of the nurses and technicians of the 9th AES and what members of my squadron were available at Clark Air Base, I reported to the 9th AES's briefing room wondering what the day's flying duties would entail and which aircraft would be used to fly to Saigon. All of the flight nurses and technicians shared coffee and conversation. Uncertainty about our prospective mission(s) to Saigon dominated the small talk while we waited for information and assignments. After what seemed a very long time, the chief nurse informed the group that an aeromedical evacuation mission would depart for Saigon and that the plane to be used would be a C-5A.

I was selected to be the Medical Crew Director of a medical crew composed of members of the 9th AES, the 10th AES, and the 65th AES (a reserve squadron from Travis AFB). There was no further information available regarding the mission. I was surprised, and felt momentarily overwhelmed by my assignment (I was a First Lieutenant at the time). Nonetheless, the five of us selected to be the medical crew hastily gathered the supplies and equipment needed for an aeromedical evacuation mission and left for the flightline and the aircraft.

After arriving at the aircraft, the medical crew and flight crew introduced themselves. Normally, the Medical Crew Director gives a briefing to the Aircraft Commander regarding the particular patient population for the mission and whether any special medical equipment will be used in flight. Likewise, the Aircraft Commander gives a briefing regarding the anticipated mission in terms of weather, altitude, and other pertinent information regarding the flight that may have an impact on patients. In this case, neither crew knew what this aeromedical evacuation mission would involve. However, C-5As were not used for aeromedical evacuation and the medical crew needed to learn the aircraft quickly. Once the mission was airborne, the flight crew provided the medical crew with a tour, a walking lesson on the features of the C-5A.

Chaos is the only word that can describe the scene on the flightline after landing at Tan Son Nhut Air Base in Saigon. Planes were everywhere: C-130s from Australia, C-130s of the South Vietnamese Air Force, U.S. planes, and planes from Europe. Aside from the chaos, the heat was stifling. The C-5A was parked just off the runway. Noise from the constant traffic on the runway blended with the hot, humid conditions of the day and the smells of jet engine fuel. Bathed in sweat, I felt as though I was eating all the grime and dirt of the airfield. From the cargo ramp of the C-5A I watched the activities swirling about the field. Even after the cargo was off-loaded from the plane, our particular aeromedical mission still eluded us. We, the medical and flight crews, waited on the flight deck while the aircraft commander and the co-pilot went into operations to find out what our mission would be. When they returned to the plane they were accompanied by an Air Force colonel who told us that we would be taking 300 people—mostly children under the age of 2—from Saigon to Clark Air Base. The children were from orphanages in the Saigon area operated by several American and international agencies.

For a second time that day, I felt overwhelmed with my responsibilities. But there was no time to hesitate and the two crews began the task of preparing the aircraft to receive many very small charges. The flight crew was actually an augmented crew, and those members of the crew who would not be performing actual flying duties on our trip back to Clark Air Base assisted the medical crew in the process of enplaning our small patients. Because of their small size, each child was carried on board, handed from one crew member to another, and secured in its seat, which, in the case of those in the cargo compartment, was a blanket on the floor. Those in the cargo compartment were secured to the floor by both litter straps and cargo tie-down straps. What I remember most about the process of loading the plane is not the sheer magnitude of the enplaning but the pathos of the moment.

Many of the children were brought to the plane by young Vietnamese women who were sobbing inconsolably as they handed the children to us, strangers and foreigners from another country, speaking a language they could not comprehend. As I took each child from the arms of each anguished woman, I, too, wanted to cry. Their pain was palpable and I wished there was some way to ease it and to assure them that I would care for these children with all the tenderness and concern that they had for them. It was with a heavy heart that I took my place along the left side of the fuselage once we had finished loading and were ready for take-off. (Just moments before take-off, our medical crew was augmented with the members of a medical crew aboard a C-141 that had landed minutes after our arrival at Tan Son Nhut. Medical crews are composed of two flight nurses and three medical technicians. Augmenting the C-5A medical crew meant that there were now four flight nurses and six medical technicians on board the aircraft.)

As we climbed to altitude, one of the adults who was accompanying the children became quite ill. Two flight nurses and one aeromedical technician went to care for her. I do not recall our discussion of what we needed to do, but we did decide to give her some medication. Because we had stowed all of the medications in the troop compartment, I had to climb the ladder to the troop compartment to obtain them. While I was in the troop compartment, we experienced a rapid decompression (RD). The effects were devastating for us and for the aircraft. At the moment of the RD, I was kneeling on the grate in the floor in the aft section of the troop compartment, talking to one of the loadmasters and closing the medications kit. It was a classic RD, and once the fog cleared and I could look down through the grate to the cargo hold below, I saw the South China Sea, a vast, sparkling prism of diamonds as the sun glinted off the water. The sight was at once beautiful and horrifying. Moments earlier, the baggage and our medical gear had been secured to the floor of the cargo bay, and the pressure wall and cargo doors had been securely fastened. Now they were gone! One medical kit seesawed precariously on the jagged edge of the floor, threatening to fall into the sea below.

Moving from my kneeling position, I turned around to look forward and saw that another of the loadmasters had followed me up the ladder, only to be caught at the gate. He was hanging onto the gate by his arm, the rest of his body dangling into the void created when the ladder was ripped out by the force of the RD. Oxygen masks were dangling in the air; the children were too small to reach them.

Crewmembers donned masks and then proceeded to pull masks to the children's faces, attempting to give each child some puffs of oxygen. The pilots began a descent to a lower altitude and once we no longer needed oxygen, we quickly reviewed the emergency procedures we would use, and moved through the troop compartment, re-securing and re-padding all of the children and the accompanying adults. We prepared for a crash landing. Those of us in the troop compartment had no way of getting downstairs to the cargo bay nor any way of getting to the flight deck, and had no way of knowing what was happening in other parts of the aircraft.

Our first impact with the ground was a hard bump and then we seemed to be airborne again. Our second impact with the ground was much more violent. Although I had secured myself to the floor near the aft section of seats in the troop compartment, I was thrown the length of the aisle, and ended up at the wall that separated the troop compartment from the aircraft environmental systems and the flight deck. Once the plane, or what was left of it, had come to a complete stop, crewmembers began to assess the children and the adults for injuries. We had crash landed in the rice paddies and everything was covered with mud.

Opening the emergency window exits and stepping outside the troop compartment, we found ourselves at ground level. A short time later, rescue helicopters began the arduous task of flying into our crash site, ferrying the survivors to Tan Son Nhut for an ambulance ride to the local hospital. Since the helicopters could not land because of the terrain, they had to hover and we had to walk backwards when bringing the children to the helicopters to protect both the children and ourselves from the aircraft debris blown about by the rotor wash. Although some of the crewmembers were uninjured or had relatively minor injuries such as cuts and bruises, some others had more serious injuries. The loadmaster who was ascending the ladder to the troop compartment when we experienced the RD was seriously injured, two of the medical technicians sustained critical injuries, one of the flight nurses had a broken collarbone, and I had the bones in my right foot broken along with a compression fracture of L3 and a puncture wound to my right leg, as well as some serious lacerations. We were taken to the Seventh Day Adventist Hospital in Saigon for initial treatment. (Of a total of 29 crewmembers on board the aircraft, 11 were killed in the crash and 5 were injured seriously enough to require hospitalization. Among the 11 killed were 2 medical technicians and 1 flight nurse.) With the exception of 1 adult, 1 child, and 1 crewmember, all those in the troop compartment and on the flight deck survived the crash. There were only 6 survivors among those who had been in the cargo area. In total numbers, there were 178 survivors and 135 fatalities in the crash of the C-5A.

By evening, the C-9 alert plane and its crew arrived in Saigon to take some of the survivors (including me) of the C-5A crash to the hospital at Clark for further treatment. Just a few minutes before midnight, the blue runway lights twinkled in the darkness as the C-9 touched down at Clark Air Base. Our arrival was greeted by security police, key officials at Clark, hospital staff, and members of the Clark Air Base family. What I remember most about that landing, aside from its smoothness and gentleness (a feat promised us by the aircraft commander), were the people who stood along the fences of the flightline in silent solidarity and unashamed grief.

I remained in the hospital at Clark until April 19, then was sent to Travis, my duty station, on a C-141 aeromedical evacuation mission to continue my convalescence. Ironically, that particular mission was one on which I previously had been scheduled to serve as Medical Crew Director. I remained with the 10th AES at Travis until August 1975, when the squadron ceased to exist. Because of my injuries, I was given non-flying duties working with the schedulers in planning C-141 missions in support of Operation New Life as well as the regularly scheduled aeromedical evacuation missions.

Research Emerging from the Context of Human Experience

The foregoing narrative recounts just one day in the total experience of Operation Babylift, and only my personal, historical experience of April 4, at that. But the tragic events of that particular day certainly had an influence, direct and indirect, on all the Operation Babylift missions that followed. No one who participated in any aspect of Babylift, whether in the air or on the ground, was left untouched by the experience.

For me, the personal costs were enormous. I lost close friends. I lost my physical well-being, albeit temporarily. I lost my flying assignment. I lost my squadron. I lost my innocence about flying itself. For a time, because of other events related to the crash, I left my Air Force Career and played at being a civilian. The time immediately after the crash and for some years later were times of great grief, intense loneliness, and spiritual wandering. I missed my friends, both those who had died in the crash and my fellow squadron members who were now scattered throughout the world in new assignments. I missed our camaraderie. I missed our light-hearted and carefree enjoyment of life even as we performed our duties as medical flight crews. I missed the sharing of our cherished dreams, our momentary disappointments, and our joys. Unable to share my feelings with those who had lived the experience with me and to learn from their stories and their insights of the experience, I felt intense loneliness and abandonment as I struggled to come to terms with what had happened. I carefully dissected every action I had taken on that day, analyzing every piece of information that I had, trying to determine if I could have done anything differently that would have changed the outcome. I wondered why I had survived and what I was supposed to do with my life because I had survived.

However, my personal losses from participation in Operation Babylift are outnumbered and overshadowed by what I have gained. Friendships that began in the tragedy of that day have endured and grown. I have learned much about myself and I have changed in positive ways because of the experience. I am less patient with pettiness, or what I perceive to be pettiness, and more patient with shortcomings. I am less hasty to judge and more willing to listen. Split-second decisions without benefit of all the facts are the rule in crisis situations and cannot be judged by "Monday morning quarterbacking."

It takes time to heal wounds, whether those wounds are physical or psychological or spiritual. In some ways, the physical wounds heal the most quickly and the least painfully. The psychological and spiritual wounds are often more painful, heal more slowly, and require more personal energy. Unlike a physical wound that can be observed and touched and felt and treated, psychological and spiritual wounds are invisible to the eye and known only to the heart. Mere words are inadequate to convey the depth of an individual's pain. Each person's pain is different because it is experienced within the context of the individual's own unique personal history that includes values, beliefs, understandings, and attitudes toward life and the world within which that life is lived.

But for all its uniqueness, the pain can be shared and healed. As I struggled within myself to heal the psycho-spiritual pain of my participation in Operation Babylift, I experienced a felt need to share in some way the whys and wherefores of my grief and loneliness, my feelings of abandonment. My initial sharings were tentative and with a selected "safe" few among my closest friends. However, it was these initial sharing experiences that led me to return to my much beloved yet painfully abandoned Air Force career. Gradually, I reached beyond my circle of intimate associates, and shared the experience with relative strangers. Finally, as an instructor at the USAF School of Aerospace Medicine, I shared the experience with students and colleagues. Each reaching out, each sharing, brought me new insights, new understandings, new ways to view the totality of the experience. I learned, too, that although my personal experience was unique, it was possible to find commonalities with others who had experienced similar pain. One day a student came to me to thank me for sharing my experiences with the class and said: "I lost my parents in a plane crash several years ago. What you shared with us today made me realize that what I have been experiencing is normal and I'm not crazy. I feel so relieved to know that it is possible to get beyond all my pain." Sharing my thoughts and feelings regarding Operation Babylift enabled me to simultaneously "re-experience" the events of that fateful day and to focus on those events in a more objective way so that I could learn and grow from both the experience itself and the process of sharing the experience with others.

The spoken word provides a different avenue for healing and learning from an experience than the written word, as I have learned from writing this article. Although I had often thought of writing about my Operation

Babylift experience, I never attempted to do so until I began this article. Trying to articulate on paper what I knew and understood in my heart was a much more difficult plumbing of the depths of my soul.

Knowledge Emerging from Human Experience: Basis for Research and Implications for Health Policy

Although the foregoing account is a personal one, the most important lesson to be learned from it and similar experiences is how to help military members involved in humanitarian missions prepare for and deal with their personal, emotional pain that results from active participation in attempts to relieve overwhelming human misery regardless of the cause. Readiness questions often revolve around what force structures are needed to support preparedness for regional conflicts and peace and humanitarian operations. But military force structure is irrelevant if the forces are not maintained in a state of readiness. This necessitates putting people before systems. Force effectiveness requires a strategy to deal with emotional and personal trauma resulting from humanitarian missions. Whatever strategy is developed, the vital first step is to recognize that the personal and personnel costs of humanitarian missions are always factors that need to be dealt with as the situation unfolds. To choose not to deal with these factors is to increase their costs.

Today, because of much research in the psychological arena of war, battle fatigue is better understood and more easily treated because it is recognized as a constant factor in wartime operations. Likewise, the chaotic and emotionally traumatic environments within which humanitarian missions occur need to be recognized so that appropriate actions can be taken to minimize the psycho-spiritual pain of these situations and to maximize the opportunities for healthy adjustment and personal growth for those who participate in these missions.

Humanitarian missions, by their very nature, expose individuals who participate in them to event, occupational and organizational stressors. Because there is some evidence that these kinds of stressors can lead to post-traumatic stress disorder (PTSD), it is imperative that organizations, such as the military, involved in these operations learn more about how individuals cope with such experiences and integrate them into their total life experiences.[1] Preventive intervention before or immediately after stress symptoms occur is critical if the cycle of events leading to severe stress reactions and PTSD is to be pre-empted. Preventive intervention means that individuals are provided with the necessary tools to cope with and overcome the trauma. If the adaptation to the situation is positive and appropriate, then the individuals have a permanently enhanced mental health.[2] Unfortunately, as Armfield states: "Preparative measures may receive less emphasis…Lessons learned are not always retained, and we can pay a high price in casualties in relearning those lessons… Prevention of severe stress reactions in the military means that society will receive more resilient individuals."[2]

I am often asked what one thing I am most grateful for or what one thing I have learned or taken from my experiences in Operation Babylift. My answer is hope. In spite of my darkest moments and most painful memories of that tragic day in April, hope regarding the ability of the human spirit to endure, to overcome, and to soar always remains. I have learned that although the darkness of winter appears invincible, it is always overcome by the gentle and warm embrace of spring.

References

1. Stuhimiller, C: Occupational meanings and coping practices of rescue workers in an earthquake disaster. Western Journal of Nursing Research 1994: 16: 268-87.

2. Armfield, F: Preventing post-traumatic stress disorder resulting from military operations. Military Medicine 1994: 159: 739-45.

Twelve Minutes Out

Originally published in 2005. Reprinted with permission of the author and of Airlift/Tanker Quarterly.

By Col Dennis "Bud" Traynor, USAF (Ret.)

Nobody panicked.

Everybody did just what they were trained to do. C-5A, 80218, was just entering the South China Sea off the coastal city of Vung Tau, Viet Nam, climbing through 23,000 feet, when an explosive rapid decompression shook the aircraft. Submitting to the 93 tons of pressure, the rear ramp and pressure door blew out, severing all flight control cables to the tail as well as lines one and two of the four hydraulic systems at the aft bulkhead.

Nobody realized until later that student Flight Engineer SSgt Donald Dionne, using an interphone cord, had been standing on that ramp near the Troop Compartment ladder monitoring the passengers and their bags. Med tech SSgt Michael Paget had been climbing the flight-deck ladder and was struck by the break-away flight deck door. Flight nurse Capt Mary Klinker, forward of the crew entry ladder, attended to Paget's injuries while the Air Force Audiovisual Service (AAVS) photographers, Joe Castro and Kenneth Nance, used their light bars to illuminate and film the evolving tragedy. Med tech TSgt Denning Johnson continued to reassure and care for the passengers in the Cargo Compartment. From the Relief Crew Compartment upstairs, Military Air Command (MAC) Mission Observer Lt Col William Willis said he would go downstairs to assist passengers and crew. Copilot Capt Edgar Melton, on his second C-5 trip, who that morning at Clark AB bought a camera and all the film he could carry, continued to document the human drama as events unfolded. The calm demeanor of Loadmasters MSgt Wendle Payne and TSgt Felizardo Aguillon, while administering oxygen and attending to the refugees in the Cargo Compartment, contributed to their reporting that most passengers were imploring them to continue to the Philippines rather than return to Saigon. TSgt William Parker, caring for the orphans in the Troop Compartment, stood up in the aisle after the first impact to successfully puncture inflating emergency slide, 4-right, only to become a second-impact casualty. He died later of his injuries. In fact, all of these true heroes died—30 years ago this April—trying to give hundreds a better chance.

It's not that another crew might not have done as well; it's that this 22MAS crew did face the challenges and demonstrated personal valor and incredible teamwork. They picked up a routine thru-flight mission in Hawaii, previously loaded with 17 howitzers at Warner Robins AFB. All were unaware that the rear-ramp lock's tie-rod assemblies had been "cannibalized," and reinstalled without re-rigging. So thirty years ago, there was this ordinary crew, who by fate and circumstance would become destined to be the first military crew to support Operation Babylift.

It would be a normal mission out of Travis AFB on March 31—an uneventful AC line check. Capt Malone, on his dollar ride, had arrived for the pre-brief wearing jungle boots—not allowed stateside—his wife had to bring him his low-quarters. Then it was on to Hickam AFB, Hawaii; Andersen AFB, Guam; Clark AB, Philippines; and Saigon, South Vietnam—with a few "routine" emergencies enroute.

None of the young and invincible crew was truly aware of the gravity of the unraveling situation in Viet Nam. None was aware that two days before, World Airways had made the last, albeit "unauthorized" evacuation from Da Nang before it fell without resistance to the Communists. None was aware during crew rest at Hickam, that Nha Trang was falling, nor while they were enroute to Guam, that Cam Rahn Bay—once the US's largest military base in South Viet Nam—had fallen, nor that World Airways was evacuating, unauthorized, 57 orphans from Saigon, as five North Vietnamese divisions were amassed some 75 miles north of the city. None realized during their crew rest at Clark that President Ford had televised his intention that "Air Force C-5As and other aircraft" would fly over 2000 Vietnamese orphans to the United States.

While this crew slept, 80218 arrived Hickam from Travis with the copilot's windshield inoperative. After being alerted for the mission, the crew was asked, due to the high-priority cargo, to carry a new windshield for installation at Guam, the next programmed crew rest. A check with weather and the risk was accepted. Upon arrival at Guam, however, the crew was told they instead would be through-flighting Guam due to the high priority howitzer cargo. Number 2 engine was shut down enroute to Clark because it exceeded MADAR vibration parameters. All in a day's work.

With the recent introduction of SA-7 shoulder-fired missiles, MAC had for months been offloading cargo at Clark for transshipment—sending C-5s back through Kadena, thereby avoiding in-country threats. It seemed odd at the time for Command Post to refuse the offer to have the loadmasters stick around to help with the offload and transfer. They then suggested we might be taking the howitzers in ourselves the next day.

The good news was we arrived just in time for Mongolian Barbeque Night at the club and a textbook good night's sleep. The bad news: I put my hat on the bed—something that I had been told was bad luck—and remember thinking, wow: I've always avoided that before—and laughed to myself about silly superstitions. The next morning, the crew was alerted and informed that the engine "inspected OK" and the windshield repair was commencing – and oh yeah, we would be taking the howitzers in to Saigon. Despite assurances about the new sealant with a one-hour cure time, I was very skeptical. About 6 AM, while eating my breakfast Blitzburger (an infamously spicy-hot Clark base-ops-snack-bar specialty), I was told 22AF Command Post needed to talk to me. Without even hinting of President Ford's televised promise, Maj Spinney and Lt Col Tonec started asking strange questions like, "How many people could we take out of Saigon, really?" SMSgt Snedegar and I went out to the aircraft and paced off the tie-down rings. Including the 73 seats upstairs in the Troop Compartment, we estimated we could accommodate at least 1,000 people.

The 22nd AF then told us to plan on floor-loading as many orphans as we could for the trip back to Clark and then asked me what we'd need to do that. I was carrying my second son's birth announcement in my flight suit pocket and my first son was two. Yes, I had an idea of what young kids needed. We emptied the BX and Commissary of Pampers, got 500 juices, 500 milks, blankets, pillows and bottles. The 22nd AF also assigned a MAC Mission Observer and alerted the standby medevac crew to accompany the flight. Flight Nurse Lt Aune and her crew were in their last hour of eligibility. First Pilot Capt Til Harp, who had flown AirEvac missions in the C-141, coordinated the details with the newest additions to our crew.

We asked for extra life rafts, a security detail and for some then-new infrared countermeasures (flare guns and harnesses for two brave crewmembers to hang out the rear troop doors and watch for missiles). Denied.

Despite being on his "dollar ride," Capt Keith Malone was a prior C-141 AC, so I elected to put him in the jump seat. I asked my relatively inexperienced copilot, Capt Melton, to buy a camera and lots of film to document our efforts.

After several false starts, we finally were told to go. We finally departed Clark at 10:13 AM. The flight into Tan Son Nhut AB (Saigon) was uneventful. Enroute we removed all of the crew bags from the Cargo Compartment downstairs and put them in the crew bunk rooms.

Arriving Tan Son Nhut, they parked us on the diagonal—taxiway 18—about 1 PM. Apparently, the orphanages weren't ready for us as only a few busloads arrived. We left #4 engine running for air conditioning. For security, TSgt Bradley was assigned to the right wheel-well area; Engineer/Scanner MSgt Lynn McAtee was assigned to the nose wheel area, and TSgt Parker was assigned to the left wheel-well area. Kids were handed up mobile airline steps bucket-brigade style to the left aft troop door. As the children greatly outnumbered the adults, we decided to put the smallest children in the 73 seats for best monitoring and care. Maximizing space, we put two kids to a seat: kid-pillow-kid, with a juice to share and a seatbelt. If the kid could open the seatbelt, he was traded for a less facile kid from downstairs.

Though we were assured that there was a manifest, it never materialized before we had to depart. We did get a list of the 43 US Defense Attaché Office (USDAO) and other employees who we were evacuating as orphan escorts. Ambassador Graham Martin, who feared the departure of large numbers of Embassy or DAO would contribute to the growing panic in South Vietnam, saw this flight as a perfect cover to begin staff withdrawal.

On the way back from filing the flight plan, we were presented with an opportunity to buy Saigon Ceramic Elephants for 50 cents each. I never liked them much, but at that price…we bought a 6-pack (extended cab pick-up truck) full. (They were all destroyed.) We still didn't comprehend Saigon's imminent danger.

For the return flight, TSgt Allen Engels was at the Engineer panel, Capt John Langford was at the Navigator panel. For loadmaster duties, TSgt Bradley was assigned to the forward Cargo Compartment, TSgt Aguillon was assigned the aft Cargo Compartment, TSgt Doughty was assigned the forward Troop Compartment and TSgt Parker was assigned the aft Troop Compartment. Each was to maintain interphone contact with the flight deck. MSgt Payne was administering an evaluation to

TSgt Aguillon as he closed the rear doors; TSgt Bradley was outside scanner. NCOIC MSgt Perkins confirmed all door warning indicator lights were out.

Everybody was at the top of their game: Everything—the offload, onload, and passenger preparations—went smoothly and professionally.

About 12 minutes out, as we were transitioned to .7 mach from 250 knots, normal climb speed, we passed through FL 230 (about 23,000 feet), just past the coastal city of Vung Tau. I had just told Check-Loadmaster SMSgt Snedegar that the book answer was "13,000 feet for 3 hours" to his question about the no-oxygen-available altitude for passengers. The unequally loaded locks on the aft ramp suddenly failed, leading to the near instantaneous departure of the entire ramp and pressure door system.

It was a classic rapid decompression—just like we all had trained for in the altitude chamber. The rudder pedals banged full right and the cockpit momentarily filled with condensation. Immediately I assumed that the copilot windshield should be in his lap (I was still unsure about the new sealant). Capt Harp, in the copilot seat, was putting on his oxygen mask. I decided that was probably best for me to do too. Jump seat had just left to hit the head. The Troop Compartment checked in first, followed by the other major crew positions. Lt Marcia Wirtz was on the rear grate upstairs in the Troop Compartment, looking straight down at the vivid blue sea. MSgt Olen Boutwell and Sgt Gmerek struggled to administer oxygen to children too short to reach the masks.

I began a slow 180-degree descending turn and dispatched SMSgt Snedegar downstairs to evaluate the doors. His report that all the flight control cables were stringing out behind the plane like spaghetti was disconcerting to say the least. The Cargo Compartment reported that there was no panic and no one seemed to be having any trouble due to lack of supplemental oxygen.

Although the flight controls felt like they were all working because artificial feel was powered by one of the remaining hydraulic systems, we would soon figure out that we only had limited roll control and absolutely no control or trim capability for any of the tail surfaces.

As we leveled out of the turn, we could look right down at the shoreline north of Vung Tau. The airspeed increased through 300 knots and the nose started to rise. It continued to rise. The vertical recovery maneuver that pilots learn in the T-38—it works in C-5s as well. This time though the pitch of the airplane was extremely nose low. But I added power in the dive to get going faster sooner. That worked: The airspeed exceeded 350 knots and we saw the red line on the airspeed indicator tapes pass by. The nose again rose furiously, but this time, I led with bank to control the pitch. We leveled off at 13,000 feet to begin a "controlled" descent.

The copilot's mask mic was cutting out; so the jump seat, Capt Malone, took over the radios. On Guard frequency, he would soon decry in frustration, caused by the Vietnamese controller's inability to grasp our plight, "Would you shut up and listen? We're going to crash land opposite direction traffic. Clear the runway."

Approaching 10,000 feet, we put down the gear handle. We only lost about 200 feet during the extension and experienced no noticeable pitch change. We then emergency-extended the nose gear. By this time, the altitude was around 7500 feet, Saigon city was in sight and we established a visual, long left base. We planned to hit the runway with max brakes, spoilers, and then full flaps after we slowed down.

I flew the power for pitch; the copilot flew the remaining aileron for bank. In the turn to final, with the gear extending, we couldn't add enough power to keep the nose up and still bank the aircraft. I told the copilot to "Take it straight ahead." Even at this point I felt we could pull out of it and try again. We were wings level coming through 1500 feet with the nose rising. We pushed the throttles to the firewall, torching the unburned fuel behind us leading some to assume that we were on fire.

Around 500 feet, I determined that we would likely impact the ground and slapped the throttles to idle. We entered ground effect and hit about 1500 feet per minute rate of descent. We seemed to glance easily back into the air; I hadn't realized that the copilot put the flaps to full soon after I pulled the throttles to idle. We skimmed over the Saigon River and impacted on top of 4 or 5 men, helplessly watching us skim the water.

After the second impact, the aircraft broke into component parts: The upper decks survived largely intact; however, the Cargo Compartment crushed and was abraded away. The tail dropped off, the wings and Troop Compartment flew up slightly, leaving the flight deck to roll inverted and skid 180 degrees. Unencumbered by the rest of the aircraft, the wings took the Troop Compartment for a relatively gentle 1000 foot skid, broke off, and proceeded further downwind and burned—away from everything and everybody.

We came to a stop. Somebody yelled fire. I undid my lap belt, swung around the yoke, cranked open the pilot's side window and stepped out.

I reached back in and grabbed my hat and put it on (I was outside). It happened to be the Nav's hat; mine was in my pocket—but that didn't occur to me at the time. Right behind me came jump-seat, the engineer, and then the copilot.

Looking back along the severed flight deck, I could see a huge fire, which I assumed at first was the rest of the aircraft. As I rounded the rear of the inverted flight deck, I realized I was really looking forward at just the burning wings. There were several people who had been thrown against the forward ramp and ended up in the inverted Flight Deck wreckage. Miraculously, six children and two adults would survive the Cargo Compartment. One of the adults was med tech Sgt Philip Wise, who had been assisting Capt Klinker with the care of SSgt Paget.

The other adult, I discovered under a blanket on the ground at the edge of the Flight Deck. I had been stepping on/over her, removing survivors and casualties from the inverted deck. After I cleared the Flight Deck of remaining bodies, I asked Sgt Wise if he was cold and needed a blanket. I picked up the blanket and there she was, molded into the dirt and wreckage. I lied to her that she was one of the better off and that we'd get her evacuated as soon as we took care of the seriously injured. I called for a Stokes litter and they flew her to the hospital.

The four crewmembers in the Relief Crew Compartment—relief navigator Maj William Wallace, SMSgt Snedegar, TSgt Bradley, and MSgt MacAtee—exited through the rear and proceeded to aid the survivors in the Troop Compartment, some 100 yards away.

Sitting on the floor between the seats in the Troop Compartment, med tech Sgt Hadley later related that having no windows, his perception was that we had landed hard, had run off the runway, run back on the runway and come to a stop. He was absolutely astonished when he opened the hatch to see grass above the opening.

The Air America and Vietnamese helicopters arrived in minutes and evacuated the survivors to Tan Son Nhut AB, a small Vietnamese hospital, the Seventh Day Adventist Hospital in Saigon, and to Thailand.

Most everyone sitting between the seats fared pretty well in the Troop Compartment. MSgt Perkins had just returned to the Troop Compartment when the door blew. Fortunately, he was reaching over the gate at the top of the ladder and did not exit the aircraft with the door; but both legs snapped in the direction of the now-gaping hole. He splinted his legs with a crutch and seatbelts and participated in the transfer of the orphans to waiting helicopters.

After all the survivors and most of the bodies were evacuated, SMSgt Snedegar and I left the scene. I picked up the 781 (maintenance record) and the MADAR tape (unfortunately in the upside-down configuration, I grabbed the spare). We intentionally left all the crew bags for another day.

We were flown to the Air America ramp on Tan Son Nhut. BG Baughn took us to his office to use the Autovon (now called DSN). We talked to 22AF/CC, MGen Gonge, with CINCMAC, Gen Carlton, listening in—or so we thought at the time. We realized only later that the Crisis action Team (CAT) was activated for Operation Babylift and several command posts across the system were patched to our discussions.

We told "Gen Gonge," everything we knew up to that point and the questions started to repeat. Back at Scott, A/TA Founding Member, Col Bob Ellington interceded on our behalf and suggested they let us go to attend to the rest of the crew. SMSgt Snedegar and I were also taken briefly to the Seventh Day Adventist Hospital for minor treatment and then to the Gray House in Saigon, an Air America contract facility where we were all billeted for the night.

A burly Air America guy with a big gold-chain bracelet took us there. He took good care of us—he even gave me a case of beer—the last thing I wanted at that point. I took my 6-ring binder out of my pocket along with my second son's birth announcement and carefully laid each page out on the Formica dresser top to dry flat, took a shower—cold water only, discovered that I had no towel, wrapped myself in the only bed sheet, observed that I was going into shock, put my feet up on the wall over the bed, and went to sleep—for a few minutes. Although it was now nighttime in Saigon, it was daylight back in "the World" at MAC headquarters. I must have been called to the CQ desk phone four or five times with anxious people asking anxious questions.

I asked permission to return to the accident site to retrieve the bodies of Capt Klinker and SSgt Paget, both pinned in the forward part of the flight deck wreckage. Permission granted. About 6AM the next morning, I caught a helicopter flight from Tan Son Nhut to the crash site and arrived to find dozens of scavengers in the area. I somehow expected there would be this silver-helmeted guard, white rope around the accident scene and all, checking crew orders for access. Nope. I found a Vietnamese soldier carrying an AR15, wearing my AF flight jacket to complement his flip-flops. After a bit of pointy-talky, we established that it was my jacket he was wearing (same name tag as my flight suit). But the contents of the rest of the crew bags remained up for grabs.

More Air America folks arrived and we began the extraction effort to free the bodies of Capt Klinker and SSgt Paget. We picked up several aircraft 10,000-pound tie-down chains, hooked them together and with the assistance of about a dozen or so locals, heave-ho'd the piece of the flight deck pinning the two remaining crewmembers and got them out. We loaded the remainder of the crew baggage on helicopters before departing the scene.

We left Saigon that afternoon for Clark about 4:15 PM on a C-141 piloted by Mort Patterson, brother of Dave Patterson (fellow 22MAS C-5 driver and current A/TA Convention Chairman). Upon arrival at Clark, we were confined to Ward C of the base hospital for two days for observation and questioning, and sent to the Oasis Hotel.

The Accident Board convened immediately at Clark. There could be no accident scene protection, and the board members had to fly back and forth every day—2.5 hours each way. The scavengers were very efficient which made the investigation exceptionally difficult. We returned to Travis nine days later on April 15th and the Accident Board reconvened there. We were released to fly again a month later.

Then came the lawsuits—some 15 years of them. At no time were any of the crew criticized, but some of us made several trips to Washington DC Federal District Court as Justice Department or plaintiff witnesses, depending on the topic. Many, many millions of dollars were paid out to adoptive families—and their lawyers!

Despite the anti-war sentiment 30 years ago that perhaps helped precipitate the end of the conflict for the U.S., a nation grateful for the crew's sacrifice awaited the children.

May we never find ourselves in this position again; but if we do, I hope that we can have a team with the professionalism displayed by the Babylift crew.

What more can I say – Great people in tragic times. 138 people died that day; but 176 survived to live the American dream…

Epilogue. At first it was thought the crash may have been attributed to sabotage but later ruled-out by the USAF. The crash investigation was headed by Maj Gen Warner E. Newby. The flight-recorder was recovered by a Navy diver on 7 April from the bottom of the South China Sea. A Pentagon spokesman said the plane had undergone minor repairs to its radio and windshield in the Philippines before flying to Saigon but added that had nothing to do with the crash. By 8 April, Operation Babylift had resumed.

At the time the USAF had taken delivery of 81 Galaxies. Wing problems had plagued this immense cargo plane but were not considered a factor in this incident. In spite of its wing problems this was only the second crash of a C-5A after over 190,000 combined flying hours by the USAF but the first crash resulting in loss-of-life.

In the end, the Accident Investigation Board attributed the survival of any on board to Captain Traynor's unorthodox use of power and his decision to crash-land while the aircraft was under some control. Captains Traynor and Harp were awarded the Air Force Cross for "extraordinary heroism and airmanship while engaged in a humanitarian mission."

Traynor and Harp were not the only heroes that day. Once the wreckage came to rest, the flight and medical crews—many of them seriously injured—performed countless acts of heroism in carrying the surviving orphans to safety. Among their number was flight nurse, Lt Regina Aune. Aune was seated on the floor of the troop compartment in the aisle near the ladder area, right next to the first row of aft facing seats bracing herself at the time of the initial impact. The second impact jolted her from her bracing position and propelled her down the entire length of the aisle. She finally came to a stop at the wall separating the troop compartment from the flight deck—near the row of seats nearest to the forward section of the troop compartment. As she slid down the aisle, she bumped into row after row of seats, sustaining multiple injuries including a serious cut to her left elbow, a bone-deep wound in her right leg and a seriously broken right foot. Bleeding heavily from the cuts in her arm and leg she never-the-less made her way to an emergency exit and began helping the crew and surviving medics remove children from the shattered aircraft.

Five minutes later, rescue helicopters began arriving. They were unable to land in the muck and mire created by the aircraft's skid, so they hovered close to the wreckage. Aune and other team members waded again and again through the mud, almost knee-deep in places, to the hovering helicopters, carrying terrified children. Finally, unable to go on, she staggered toward an approaching officer. She managed to stand straight and said, "Sir, I request to be relieved of my duties since my injuries prevent me from carrying on." She then passed out. Later, at a Saigon hospital, it was discovered that, in addition to her broken foot, she had a compression fracture of the third lumbar vertebra. Despite her injuries she had helped carry 149 children to safety. She was later awarded the Cheney Award for 1975, recognizing an act of valor "in a humanitarian interest performed in connection with aircraft."

All in all, thirty-seven medals were awarded to Air Force crew members or their next of kin, including an Airman's Medal posthumously awarded to Capt Mary Klinker, the last U.S. servicewoman to die in the Vietnam conflict.

But, Air Force personnel were not the only heroes, or more aptly, heroines, on board. Thirty-five civilian women who were selflessly working for various U. S. government agencies in Saigon at the time of their death, were on board helping to take care of the children. They were: Barbara Adams, Clara Bayot, Nova Bell, Arleta Bertwell, Helen Blackburn, Ann Bottorff, Celeste Brown, Vivienne Clark, Juanita Creel, Mary Ann Crouch, Dorothy Curtiss, Twila Donelson, Helen Drye, Mary Lyn Eichen, Elizabeth Fugino, Ruthanne Gasper, Beverly Herbert, Penelope Hindman, Vera Hollibaugh, Dorothy Howard, Barbara Kauvulia, Barbara Maier, Rebecca Martin, Sara Martini, Martha Middlebrook, Katherine Moore, Marta Moschkin, Marion Polgrean, June Poulton, Joan Pray, Sayonna Randall, Anne Reynolds, Marjorie Snow, Barbara Stout, and Doris Jean Watkins. Three other Americans were among those killed in the crash: Theresa Drye (a child), Laurie Stark (a teacher) and Sharon Wesley, who had previously worked for both the American Red Cross and Army Special Service, and chose to stay on in Vietnam after the pullout of U.S. military forces in 1973.

In commemoration of that eventful time, World Airways has arranged a special flight—Operation Babylift – Homeward Bound. On board the World Airways MD-11 will be 20 of the former orphans, many of whom have never had the opportunity to return to Vietnam and see their homeland. Randy Martinez, World's president and chief executive officer, and several invited guests will travel with the group. The flight will leave Atlanta, Georgia, on 12 June 2005, fly to Oakland, California, and then on to Ho Chi Minh City for a two-day visit. The guests will tour the city and will be honored at a special banquet in the Unification Palace. The trip will no doubt be a very emotional and fulfilling voyage for the adoptees, their family members, World Airways employees, and the impressive list of invited guests.

But that's another story…

Author's Notes

Certain aspects of this book require some explanation for the sake of clarity:

Much of the information is taken from the two newspapers published in Honolulu at the time. Because the International Date Line passes between Southeast Asian locations and Honolulu, articles published on, for example, Tuesday might be describing as happening "today" events that happened on Wednesday in Vietnam. The same confusion occurs when writing dates—when an event was reported as having happened on April 5 in Saigon, the date was still April 4 in Honolulu. I have not attempted to manipulate these day/date reports. One article might report the Daly flight as occurring on April 3, another as April 4. I didn't attempt to reconcile or clarify; I simply quoted them as they were published.

The two newspapers had different policies regarding capitalization in headlines. One capitalized all important words; the other capitalized only the first word. For the sake of consistency, I have followed the former practice.

One more note on the newspapers—*The Honolulu Advertiser* capitalized the word 'the' as part of the title, and the *Honolulu Star-Bulletin* did not. That is an inconsistency with which I have learned to live. On Sundays, though, there was the single newspaper, *The Sunday Star-Bulletin and Advertiser*, a combination much like the current single Honolulu newspaper.

All the stories are told in the words of the people who lived them whenever possible. I used every word of Jean Fox Holland's journal, and in the Appendices, I have included Aune's and Traynor's articles exactly as they were previously published. The stories of the volunteers are direct quotes in most instances, taken from interview transcripts or emails as I received them, and some stories were written for this book by those who lived them.

Readers may become confused by the reports of varying numbers of orphans transported. The total is very hard to pin down, and in truth, there appears to be no definitive number. Some are military numbers that do not include those privately transported, or those carried out by

Australians or others. Some include all who went to the U.S., including those taken by Holt International and other private groups, but none who went to other countries.

It seems impossible that there can be no precise number agreed upon by everyone involved—all flights had manifests, after all, but as the month wore on and confusion reigned, they may not have been as accurate as they would have been in optimal circumstances. The manifest for the C-5A is at the bottom of the South China Sea, and even had it survived, it would have been incomplete. Air Force survivors of the crash and civilian friends of those aboard, as well as the orphanage workers, gradually put together a list of those lost, as best they could.

To this day, it is possible to find different numbers in different sources. Perhaps the total number of orphans transported out of Vietnam is less important than the lives of the individual children saved; a number, after all, is only a number. A child is one of us.

A spelling issue emerged early on. Many of the words were actually two words at one time. Saigon was Sai Gon; Hanoi was Ha Noi; Vietnam, Viet Nam; Babylift, Baby Lift. As time wore on, these names became single words in print. For simplicity, I have chosen to use those and other single-word spellings.

There is little agreement on the number of miles these children were transported. Going all over the world as they did, there actually are many numbers. I chose "7,000" for the title because somewhere along the line I read in a newspaper that Saigon is 6,999 miles from the destination in California. How anyone can be that precise is beyond imagining; I chose to round it up to a memorable figure for the title.

Because this book has a particular focus on the journey, I have not attempted to follow the lives of many of the orphans as they lived them after Babylift. The end of Babylift spelled the beginning of new lives for the children. Those stories happened in other places in other days, and there are thousands of them. I leave the telling of the lives after Babylift to another time.

Acknowledgements

Storytellers have been a part of the human experience since the times when stories were carved into the walls of caves and histories were sung around the fires of earliest man. But no storyteller, then or now, tells or sings or writes in a vacuum. The lucky ones find the people who know the stories and will tell them, to be passed on together and to become part of the story of a people, a nation, a world. I have been one of the lucky ones to find some of the people who know some of the stories of Babylift.

After initial interviews in 2008 and 2009, I began writing the true story of the adoption experience of the Bill and Ann Say family, who lived in Honolulu, Hawaii in 1975 and who told their story so willingly.

The Honolulu State Library provided me the contact information for researcher Lesley Agard. I am eternally grateful for the hours Lesley spent in the library's newspaper archive, locating and printing everything published in the two Honolulu newspapers on the subject of Babylift during the month of April, 1975. When the printed articles arrived in the mail I realized that there was a story to be told that was much broader than that of the Say family, and many stories within it. The 56 newspaper articles became the chronology for the story of Operation Babylift and of the journey through aircraft and air bases, over islands and oceans and ultimately to faraway homes.

Eventually, following a long and winding path with intermittent success over a period of years, I found some of the people who were there in Hawaii, Vietnam, and the Philippines in 1975 – people who were part of the courageous, compassionate, and generous effort.

Key among these people and the source for names of others was Lt General LeRoy J. Manor, U.S. Air Force (Ret.), who was introduced to me by Col Jack J. Gardner, U.S. Army (Ret.), and his wife Bonnie in 2011. Col Gardner and Bonnie have opened their home many times for interview trips to Florida and have offered consistent encouragement and a sense of excitement about the story and the people in it. For this and for being who they are, I thank them once again.

"Thank you" is an expression inadequate to share my feelings for the following tellers of their own stories:

Lt Gen Manor provided not only his own memories and documents, but information leading to members of the 1st Test Squadron and others in the military in Saigon, Vietnam, and at Clark Air Base in the Philippines in 1975. These families contributed all that they could to the success of Operation Babylift as it happened, and to the completion of this writing today. With one telephone call, Manor introduced me to Rose Marie and Rocket Rakocy, who led me to other members of their Air Force squadron. It was Manor as well who 'found' Col Regina Aune of the C5-A, and Aune who knew of other crew members on that flight. Without Lt Gen Manor, there would be no Babylift journey book.

Information and insights provided by the Folts family added dimensions that could have come from no one else. Col L. Douglas Folts, his wife, Patricia, and his family, including sons Mike and Kelly, were stationed at Clark at the time, and all were involved in Babylift. In addition, Patricia's mother, Jean Fox Holland, lived with the family and kept a careful and vivid daily journal of the events in which she participated and those that she observed throughout the month. I have included every word of her journal in this book. Though she has been gone since 1983, she lives on in her words. I am indebted to her especially for the most visual line in her poem, which I have used as the title of the book.

It is also through the Folts family that I obtained from Hong T.T. Nguyen the perspective of a child old enough to remember her extraction from her collapsing country. I thank her for sharing those memories.

Members of the 1st Test Squadron, 405th Fighter Wing, Clark Air Base, Republic of the Philippines, offered immediate assistance in putting together a narrative of the events at Clark during that fateful April. Capt Parker (Rocket) Rakocy and Rose Marie provided contact information for each of the couples, after getting them on board for the book. Rosie was particularly helpful in encouraging everyone to respond to my first emails and phone calls.

Capt Fred Aldrian and Kathy, Maj Anthony P. Callanan and Virginia, Maj Franklyn R. Johnson and Betsy, Maj Thomas P. McAtee and Ann, Lt Col Frank McReynolds and Carolyn, all of the 1st Test Squadron, willingly, even eagerly, offered their memories by interview and email, in several cases saying, "This story needs to be told. Please don't give up."

Also stationed at Clark were Col Albert M. Navas and Barbara; her interview, and information from their daughter, Virginia, added another story to the accumulating details of the events there. In addition, SMSgt Tom Pearson and Mavis worked tirelessly through the month, Tom for the Aerial Port Squadron, where all aircraft were processed for flight, and Mavis as a civilian spouse working for the 374th Wing Commander. Her vivid story offers a glimpse into the frantic hours after the crash and the impact of the children on the volunteers.

Col Regina Aune, Col Dennis Traynor, and SMSgt Ray Snedegar graciously gave me powerful and detailed information about the crash of the C-5A in Saigon, based on their experiences as survivors. All are storytellers themselves, and all were willing to share, both in writing and in interviews, memories of that day that are painful even now. No news report, no secondary source of any kind, could have brought to life the stories that these people told. The articles written by Aune and Traynor appear in their entirety in the Appendices of this book. For allowing that, I sincerely thank them and their publishers.

Col Aune also offered valuable assistance in scheduling a tour of the C-5A at the 433rd Airlift Wing Headquarters, Lackland AFB, San Antonio, Texas. I deeply appreciate Maj Timothy Wade, PA officer at Lackland, who facilitated the tour, and both Maj Federico Mendoza and Lt Thomas Fedesna, pilots of the aircraft, who led our group through the entire airplane. There, Aune described details of the events before, during, and after the crash, details that became visceral and immediate in ways that the imagination could never create. I have tried to offer words to bring those events to life.

Award-winning history teacher Joanne Pfannenstiel Emerick, Historian of the WW II 31st Bombardment Squadron and author of *Courage Before Every Danger, Honor Before All Men*, deserves a special thanks. Her encouragement from the very beginning, her suggestions and assistance in locating sources, and her generous invitation allowing me to join her group of veterans on their travels to Hickam Air Force Base, Hawaii, in December 2011 all were invaluable in this years-long effort to find the truth in the story of the unique journey.

United States Air Force History Offices offered as much information as possible, given that the operation was so brief and chaotic, and the record-keeping so difficult. I am indebted to Jenny Krider, Historian, 15th Wing History Office, Hickam AFB, Hawaii, 2011, who not only gave me access to records in the office, but later scanned many pages and sent them to me in Kansas; to Paul Hibbeln, Historian, 15th Wing History Office, Hickam AFB, Hawaii, 2012, who was Jenny's follow-on in the history office; and to Judith Taylor, Historian, Air Force Medical Services, San Antonio, Texas, 2012, who sent the relevant pages from the Torma article and the Haulman book that I have cited as sources. All came forward to assist a complete stranger in the request for documents and information that, as Jenny Krider remarked, "belong to the people of the United States." Jim Boyd, USAF RAO Director, U.S. Embassy Warden, Angeles City, Philippines 2013, offered information and corrections on the history and ultimate fate of Clark Air Base.

In addition to the above historians, Jessie Higa, Volunteer Historian at Hickam AFB, deserves my profound thanks for her successful efforts to acquire permission for me to tour Hickam with the group of veterans led by Joanne Emerick. It was only through the encouragement and efforts of Emerick and Higa that I was able to attend December 7, 2011 commemorative ceremonies, tour the base, and spend time in the history office there.

Charlotte Hinger, award-winning novelist and Kansas historian, has been in my corner from the beginning with advice on everything from query letters to proposals, documentation, and marketing. She has my deep and eternal gratitude.

Among those who volunteered or supported Operation Babylift and the journeys of the children in various ways were a great many civilians at all the locations. I was able to locate only a few of these people. Dr. Wayne McKinny offered background information, as well as vivid and critical details about his experiences, both in Saigon and aboard the aircraft. Joseph W. Knowland, publisher and editor of the *Oakland Tribune* when Babylift occurred, was most generous in his willingness to share his iconic editorial. Bill Kurtis offered encouragement from his first reading, and gave permission to use not only his stunning photographs, including the one on the cover, but also his personal story of "the baby in pink." Bill was on assignment for CBS in Saigon at the time. To all of these people, I offer my deepest gratitude.

Key among the civilians are Bill and Ann Say, the volunteers and adoptive parents whose story inspired the writing of this book. From the first interview in the fall of 2008 to a meeting in late 2014, they have patiently waited through the long process and offered encouragement in reading early versions, from the first attempted magazine article to a recent version of the book that grew out of that attempt. I am so grateful for their help and their patience.

Marcie Say, the baby of the flight bag, who naturally remembers nothing of the events, belongs in this list as an enthusiastic follower of the story and a young woman who understands her place in it. I thank her for her views on her family, her life, and her place in this story.

Friends and family inevitably become involved in a project that arouses so much interest and so many questions over so many years. Karen James Torline tipped me off years ago about the interesting couple who lived next door to her — a couple who had adopted a Vietnamese baby who came from Operation Babylift in 1975. Recognizing a good story when she heard one, and remaining in touch with the Say family, she eventually went with me to Missouri for the initial interview in 2008. I owe her my thanks for her intuitive recognition of a good story and her belief in my ability to write it.

Among other friends and family who assisted in locating people and information are Jarrod Deines, Command Master Chief, U.S. Navy, who located additional information and contacts while he was at Hickam; Colleen Milleson, who followed a hunch and found the good doctor; Bill Milleson, who long ago wrote letters home from Vietnam describing and remembering the orphanages; and Vincente Vasquez, who shared his extensive knowledge of and experience with the C-141.

Mark and Elizabeth James, Cindy Schnelle, Joanne Emerick, and Charlotte Hinger all read various versions of the book and offered perceptive and helpful comments. Vickie Deines was captive audience to an oral reading of an early version of the book on a long drive across Kansas and named what was, to her, the best story. Ann and Bill Say read a nearly finished version, and their satisfaction and praise were effective in providing impetus for the ongoing project. Sueanne Hill waded through the list of sources and the endnotes searching for errors (and finding them). For the consistent encouragement of all these people, I am forever grateful.

It is essential that I thank here my tech support guy and general life-saver and sanity-preserver, who kept me from outright panic on several occasions. Tyrell Spillman at Rejuvitech in Hoxie, Kansas, has more patience than I deserve, and he kept the technology from collapsing and the whole project on track without even knowing what the book was about. I am thankful daily for his expertise.

Any acknowledgment of assistance and encouragement would be incomplete without expressing my deep appreciation and affection for the late Helen Hadley Lambert, who traveled the writing journey with me for many years, through poetry both personal and published, through Babylift searches and stories and successes. No friend has ever been more true.

To my deep regret, I was never able to locate the compassionate, courageous stewardess, Doris Witt, who above all people exemplified the spirit of Babylift when she made a personal decision at a moment's notice and saved a single infant who would become Marcie Say. Wherever she is, although I cannot thank her for information about Babylift, I do thank her, from my heart, for her part in it.

Myrna James Yoo at Blueline Publishing took a chance on a book about an esoteric and limited subject when she agreed to publish *Angels Flying Out of Hell*. The book is not only a story in itself; it is a conduit for many stories. With great perception, Yoo recognized the need for true stories, the hunger for them in our world. No expression of gratitude is adequate for such awareness, nor for the assistance offered by Yoo and her team at Blueline Publishing. I especially appreciate the expertise of designer Paul Rodriguez in preparing the beautiful cover and final document for printing, and of Greg Cradick for his fine photography.

Chapter Endnotes

The Prologue
1 Adamski, Refugee Airlift Finish Seen in 48-72 Hours…, *Honolulu Star-Bulletin*.
2Ann Say, interview Oct. 4, 2008.

Chapter 1 The Beginning
1 Tobin, *Last Flight from Saigon*, p. 19.
2 Ann Say, interview Oct. 4, 2008.
3 McKinny, interview Aug. 27, 2012.
4 Milleson, interview Oct. 6, 2013.
5 Milleson, letters from Vietnam.
6 Nelson, 17 Children Escape the Suffering…, *Honolulu Star-Bulletin*.
7 Kelly, Agency Speeds up Rescue…, *The Honolulu Advertiser*.
8 Bill Say, interview June 10, 2009.
9 McKinny, interview Aug. 27, 2012.
10 McKinny, interview Aug. 30, 2012.
11 Northshield, *The Sins of the Fathers*.
12 Northshield, NBC Reports: *The Sins of the Fathers*.

Chapter 2 Vietnam: A Country in Transition
1 Karnow, *Vietnam: A History*, p. 684.
2 Karnow, p. 688.
3 Karnow, p. 684.
4 Karnow, p. 676.
5 Karnow, p. 685.
6 Ann Say, interview Oct. 4, 2008.
7 Tobin, p. 17.
8 Tobin, p. 18.
9 Ann Say, interview Oct. 4, 2008.
10 Nelson, 17 Children Escape the Suffering…, *Honolulu Star-Bulletin*.
11 Islanders Open Homes…, *Honolulu Star-Bulletin*.

12 Islanders Open Homes...

13 Cross, MAC and Operation Babylift, Airlift.

14 Cross, MAC and...

15 Islanders Open Homes...

Chapter 3 The Daly Flight

1 Zeitlin, Evacuation of Orphans..., *Honolulu Star-Bulletin*.

2 Ibid.

3 Kloss, To Vietnam's Orphans..., *Honolulu Star-Bulletin*.

4 Zeitlin, Evacuation...

5 Arnett, Pilot Ignores Order, *Honolulu Star-Bulletin*.

6 Ibid.

7 Manor, interview Nov. 6, 2011.

8 World Airways Cargo Back to Saigon 1975, online.

9 Adamski, Tiny Crash Victim..., *Honolulu Star-Bulletin*.

10 Kloss, To Vietnam's Orphans...

11 Arnett, Pilot ignores...

12 Ibid.

13 Minetree, *People Magazine* Archive, online.

14 Washington Post Service. Viet Aid Offers Skyrocket.

15 World Airways Cargo...

16 How Many Passengers Can Fit in a 727? From the flight deck.com, online.

17 Arnett, Pilot Ignores...

18 Ibid.

19 Zeitlin, Evacuation of Orphans Vowed...

20 Arnett, Saigon Tots..., *Honolulu Star-Bulletin*.

21 Minetree.

Chapter 4 President Ford and the Commitment to Babylift

1 Cross, MAC and...

2 Bulletin, Orphan Plane Crashes, *The Honolulu Advertiser*.

3 Washington Post Service. Viet Aid Offers..., *The Honolulu Advertiser*.

4 Ibid.

5 Vietnam Donation Agencies Listed, *Honolulu Star-Bulletin*.

6 Immigration Pleas Speeded Up Here, *Honolulu Star-Bulletin*.

7 Ong, Hawaii's Help Us Roster..., *The Honolulu Advertiser*.

8 Bulletin, Orphan Plane..., *The Honolulu Advertiser*.

9 Cunningham, Viet Kin Target..., *The Honolulu Advertiser*.

10 Ibid.

11 Evacuate Kin First…, *Honolulu Star-Bulletin*.

12 Cunningham.

13 Kelly, Agency Speeds up, *The Honolulu Advertiser*.

14 Manor, personal interview April 4, 2012.

15 Order of the Sword: Quotation, PACAF Hdq.

16 Reinlie, *Fort Walton Beach FL Daily News*.

17 Manor, telephone interview Nov. 17, 2011.

18 Manor, personal interview April 4, 2012.

19 McAtee, email April 26, 2012.

20 Pearson, email April 12, 2014.

21 Fact sheet, C-5 Galaxy, Official Site of the USAF, online.

22 Manor, email Feb. 8, 2012.

23 Johnson, email April 8, 2012.

Chapter 5 Preparations Everywhere by Everyone

1 Tobin, p. 43.

2 Thieman, email Sept. 4, 2012.

3 Gathering of Eagles Foundation, online.

4 Snedegar, email Sept. 4, 2014.

5 Aune, "Reflections…" *Military Medicine*.

6 Aune, interview Aug. 5, 2014.

7 Aune, interview Aug. 6, 2014.

8 Traynor, "Operation Babylift," *Airlift/Tanker Quarterly*.

9 Aune, interview Aug. 5, 2014.

10 Aune, "Reflections…"

11 Aune, interview Aug. 6, 2024.

12 Traynor, "Operation Babylift."

13 Budznya, Two Air Force Nurses Heroes…online.

14 Aune, interview Aug. 7, 2014.

15 Snedegar, email Sept. 9, 2014.

16 Traynor, interview Aug. 20, 2014.

17 Aune, "Reflections…"

18 AP, Saigon. In Crash, Many Die, *Honolulu Star-Bulletin*.

19 Torma, Operation Babylift, USAF Medical Service Digest.

20 Pearson, email April 12, 2014.

21 Patricia Folts, interview May 12, 2012.

Chapter 6 Devastating Heartbreak

1 Tobin, p. 29.

2 Traynor, interview Aug. 20, 2014.

3 Aune, "Reflections…"

4 Orphan Tots Die in Crash, *Honolulu Star-Bulletin*.

5 Ibid.

6 Traynor, "Operation…"

7 Ibid.

8 Aune, "Reflections…"

9 Pearson, email April 12, 2014.

10 Pearson, email May 5, 2014.

11 Tobin, p. 29-30.

12 Traynor, "Operation…"

13 Orphan Tots Die in Crash.

14 Aune, interview Aug. 7, 2014.

15 Traynor, "Operation…" Epilogue.

16 Frisbee, online.

17 100 Orphans Survive Air Disaster, *The Honolulu Advertiser*.

18 Snedegar, email Sept. 9, 2014.

19 Traynor, "Operation…"

20 Aune, "Reflections…"

21 Aune, interview Aug. 6, 2014.

22 Traynor, "Operation…"

23 100 Orphans Survive…

24 Orphan Tots Die in Crash.

25 Ibid.

26 100 Orphans Survive…

Chapter 7 Speculation

1 Cross, Mac and Operation Babylift…

2 Orphan Tots Die...

3 Traynor, "Operation…"

4 Snedegar, email Sept. 4, 2014.

5 Washington: Sabotage Suspected, *Honolulu Star-Bulletin*.

6 100 Orphans Survive…

7 Orphan Tots Die...

8 Traynor, "Operation Babylift."

9 100 Orphans Survive…

10 Orphan Tots Die...

11 Manor, interview April 4, 2012.

12 Manor, interview Nov. 6, 2011.

13 Manor, interview Aug. 6, 2014.

14 Mullen, For Adoptive Parents, *The Honolulu Advertiser*.

15 Ibid.

16 Thieman, email Sept. 4, 2012.

17 Mullen, For Adoptive Parents…

18 Ibid.

19 Ibid.

20 Babylift is Still a Go, UPI Washington, *The Honolulu Advertiser*.

21 Ibid.

22 Immigration Pleas Speeded up…, *Honolulu Star-Bulletin*.

Chapter 8 Carrying On: The Morning After

1 Vasquez, email Sept. 2, 2014.

2 AP Saigon, More Tots Leave Saigon, *Honolulu Star-Bulletin*.

3 Ibid.

4 Lazarus, "The New Colossus."

5 Aldrian, interview May 2, 2012.

6 Manor, interview Nov. 17, 2011.

7 Manor, interview Nov. 6, 2011.

8 McAtee, email April 26, 2012.

9 McReynolds, email June 9, 2012.

10 Wolf, 407 Viet Tots…, *The Sunday Star-Bulletin and Advertiser*.

11 Ibid.

12 Ibid.

13 Ibid.

14 McKinny, interview Aug. 27, 2012.

15 Virginia Callanan, interview April 20, 2012.

16 Ibid.

17 Navas, interview May 25, 2012.

18 Parker Rakocy, email July 16, 2012.

19 McAtee, email April 26, 2012.

20 Parker Rakocy, email July 16, 2012.

21 McAtee, email April 26, 2012.

Chapter 9 Moment by Moment, Day by Day

1 Manor, interview Nov. 6, 2011.
2 Pearson, email April 12, 2014.
3 Patte Folts, interview May 12, 2012.
4 Pearson, email April 12, 2014.

Chapter 10 The Orphans

1 McAtee, email April 26, 2012.
2 Adamski, Tiny Crash Victim…
3 Bowman, New Life, *Honolulu Star-Bulletin*.
4 Ibid.
5 Ibid.
6 UPI, 286 Orphans Arrive…, *The Honolulu Advertiser*.
7 Wolf, Tots Sparkle under Tripler Care, *The Honolulu Advertiser*.
8 Shriners' Hospital…, *Honolulu Star-Bulletin*.
9 Parish & McNerney, A Message from National Association, Blue Shield Plans.

Chapter 11 Hiatus and Criticism

1 AP, Saigon Halts Large-Scale Orphan Lift, *Honolulu Star-Bulletin*.
2 UPI, Saigon: Fate of War Orphans in Doubt, *The Honolulu Advertiser*.
3 AP, Saigon Halts…
4 Adamski, Tiny Crash Victim…
5 AP, Saigon Halts…
6 Ibid.
7 Ibid.
8 Ibid.
9 Cuneo, South Vietnam Ends Babylift, *The Honolulu Advertiser*.
10 Virginia Callanan, interview April 20, 2012.
11 Johnson, email June 7, 2014.
12 Cuneo.
13 UPI, VC Shelling Suburbs…, *The Honolulu Advertiser*.
14 UPI, North Viets Bombard…, *The Honolulu Advertiser*.
15 UPI, 286 Orphans Arrive…
16 AP, Eugene, OR. Political Use of Orphans…, *Honolulu Star-Bulletin*.
17 Ibid.
18 Ibid.
19 Pearson, interview April 4, 2014.

Chapter 12 Resumption of Flights

1 Wagnerites Join in 'Baby Lift,' online.

2 Mike Folts, interview Aug. 15, 2012.

3 Kelly Folts, email Sept. 15, 2014.

4 Doug Folts, letter to Andrea…

5 Patte Folts, interview May 12, 2012.

6 Anonymous Student, Operation Baby Lift: WHS students…online.

7 Pearson, email April 12, 2014.

8 Manor, interview Sept. 1, 2013.

9 Jordan, "Diary of an Air Force Chaplain at Wake," *History of the 15th Air Base Wing.*

10 Lee & Haynesworth, White Christmas in April, p. 4-5.

Chapter 13 Getting Around the Red Tape

1 Tobin, Last Flight from Saigon, p. 44.

2 Tobin, p. 21.

3 Tobin, p. 20.

4 Tobin, p. 21.

5 Tobin, p. 50.

6 Tobin, p. 50.

7 Doug Folts, "Vietnam Evacuation." Personal narrative.

8 Doug Folts, interview Aug. 17, 2012.

9 Hong, interview Sept. 22, 2013.

10 McKinny, interview Aug. 27, 2012.

Chapter 14 Angry Opposition

1 Flaste, Airlift of Orphans Outrages Some, *Honolulu Star-Bulletin.*

2 Hostetler, Operation Babylift Mistake…, *The Honolulu Advertiser.*

3 Westfall, A Soldier's Choice, *People*, p. 80.

4 Waskul, American Orphans Too, *The Sunday Star-Bulletin and Advertiser.*

5 Now They'll Have Love, Honolulu Star-Bulletin.

6 Flaste.

7 Ibid.

8 Combined News Services. Babylift Ends, *The Honolulu Advertiser.*

9 Ibid.

10 UPI, Fraud Reported in Orphan Airlift, *The Honolulu Advertiser.*

11 Knoefler, Joy Was Seeing Their Children Go, *Honolulu Star-Bulletin.*

12 Zeitlin, A Mother Says Goodbye, *Honolulu Star-Bulletin.*

13 UPI, Fraud Reported…, *The Honolulu Advertiser.*

14 AP, Frauds in Babylift Reported, *Honolulu Star-Bulletin*.

15 AP, Children Without Country, *Honolulu Star-Bulletin*.

16 Chancellor and Quinn Online.

17 AP, It's 'Phony Issue' Say Diplomats, *Honolulu Star-Bulletin*.

18 AP, Most Are Actually 'Half-Orphans,' *Honolulu Star-Bulletin*.

19 AP, U.S. Has Thousands of Its Own, *Honolulu Star-Bulletin*.

20 AP, 300 More Set to Leave Tomorrow, *Honolulu Star-Bulletin*.

21 Manor, interview Nov. 6, 2011.

22 Manor, interview Sept. 1, 2013.

23 Barnes, email Feb. 15, 2015.

24 Parish & McNerney.

25 Bartoloni, email Feb. 15, 2015.

Chapter 15 Volunteers and Adoption Policies

1 Ann Say, interview Oct. 4, 2008.

2 Islanders Open Homes, *Honolulu Star-Bulletin*.

3 State Queried on Processing, *The Honolulu Advertiser*.

4 McKinny, interview Sept 4, 2012.

5 Bill Say, interview June 10, 2009.

6 UPI, Babylift Resumed, *The Honolulu Advertiser*.

7 Ibid.

8 Lueras, No Longer Orphans, *The Sunday Star-Bulletin and Advertiser*.

9 Ibid.

10 Nelson, New Parents Greet Orphans, *Honolulu Star-Bulletin*.

11 Johnson, email April 8, 2012.

12 Johnson, email April 5, 2012.

13 Aldrian, interview May 4, 2012.

14 McAtee, email April 26, 2012.

15 Navas, interview May 25, 2012.

16 Jordan, History of the 15th Air Base Wing.

17 Washington Post Service. Health Threat Reported, *The Honolulu Advertiser*.

18 UPI, Washington, INS to Probe Reports…, *The Honolulu Advertiser*.

19 Lueras, Saigon Catholics Oppose…, *The Honolulu Advertiser*.

20 Manor, interview Nov. 17, 2011.

21 Tobin, p. 67.

22 Tobin, p. 67-68.

23 Tobin, p. 62-63.

24 Manor, interview Aug. 5, 2014.

25 Tobin, p. 68.

26 Tobin, p. 69.

27 Haulman, The United States Air Force and Humanitarian
Operations, p. 432-433.

Chapter 16 The Last Flights

1 Kurtis, email Jan. 22, 2015.

2 Adamski, Refugee Airlift Finish Seen, *Honolulu Star-Bulletin*.

3 Adamski, Tiny Crash Victim…

4 Tong, Montagnard Orphan Flight…, *The Honolulu Advertiser*.

5 Adamski, Refugee…

6 Tong.

7 Adamski, Refugee…

8 Tong.

9 Tong.

10 Pearson, email April 12, 2014.

11 Nguyen, *The Unwanted*, p. 342-343.

12 Tobin, p. 74-79.

13 Pearson, interview April 4, 2014.

14 Lee & Haynsworth, p. 5.

15 Tobin, p. 110.

Chapter 17 A Year of Miracles

No Notes Ch. 17

Chapter 18 The Bases and The Aircraft: What Happened Next

1 Wilson, "Generals Note Base Efforts," *Philippine Flier*.

2 Manor, interview Sept. 1, 2013.

3 Ibid.

4 Boyd, email June 21, 2013.

5 Cordero-Fernando and Ricio, Turn of the Century.

6 Boyd.

7 Aune, interview March 4, 2014.

8 A World of Difference: Heritage, online.

9 Mendoza, email Nov. 21, 2014.

10 Mendoza, email Dec. 6, 2014.

11 Vasquez, interview Sept. 26, 2014.

12 Air Mobility Command: C-141B Starlifter, online.

13 Fact Sheet, C-9 Nightingale, online.

Chapter 19 The People: Where They Are Now

1 Barron, Ed Daly Dies, *The New York Times* online.

2 Manor, interview Sept. 1, 2013.

3 Reinlie, From D-Day to Son Tay, *Fort Walton Beach Florida Daily News*.

4 Herson, Letter of Notification.

5 Manor, telephone interview.

6 Humphrey,Northwest *Florida Daily News*.

7 Doug Folts, email May 23, 2014.

8 Hong T.T. Nguyen, interview May 15, 2014.

9 Doug Folts, letter Sept. 5, 2013.

10 Traynor, "Operation Babylift."

11 Frisbee, "Valor: The Lady Was a Tiger," online.

12 Gathering of Eagles Foundation, Online.

13 Aune, "Reflections…

14 Aune, interview Aug. 5, 2014.

15 Snedegar, email Sept. 4, 2014.

16 Parker L. 'Rocket' Rakocy, Obituary, *The Northwest Florida Daily News*.

17 Rose Marie Rakocy, interview Aug. 1, 2014.

18 Johnson, email April 8, 2012.

19 McAtee, email May 29, 2014.

20 Johnson, email June 24, 2014.

21 McReynolds, email June 23, 2014.

22 Aldrian, interview July 2, 2014.

23 Tony Callanan, interview July 4, 2014.

24 Pearson, email May 22, 2014.

25 Pearson, interview March 27, 2014.

26 Navas-Heine, interview July 10, 2014.

27 McKinny, interview Aug. 27, 2012.

28 Ibid.

29 Knowland Website, online.

30 Knowland, interview May 15, 2014.

31 Kurtis, email Jan. 22, 2015.

32 Bartoloni, email Feb. 15, 2015.

33 Barnes, email Feb. 15, 2015.

34 Ann Say, interview Aug. 19, 2014.

35 Marcie Say, email March 27, 2014.

36 Doug Folts, interview Aug. 17, 2012.

The Epilogue

1 Aune, "Reflections…"
2 Snedegar, email Sept. 4, 2014.
3 Kien Nguyen.
4 Jordan.

Sources by Category

Interviews

Aldrian, Kathy, telephone interviews, May 2, 4, July 2, 2012.

Anonymous source active in Babylift, 1975, telephone interview, Nov. 12, 2012.

Aune, Col Regina (Ret.), telephone interview, March 4, 2014.

Aune, Col Regina (Ret.), personal interviews, San Antonio, Texas, Aug. 5, 6, 7, 2014.

Callanan, Virginia, telephone interview, April 20, 2012.

Callanan, Maj Anthony (Ret.), telephone interview, July 4, 2014.

Folts, Col L. Douglas (Ret.), telephone interview, Aug. 17, 2012.

Folts, Mike, telephone interview, Aug. 15, 2012.

Folts, Patricia and L. Douglas, telephone interview, May 12, 2012.

Knowland, Joseph W., telephone interview, May 15, 2014.

Kurtis, Bill, telephone interview, Jan. 28, 2015.

Manor, Lt Gen LeRoy (Ret.), telephone interviews, Nov. 6, 17, 2011; March 1, 2015.

Manor, Lt Gen LeRoy (Ret.), personal interviews, Shalimar, FL, April 4, 2012; Sept. 1, 2013.

Manor, Lt Gen LeRoy (Ret.), personal interviews, San Antonio, TX, Aug. 5, 6, 7, 2014.

McKinny, Dr. Wayne R., telephone interviews, Aug. 28, 30; Sept. 4, 2012.

Mendoza, Maj Federico R., USAF AFRC 68 AS/DOP, interview and C-5A tour, San Antonio, TX, Aug. 6, 2014.

Milleson, William J., personal interview, North Platte, NE, Oct. 6, 2013.

Navas, Barbara, telephone interview, May 25, 2012.

Navas-Heine, Virginia, telephone interview, July 10, 2014.

Nguyen, Hong T. T., telephone interview, May 15, 2014.

Pearson, Mavis, telephone interviews, March 27, April 4, 2014.

Rakocy, Rose Marie, personal interview, Shalimar, FL, April 4, 2012; telephone interview, Aug. 1, 2014.

Say, Ann, personal interview, Lake Ozark, MO, Oct. 4, 2008; telephone interview, Aug. 19, 2014.

Say, Bill, telephone interview, June 10, 2009.

Snedegar, CMSgt Ray (Ret.), telephone interview, Sept. 2, 2014.

Traynor, Col Dennis (Ret.), telephone interview, Aug. 20, 2014.

Vasquez, MSgt Vincente (Ret.), personal interview, North Platte, NE, Sept. 26, 2014.

Correspondence

Aune, Col Regina (Ret.), email to author, March 4, 2014.

Barnes, Geraldine, email to author, Feb. 15, 2015.

Bartoloni, Jennifer, email to author, Feb 15, 2015.

Boyd, Jim, email to author, June 21, 2013.

Callanan, Major Anthony (Ret.), emails to author, July 16, 2012; July 4, 2014.

Folts, Kelly, email to author, Sept. 15, 2014.

Folts, Col L. Douglas (Ret.), letter to author, Sept. 5, 2013.

Folts, Col L. Douglas (Ret.), email to author, May 23, 2014.

Folts, Col L. Douglas (Ret.), Letter to Andrea and Nhu, June 14, 2003.

Herson, James P. Jr., Ph.D. Command Historian, DAFC, United States Special Operations Command. Letter of Notification to Lt Gen LeRoy J. Manor concerning his selection to the Commando Hall of Honor. MacDill Air Force Base, Tampa, FL. March 13, 2014. Sent to author by Manor March 27, 2014.

Johnson, Betsy, emails to author, April 8, 25, 2012; June 24, 2014.

Kurtis, Bill, email to author, Jan. 22, 2015.

Manor, Lt Gen Leroy (Ret.), email to author, Feb. 8, 2012.

McAtee, Major Thomas P. (Ret.), emails to author, April 26, July 6, 2012; May 29, 2014.

McReynolds, Carolyn, emails to author, June 9, 2012; June 23, 2014.

Mendoza, Maj Federico R., USAF AFRC 68 AS/DOP, emails to author, Nov. 21, 2014; Dec. 6, 2014.

Milleson, William J., letters to author from Vietnam, Oct. 4, 1965; Dec. 6, 1965.

Pearson, Mavis, emails to author, April 12, May 5, 22, 2014.

Rakocy, Capt Parker (Ret.), email to author, July 16, 2012.

Say, Marcie, email to author, March 27, 2014.

Snedegar, CMSgt Ray (Ret.), emails to author, Sept. 4, 9, 2014.

Thieman, LeAnn, email to author, Sept. 4, 2012.

Tierney, J., letter to Commander 13th Air Force, May 18, 1975. Forwarded to author by Col L.D. Folts, Jan. 2, 2015.

Traynor, Col Dennis (Ret.), emails to author, Aug. 19, 20, 2014.

Vasquez, Msgt Vincente (Ret.), email to author, Sept. 2, 2014.

Books

Cordero-Fernando, Gilda, and Nik Ricio. *Turn of the Century*. GCF Books, Quezon City, Philippines, 1978.

Cross, Coy F. II. *MAC and Operation Babylift: Air Transport in support of Noncombatant Evacuation Operations*. USAF Military Airlift Command Office of History Monograph. Scott Air Force Base, IL. 1989.

Haulman, Daniel L. *The United States Air Force and Humanitarian Operations, 1947-1994*. Air Force History and Museum Program, Washington, D.C. 1998.

Jordan, Kaye A., Historian, 15th Air Base Wing. *History of the 15th Air Base Wing, Office of the Chaplain. 1 April – 31 July, 1975*. Hickam Field, Honolulu, Hawaii. Pacific Air Forces, United States Air Force. Publication date unavailable.

Karnow, Stanley. *Vietnam: A History*. Viking Press, New York. 1983.

Lee, Edward J. and Toby Haynsworth, Eds. *White Christmas in April: The Collapse of South Vietnam*. Peter Lang Publishing, Inc., New York, 1999.

McKelvey, Robert S. *The Dust of Life: America's Children Abandoned in Vietnam*. University of Washington Press, Seattle and London. 1999.

Nguyen, Kien. *The Unwanted*. Little, Brown and Company, New York. 2000.

Tobin, Lt Col Thomas G.; Lt. Col. Arthur E. Laehr; and Lt. Col. John F. Hilgenberg. *Last Flight from Saigon*. USAF Southeast Asia Monograph Series, Vol. IV, Monograph 6. Washington D.C.: Office of Air Force History, United States Air Force. 1978. New Imprint 1985.

Warren, Andrea. *Escape From Saigon: How a Vietnam War Orphan Became an American Boy*. Farrar, Straus, and Giroux, Sunburst Edition, 2008.

Online articles

Air Mobility Command. "C-141 Starlifter." www.amcmuseum.org/exhibits_and_planes/c-141b.php. (Accessed Sept. 3, 2014.)

Anonymous Student. 1975. "Operation Baby Lift: WHS students offer the personal touch." *Falcon Crier*. April 11. www.whoa.org/publications/criers/750411/0607.jpg. (Accessed July 1, 2013.)

"A World of Difference: Heritage." www.worldairways.com/heritage.php. (Accessed May 6, 2014.)

Barron, James. 1984. "Edward Daly Dies; Airline Chairman." *The New York Times*. Jan. 24. www.nytimes.com/1984/01/24/obituaries/edward-daly-dies-airline-chairman.html. (Accessed July 18, 2013.)

Boyd, Jim. USAF RAO Director, U.S. Embassy Warden. Angeles City, Philippines. http://www2.mozcom.com/~rao_cabr. (Accessed May 21, 2013.)

Budznya, Tom. "Two AF Nurses Heroes of 'Operation Babylift.'" Official Site of the U. S. Air Force, News page. http://www.af/mil/news/story. (Accessed May 14, 2013.)

Fact Sheet, "C-5 Galaxy." Official site of the U.S. Air Force. http://www.af.mil/AboutUs/FactSheets/Display/tabid/224/ Article/104492/c-5-abc-galaxy-and-c-5m-super-galaxy.aspx (Accessed Sept. 3, 2014.)

Fact Sheet, "C-9 Nightingale." Official site of the U.S. Air Force. www. af.mil/AboutUs/FactSheets/tabid/131/Default.aspx?Search=C-9+Nightingale. (Accessed Sept. 3, 2014.)

Frisbee, John L. "Valor: The Lady Was a Tiger." www.airforcemag.com/ MagazineArchive/Pages/1986/June 1986. (Accessed Feb. 22, 2014.)

Gathering of Eagles Foundation. "Eagle Biography, Colonel Regina C. Aune." http://goefoundation.org/index.php/eagles/biographies/a/ aune-regina-c/. (Accessed Feb. 22, 2014.)

"How Many Passengers Can Fit in a 727?" www.fromtheflightdeck.com/ reviews/727/World727. (Accessed Oct. 9, 2013.)

Knowland, Joseph W., www.deeknowland.com. (Accessed May 20, 2014.)

L'Ecluse, Kathleen. "Babylift Revisited: Remembering the Crash." http://babyliftrevisited.typepad.com/babylift_revisited/2006/04. (Accessed July 21, 2013 and Sept. 3, 2014.)

Minetree, Harry. *People* Archive, June 16, 1975, Vol. 3, No. 23. www.people.com/people/archive/article/0,,20065348,00.html. (Accessed June 28, 2013.)

Northshield, Robert. *NBC Reports: The Sins of the Fathers*. Stock Footage and summary. http://nbcuniversalarchives.com/nbcuni/ clip/5112769389_s01.do. (Accessed Oct. 1, 2014.)

Traynor, Col. Dennis "Bud," (Ret.). www.facebook.com/groups/ C5.babylift/photos/. (Accessed Aug. 19, 2014.)

UPI. "Vietnam Passage. The Stories: Trung." www.pbs.org/ vietnampassage/Stories/stories.trung.02.html. (Accessed July 1, 2013.)

"Wagnerites Join in 'Baby Lift'." 1975. *Falcon Crier*, April 11. www.whoa. org/publications/criers/750411/01.jpg. (Accessed July 1, 2013.)

"World Airways Cargo Back to Saigon Babylift, 2005." Luchtzak Aviation. April 2. http://www.luchtzak.be/forums/viewtopic. (Accessed July 1, 2012.)

Periodicals

Aune, Col Regina C. (Ret.). USAF NC." Reflections on a Humanitarian Mission 20 Years Later: Operation Babylift." *Military Medicine: International Journal of AMSUS*. Vol. 160. Nov. 1995.

Cross, Coy F. II. "MAC and Operation Babylift." *Airlift*. Spring 1990.

Torma, Brig Gen Michael J., MC, and George M. Watson Jr., Ph.D. "Operation Babylift." *USAF Medical Service Digest*. Summer, 1990.

Traynor, Col Dennis (Ret.). "Operation Babylift" *Airlift/Tanker Quarterly*. Vol. 13, Number 2, Spring, 2005.

Westfall, Sandra Sobiera and Kathy Free. "A Soldier's Choice." *People*. Nov. 18, 2013.

Personal Diaries and Narratives

Holland, Jean Fox. Diary: *Operation Babylift, April 1975, Clark Air Base, Philippines*.

Folts, Col L. Douglas (Ret.). "Vietnam Evacuation." Personal narrative sent to author Sept. 2013.

Other Sources

Benson, Jay, Producer. *The Children of An Lac*. 1980. Full Movie. Directed by John Llewellyn Moxey. http://www.imdb.com/video/hulu/vi986972697/ (Accessed April 4, 2014).

Chancellor, John and Charlie Quinn. "Cambodian Children in the United States/Legal Complications." *NBC Evening News*, Wednesday, April 16, 1975. Two-minute DVD obtained from http://tvnews.vanderbilt.edu/program.pl?ID=482252. (Accessed Oct. 1, 2014.)

Lazarus, Emma. From "The New Colossus." 1883.

Order of the Sword: Quotation from a plaque honoring Major General Leroy Manor's PACAF designation to Order of the Sword. United States Air Force Headquarters of Pacific Air Forces building, Joint Base Pearl Harbor/Hickam, Honolulu, Hawaii.

Parish and McNerney. "A Message from the National Association of Blue Shield Plans and the Blue Cross Association to All Blue Cross and Blue Shield Chief Plan Executives." April 7, 1975.

Newspapers

Adamski, Mary. 1975. "Refugee Airlift Finish Seen in 48-72 Hours." *Honolulu Star-Bulletin*, April 26.

Adamski, Mary. 1975. "Tiny Crash Victim Joins Island Family." *Honolulu Star-Bulletin*, April 8.

AP Eugene, OR. 1975. "Political Use of Orphans Deplored." *Honolulu Star-Bulletin*, April 9.

AP Leesburg, VA. 1975. "Children Without Country." *Honolulu Star-Bulletin*, April 16.

AP Phnom Penh. 1975. "It's 'Phony Issue' Say Diplomats." *Honolulu Star-Bulletin*, April 10.

AP Saigon. 1975. "In Crash, Many Die." *Honolulu Star-Bulletin*. April 4.

AP Saigon. 1975. "Most Are Actually 'Half-Orphans'." *Honolulu Star-Bulletin*, April 10.

AP Saigon. 1975. "300 More Set to Leave Tomorrow." *Honolulu Star-Bulletin*, April 10.

AP Saigon. 1975. "More Tots Leave Saigon." *Honolulu Star-Bulletin*, April 5.

AP Saigon. 1975. "Orphan Tots Die in Crash." *Honolulu Star-Bulletin*, April 4.

AP Saigon. 1975. "Saigon Halts Large-Scale Orphan Lift." *Honolulu Star-Bulletin*, April 7.

AP San Francisco. 1975. "Frauds in Babylift Reported." *Honolulu Star-Bulletin*, April 14.

AP Washington. 1975. "Sabotage Suspected." *Honolulu Star-Bulletin*, April 4.

AP Washington. 1975. "U.S. Has Thousands of Its Own." *Honolulu Star-Bulletin*, April 10.

Arnett, Peter. 1975. "Pilot Ignores Order, Flies Orphans Out." *Honolulu Star-Bulletin*, April 2.

Arnett, Peter. 1975. "Saigon Tots Sample U.S. Delights." *Honolulu Star-Bulletin*, April 3.

Bowman, Pierre. 1975. "New Life." *Honolulu Star-Bulletin*, April 8.

Bulletin. 1975. "Orphan Plane Crashes." *The Honolulu Advertiser*, April 4.

Combined News Services San Francisco. 1975. "Babylift Ends." *The Honolulu Advertiser*, April 15.

Cuneo, Alice Z. 1975. "South Vietnam Ends 'Babylift'." *The Honolulu Advertiser*, April 7.

Cunningham, James F. 1975. "Viet Kin Target of Local Aid." *The Honolulu Advertiser*, April 4.

"Evacuate Kin First." 1975. *Honolulu Star-Bulletin*, April 14.

Flaste, Richard. 1975. "Airlift of Orphans Outrages Some." *Honolulu Star-Bulletin*, April 9.

Hostetler, Harold. 1975. "Operation Babylift Mistake in Long Run." *The Honolulu Advertiser*, April 15.

Humphrey, Kelly. 2015. "His Honors Are Legion." *Northwest Florida Daily News*, March 20.

"Immigration Pleas Speeded Up Here." 1975. *Honolulu Star-Bulletin*, April 4.

"Islanders Open Homes." 1975. *Honolulu Star-Bulletin*, April 4.

Kelly, Peter M. 1975. "Agency Speeds Up Rescue of Viet Orphans." *The Honolulu Advertiser*, April 4.

Kloss, James. 1975. "To Vietnam's Orphans, He's Top Flight." *Honolulu Star-Bulletin*, April 9.

Knoefler, Tammy. 1975. "Joy Was Seeing Their Children Go." *Honolulu Star-Bulletin*, April 11.

Knowland, Joseph W. 1975. "Tribune Editorial." *The Oakland Tribune*. April, (date unknown). Permission granted by Knowland to reprint full editorial.

Lueras, Leonard. 1975. "No Longer Orphans." *The Sunday Star-Bulletin and Advertiser*, April 13.

Lueras, Leonard. 1975. "Saigon Catholics Oppose Massive Babylifts, Bishop." *The Honolulu Advertiser*, April 25.

Mullen, Donald E. 1975. "For Adoptive Parents, It's an Agonizing Wait." *The Honolulu Advertiser*, April 5.

Nelson, Lyle. 1975. "New Parents Greet Orphans at Hickam." *Honolulu Star-Bulletin*, April 24.

Nelson, Lyle. 1975. "17 Children Escape the Suffering in Vietnam." *Honolulu Star-Bulletin*, April 2.

"Now They'll Have Love." 1975. *Honolulu Star-Bulletin*, April 18.

Ong, Vickie. 1975. "Hawaii's 'Help Us' Roster Arrives in Vietnam Today." *The Honolulu Advertiser*, April 8.

Rakocy, Parker L. 'Rocket.' 2013. Obituary. *The Northwest Florida Daily News*, Oct. 21.

Reinlie, Lauren Sage. 2014. "From D-Day to Son Tay." *Fort Walton Beach Florida Daily News*, Dec. 31.

Saigon. 1975. "100 Orphans Survive Air Disaster." *The Honolulu Advertiser*, April 5.

"Shriners' Hospital Will Take Orphans." 1975. *Honolulu Star-Bulletin*, April 25.

"State Queried on Processing." 1975. *The Honolulu Advertiser*, April 4.

"Stopovers Scheduled in Isles." 1975. *The Honolulu Advertiser*, April 5.

Tong, David. 1975. "Montagnard Orphan Flight Lands Here." *The Honolulu Advertiser*, April 26.

UPI. 1975. "286 Orphans Arrive on What May Be Last Flight." *The Honolulu Advertiser*, April 9.

UPI Saigon. 1975. "Babylift Resumed." *The Honolulu Advertiser*, April 12.

UPI Saigon. 1975. "Saigon: Fate of War Orphans in Doubt." *The Honolulu Advertiser*, April 8.

UPI Saigon. 1975. "North Viets Bombard Key Targets." *The Honolulu Advertiser*, April 15.

UPI Saigon. 1975. "VC Shelling Suburbs of Viet Capital." *The Honolulu Advertiser*, April 7.

UPI San Francisco. 1975. "Fraud Reported in Orphan Airlift." *The Honolulu Advertiser*, April 14.

UPI Washington. 1975. "Babylift Is Still a Go." *The Honolulu Advertiser*, April 5.

UPI Washington. 1975. "INS to Probe Reports of 'Babylift' Bribery." *The Honolulu Advertiser*, April 18.

"Vietnam Donation Agencies Listed." 1975. *Honolulu Star-Bulletin*, April 4.

Washington Post Service. 1975. "Health Threat Reported from Orphan Flights." *The Honolulu Advertiser*, April 18.

Washington Post Service, Washington. 1975. "Viet Aid Offers Skyrocket." *The Honolulu Advertiser*, April 3.

Waskul, Greg. 1975. "American Orphans Too." *The Sunday Star-Bulletin & Advertiser*, April 20.

"WHS Fathers Die in C-5A Crash." *Falcon Crier*, Wagner High School, Clark Air Base, PI. April 11, 1975.

Wilson, Gen. Louis L., Commander in Chief of Pacific Air Forces 1975. "Generals Note Base Efforts." *The Philippine Flyer*, April 25. Sent in an email to the author by Lt. Gen. Leroy J. Manor, Feb. 8, 2012.

Wolf, Janice. 1975. "Tots Sparkle Under Tripler Care." *The Honolulu Advertiser*, April 10.

Wolf, Janice. 1975. "407 Viet Tots on Their Way to a New Life." *The Sunday Star-Bulletin and Advertiser*, April 6.

Zeitlin, Arnold. 1975. "A Mother Says Goodbye…and a Mother Remembers." *Honolulu Star-Bulletin*, April 15.

Zeitlin, Arnold. 1975. "Evacuation of Vietnam Orphans Vowed." *Honolulu Star-Bulletin*, April 1.

Recommended Reading

Aune, Regina C. and Aryn C. Lockhart. *Operation Babylift: Mission Accomplished – A Memoir of Hope and Healing*

Clark, Cherie. *After Sorrow Comes Joy: One Woman's Struggle to Bring Hope to Thousands of Children in Vietnam and India*

Karnow, Stanley. *Vietnam: A History*

Lee, J. Edward and Toby Haynsworth. *White Christmas in April: The Collapse of South Vietnam, 1975*

McKelvey, Robert S. *The Dust of Life: America's Children Abandoned in Vietnam*

Nguyen, Kien. *The Unwanted*

Peck-Barnes, Shirley. *The War Cradle: Vietnam's Children of War, Operation Babylift—The Untold Story*

Sachs, Dana. *The Life We Were Given: Operation Babylift, International Adoption, and the Children of War in Vietnam*

Taylor, Rosemary. *Orphans of War: Work With the Abandoned Children of Vietnam 1967-1975*

Thiemann, Leann. *This Must Be My Brother: The Daring Rescue of Innocent Children in the Final Desperate Hours of the Vietnam War*

Warren, Andrea. *Escape from Saigon: How a Vietnam War Orphan Became an American Boy*

Index

Folts, Patricia 98, 110

Ford, President Gerald 24, 31, 33 34, 35, 40, 48, 55, 61, 62, 90, 124, 134, 158, 194, 195

Friends of Children of Vietnam (FCVN) 15, 16, 18, 19, 23, 25, 29, 36, 38, 39, 69, 82, 83, 88, 127, 128, 131. 132, 134, 153, 154, 157, 158

Gonge, John F. 57, 200

Grimes, Larry 103

Guam 33, 40, 68, 103, 137, 139, 145, 154, 162, 181, 183, 194

Ha, Huong Thi Cam 125

Hadley, Jim 50, 199

Healy, Ken 31

Heninger, Mike 145

Hensley, Dale 105

Hickam Air Force Base 33, 37, 38, 40, 44, 46, 58, 59, 61, 65, 67, 69, 75, 78, 81, 83, 84, 88, 128, 133, 135, 137, 144, 145, 162, 163, 181, 182, 183, 194

Hilderbrand, Dr. Gene 30

Holland, Jean Fox 11, 44, 47, 64, 65, 63, 74, 76, 77, 78, 79, 80, 87, 93, 94, 102, 103, 106, 140, 141, 146, 149, 151, 167, 168, 169, 181

Hurley, Bishop Mark 138

International Disaster Relief Center 34

Johnson, Betsy 89, 135

Johnson, TSgt Denning 57, 180, 193

Johnson, Franklyn R. 89, 135, 172

Kane, Robert 30, 82, 134

Keating, Bill 31

Klinker, Mary 40, 43, 54, 57, 170, 180, 193, 199, 200, 201, 203

Knowland, Joseph W. 30, 32, 175

Krall, John 123

About the Author

Bette Milleson James writes both prose and poetry following a career teaching English in Western Kansas, where she lives on the family farm. She holds a B.A. in English and an M.S. in Literature. Her work has been published in several anthologies, including *I Am Wherever You Are* with artist N.A. Noel. James has worked as copy editor for a Colorado-based periodical and has edited children's books. In addition, several volumes of her work have been published: *Christmas Dreams*, a book of seasonal poetry, *Bless the Children*, a book of poems about children, and *Colorado Cravings*, a cookbook reflecting history and lifestyle, all from Blueline Publishing of Denver, Colorado. James' most recent publication is *Introspection and Environment*, a collaboration with her son, Mark.